MW01623677

THE UNIVERSAL LANGUAGE DISC REFERENCE MANUAL

By Bill J. Bonnstetter & Judy I. Suiter

"You can get everything you want in life by helping others get what they want!"
–Zig Ziglar

18TH PRINTING
www.TTISI.com

© 1993-2018 Target Training International, Ltd.

© 1993, 2001, 2004, 2007, 2009, 2011, 2013, 2016, 2018 by Target Training International, Ltd. All rights reserved.

Original version © 1984 by Target Training International, Ltd. Revised periodically.

Reproduction in any form is prohibited.

ISBN 978-0-9707531-4-4

Internet Delivery Service® (IDS) is a registered patent of Target Training International, Ltd. The following are registered trademarks of Target Training International, Ltd. Any use must acknowledge ownership by Target Training International, Ltd.: Style Insights®, Motivation Insights®, Managing for Success®, TTI Success Insights®, Success Insights Wheel® and TriMetrix®.

ABOUT THE AUTHORS

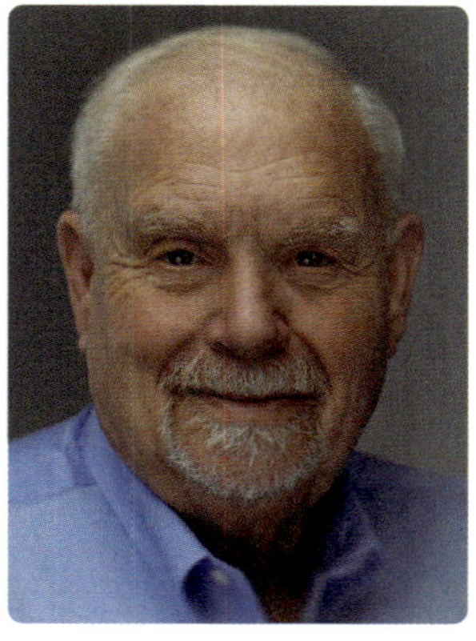

Bill J. Bonnstetter, 1938 - 2016
Chairman of the Board
Target Training International, Ltd.
and TTI Success Insights

A true thought leader impassioned by human behavior and an improved understanding of how individuals think, behave and work, Bill J. Bonnstetter is the co-founder of Target Training International, Ltd. (TTI) and TTI Success Insights. Established in 1984, TTI develops and markets research-based, validated assessments and products available in more than 90 countries and 40 languages.

In 1964, Bonnstetter earned his bachelor's degree in business with an emphasis in marketing and in 1969 a master's degree in business education from the University of Northern Iowa.

After working many years in the sales industry studying the buying styles of farmers, he and his son, David, formed Target Training International, Ltd. Bonnstetter is considered one of the pioneers in the assessment industry because of his significant contributions to the research and study of human behavior. He was the first to computerize the DISC assessment, making reports available via his patented Internet Delivery Service® (IDS). He was also the first to produce a computerized motivators assessment based on Eduard Spranger's personality model. Bonnstetter has received patents for TTI's job benchmarking process, which matches the right person with the right job, and for developing personalized reports integrating motivators and behaviors.

© 1993-2018 Target Training International, Ltd.

Bonnstetter's other accomplishments include the invention of the TTI Success Insights® Wheel, which visualizes an individual's natural versus adapted personality style and personal versus work behaviors. Bonnstetter was a thought leader in this regard and was the first to provide a visual display of individual behavioral graphs.

An international speaker and author of *If I Knew Then* and several articles and white papers, Bonnstetter's most recent research has focused on normal behavior of sales people, managers and leaders, college freshmen, superior performers and entrepreneurs. Two of his most impassioned research pursuits are in the realms of education and serial entrepreneurship.

Driven by his passion to help others, Bonnstetter and TTI emphasize excellent customer support provided to associates and employees. In an effort to give back to the greater community, each year TTI donates $1 million worth of assessments and services to educational organizations and non-profits that could not otherwise afford them.

Judy I. Suiter,
Founder & President
Competitive Edge, Inc.

"Learning is directly proportional to the amount of fun people have." Thus goes the philosophy of Judy Suiter, founder and president of Competitive Edge, Inc., a top human resources training and consulting company that specializes in building high performance teams, executive coaching and sales training. An internationally recognized organization, Competitive Edge, Inc. has been in business since 1981.

Judy's 30 years of experience is extensive. She has a BS in Industrial and Personnel Psychology from Middle Tennessee State University, a minor in Business Administration and over 680 hours in advanced behavioral and organizational development training. Ms. Suiter has designed and conducted training programs for over 60,000 people in numerous organizations throughout the United States, Puerto Rico and Europe. She is the author of *Energizing People, Unleashing the Power of DISC; Exploring Values, Releasing the Power of Attitudes; The Ripple Effect, How the Global Model of Endorsement Opens Doors to Success; The Sea of Change, Solutions for Navigating the Disconnects in the Workplace,* and *The Journey, Quotes to Keep Your Boat Afloat!* which she published in response to numerous requests for copies of her widely used quotations.

Some of Competitive Edge, Inc.'s current clientele includes multiple federal agencies with law enforcement responsibilities, global manufacturing facilities and financial service organizations.

© 1993-2018 Target Training International, Ltd.

The Institute of Management Consultants has designated Judy as a Certified Management Consultant; less than 1% of management consultants in the USA have earned this designation. In January, 2005, she was presented with the first Lifetime Achievement Award for TTI Performance Systems, Ltd. and has been a member of TTI's Chairman's Club since its inception. It is no wonder that her credo is, "Be daring, be first, be different."

TABLE OF CONTENTS

© 1993-2018 Target Training International, Ltd.

INTRODUCTION

Since 1979 the founders of TTI have been doing research on what makes normal people unique. The research has proven the value of understanding people's behavior. "Behavior" refers to **HOW** people do what they do. This research has also proven the need for understanding **WHY** people do what they do as well as looking at skills, or **WHAT** people do.

Research has proven that understanding a person's behavior is important, but it by no means is the only thing that you should take into consideration when looking for solutions to people challenges.

To better understand what people bring to the workplace, take a look at **TTI's Dimensions of Superior Performance™.**

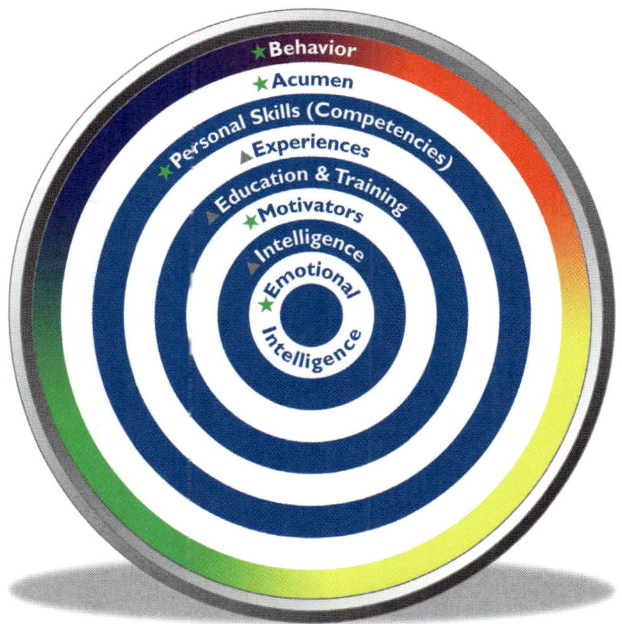

©2013 Target Training International, Ltd.

★ TTI MEASURES:
- Behavior
- Acumen
- Personal Skills (Competencies)
- 12 Driving Forces (Motivators)
- Emotional Intelligence

▲ TTI ACKNOWLEDGES:
- Experiences
- Education & Training
- Intelligence

Many organizations think they can solve all of their problems with DISC alone. DISC is not a measurement of a person's intelligence, motivators, experience, education and training, personal skills or emotional intelligence. This reference manual will not go into depth in all of these areas; but occasionally we may point out the value of collecting information from one or more of these areas to provide a complete solution for solving people problems.

Let's briefly explore TTI's Dimensions of Superior Performance. Emotional Intelligence is an important issue leading to performance. However, it's difficult for some people to appreciate and understand the value of controlling their emotional intelligence. A person can have all the talent in the world to match a particular job, but fail to be a superior performer by not using proper emotional intelligence.

Intelligence is also center core in our model; however, there is not enough research to prove or disprove that superior intelligence by itself will always lead to success.

People are hired for skills and fired for attitude. Attitudes are key to job satisfaction, performance, the WHY behind the enjoyment. Motivators help people discover their purpose and direction in life.

There are times when people are hired based only on previous experience. If experience always led to success, then all experienced people would be successful!

Training and education are also key elements to what a person brings to the job. TTI does not measure these, however, recognizes their importance to superior performance and job alignment.

Many organizations have recognized the importance of personal skills (competencies). TTI has conducted research, which has proven that superior performance in any career always includes an abundance of personal skills along with other dimensions of superior performance.

We have case studies showing a person has had a job match with all the other dimensions but their world view/acumen. This had led to inferior performance. By acumen, we are referring to their judgment based on intrinsic, extrinsic and systemic views, or the filters through which a person views the world.

We have positioned behavior on the outside of our Dimensions of Superior Performance for a very specific reason: A person's behavior is totally observable. The other dimensions are basically unobservable. We sit in a public location and observe people's behavior by the way they walk, talk, their facial expression, or how they stand in line. This manual is all about understanding people's behavior —DISC.

"TTI SI has distribution of its model in over 90 countries, and computerized personal reports are available in 40 languages."

© 1993-2018 Target Training International, Ltd.

Our research has indicated that behavior (DISC) is truly a universal language throughout the world. There are no borders! TTI has distribution of its model in over 90 countries, and computerized personal reports are available in 40 languages.

Here are some questions we've used throughout the world to help us understand the application worldwide.

Have you ever met someone you didn't like?
100 percent of people throughout the world have had this experience.

How soon can you tell if you dislike a person?
The majority of people claim they can identify people they dislike in two minutes or less. This proves that behavior is observable because how could you possibly analyze a person's intelligence, motivators, education, acumen and personal skills in such a short period of time.

Have you ever been mismanaged?
When you were mismanaged, did you take time to discuss it with the person who mismanaged you? 95% said they were mismanaged but did not talk with the person who was mismanaging them.

Have you ever left a store vowing NEVER to return?
Was it because of the way you were treated? Again, 95% said YES, they have left a store vowing never to return, and it was because of the way they were treated.

Have you ever met a salesperson you did NOT like?
Did you buy from that salesperson? Most people polled said they have met a salesperson they did NOT like and did NOT buy their product. Others said they only bought the product because they couldn't get it anywhere else.

If your desire is maximum effectiveness in your people interactions, this book is for you. You must learn the universal, observable language of behavior, DISC. This book is a reference manual to help you in learning the DISC language. Providing you with all you need to know, it is the most comprehensive, complete book about DISC on the market today.

Every day we live in a laboratory where we have the unique opportunity to learn about people. **By developing a strong command of the DISC language, you will:**

1. **Know your behavioral style.**
2. **Recognize the behavioral style of others.**
3. **Adapt and blend your style for greater, more effective communication and relationships!**

© 1993-2018 Target Training International, Ltd.

The DISC language was used to write this book. Many people were surveyed and asked what causes them to read or not read a book.

Here are some responses of what people said they wanted in a reference manual:

The DISC language, although not always known as DISC, has been in existence since people began watching people. By learning the language and opening your "behavioral eyes," you will take a quantum leap into the effectiveness of your interpersonal communications as you interact daily with people. Our wish, as authors, is for you to learn this unique language and use it to bring out the best in those around you, creating win/win situations.

All the best to each of you as you study!

© 1993-2018 Target Training International, Ltd.

WHAT IS DISC? 1

Chapter Objective

To define and establish the parameters of the DISC language:

A. What DISC is NOT
B. What DISC IS

To explain maximum use of the language and prevent abuse or overextension of the model.

Chapter Contents

- DISC Defined
- What DISC is NOT
- What DISC IS
- DISC Language Rules
- Objectives Revisited

"Communication is EVERYTHING!"

–Lee Iacocca in *Iacocca*

© 1993-2018 Target Training International, Ltd.

DISC DEFINED

Once upon a time, in a faraway land, a man (of unknown name or origin) was sitting on a rock, watching people. We're not sure why he was watching people, but one thing we do know for sure, he was content watching for hours.

As he watched, an unusual thing began to happen, he began to notice incredible similarities in the people who passed by. Although each one physically looked different, there were great similarities in how they acted. Some seemed talkative and friendly, while others were all business. Some talked more than they listened while others just listened. He was fascinated and was learning so much about people just by watching.

Then an idea popped into his mind, *"If I become like the person I am talking to, maybe I can get to know more people and really make a difference in their lives. Hmm! Will it work?"*

Methodically, he jotted down all the similarities and found four ways people acted. He wrote detailed descriptors for each one (not knowing what a descriptor was, he simply wrote down what he saw):

1. **Some people were forceful, direct, and results-oriented**
2. **Some were optimistic,fun, talkative**
3. **Some were steady, patient, relaxed**
4. **Some were precise, accurate, and detail-oriented**

He found that many people had characteristics of two or even three of the behaviors, but one behavior seemed to be the strongest. To test his theory, he was outgoing and friendly to the talkative, fun people. He put on a serious face and discussed the deep details of life with those of precise, accurate behavior. To those who were direct, he picked up his pace and got right to the point. Last of all, to those of steady, patient behavior, he laid back, relaxed and listened. Incredible! Fantastic! He noticed his communication became more and more effective and people began to seek him out!

He soon realized that a man who understood people was in great demand. To make a long story short, he became a well-respected citizen of the community, making many contributions to better the lives of the people around him. One thing people always said about him was that they felt so good when talking to him. Later in life as he pondered his accomplishments, he smiled and said, *"All this I have done just because I took the time to open my eyes and watch people."*

DISC is the universal language of observable human behavior. Just watching people proves its validity. Every day we live in a wonderful laboratory where we can observe people and learn how to communicate better. Scientific research has proven that people, in terms of "how they act" universally, have similar characteristics. By learning these characteristics, we can increase communication and, therefore, increase our understanding of each other. The focus of this chapter is to define the parameters of what DISC is and what it is not. To define DISC, we will first define what DISC is NOT.

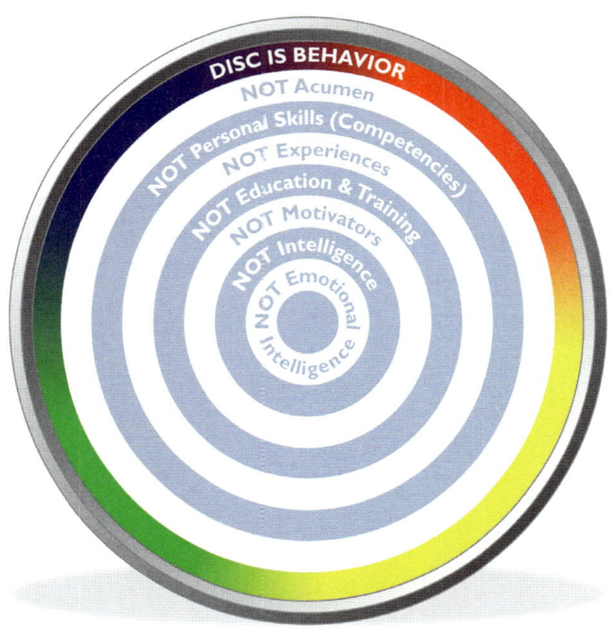

© 1993-2018 Target Training International, Ltd.

What DISC is NOT

1. **DISC is NOT a measurement of a person's EMOTIONAL INTELLIGENCE.**
   TTI has a validated assessment to measure Emotional Intelligence.

2. **DISC is NOT a measurement of a person's INTELLIGENCE.**
   Intelligence is very difficult to measure, if it can be measured at all. The DISC language gives us no indication of a person's intelligence. TTI acknowledges the importance of intelligence; however, DISC does not measure it.

3. **DISC is NOT an indicator of a person's MOTIVATORS.** Motivators are the why of a person's behavior! Why do we do what we do? Motivators are not observable. TTI has a validated assessment that measures a person's motivators based on Eduard Spranger's model.

4. **DISC does NOT measure EDUCATION & TRAINING.** Many employers base their selection and promotion on education and training. Again, this is outside the realm of the DISC model! TTI acknowledges the importance of education and training; however, DISC does not measure it.

© 1993-2018 Target Training International, Ltd.

5. **DISC is NOT a measurement of EXPERIENCE.**
   Experiences are one of the primary focuses of an employer indicating the details of a professional journey. TTI acknowledges the importance of experience; however, DISC does not measure it.

6. **DISC does NOT measure someone's PERSONAL SKILLS.**
   TTI has an assessment that does measure 25 job-related skills.

7. **DISC does NOT measure a person's ACUMEN.**
   To gain insights into a person's world view/acumen, TTI uses a validated assessment based on axiology.

DISC is none of the above; and yet, as we shall see, DISC has an inescapable bearing on all of the above. An awareness and proper application will affect all of the above areas. So, what is DISC and why is it so important?

DISC IS A UNIVERSAL LANGUAGE

DISC is the universal language of HOW you do what you do! Research has consistently shown that behavioral characteristics can be grouped together into four quadrants, or styles. People with similar styles tend to exhibit specific types of behavior common to that style—this is not acting. **A person's behavior is a necessary and integral part of who they are.** In other words, much of our behavior comes from "nature" (inherent), and much comes from "nurture" (our upbringing). The DISC model merely analyzes behavioral style; that is, a person's manner of doing things.

DISC IS AN OBSERVABLE LANGUAGE

Everything learned in the DISC language is totally observable. Often those who have taken the Style Insights® instrument are amazed at the accuracy of the information in the resulting report. Still, we are only looking at observable behavior. By applying the DISC language, we stand a greater chance of learning about a person's beliefs, skills and experience, education and training, and even intelligence; but the scope of the DISC language extends only to behavior.

The DISC model categorizes how we act — period! To extend it beyond its scope is to abuse a very powerful communication tool. Conversely, not to give it credence is to guarantee continued communication problems. In the building industry, tools allow for better and more efficient work. In the people business, which we all are in, the DISC language is a powerful tool for increasing communication effectiveness.

DISC IS A UNIVERSAL LANGUAGE

In every culture studied, the DISC model has been found to be valid. Reports are now available in many different languages. It is a universal language. **This is easily observed by asking a few questions:**

1. Have you encountered people of a certain cultural background who are expressive, animated, out going, verbal or "touchy-feely?"

2. Have you encountered people of a certain cultural background who seem to be cool, aloof, hard to read, introverted or analytical?

DISC IS A NEUTRAL LANGUAGE!

This point is so important that we are asking you to **repeat it three more times:**

1. **DISC IS A NEUTRAL LANGUAGE!**

2. **DISC IS A NEUTRAL LANGUAGE!**

3. **DISC IS A NEUTRAL LANGUAGE!**

Right and wrong has nothing to do with the DISC language. DISC is a NEUTRAL language only describing the differences in how people approach problems, other people, pace and procedures. Winners come from all styles of behavior.

Michael Jordan has a dominant behavior style on the basketball court, and people view him as a role model not because he is a dominant player, but because of his motivators.

Interestingly enough, the behavioral style people prefer is usually similar to their own — "Birds of a feather flock together." In extreme cases, we have seen heads of organizations not hire someone based on the applicant's behavioral style. Having nothing to do with a bona fide job selection process, the people making the hiring decisions simply did not like certain behavioral styles and wanted only people around who were like them. **This is called "behavioral blindness."** The thinking behind this point of view is narrow-minded, but can be changed by learning the DISC language.

"It's not what style you are; it's what you do with what you are."

–Bill J. Bonnstetter

A person's behavioral style is NOT what makes them good or bad, right or wrong. It is their beliefs and motivators only that have everything to do with good or bad, right or wrong.

© 1993-2018 Target Training International, Ltd.

Pursuing this further, why would a person mistreat another person? Only two answers are possible:

1. Lack of awareness of their behavior!

2. Awareness of their behavior, but not caring.

Lack of awareness of their behavior is simply solved by making the person aware of their behavior. If they then correct their behavior, you know they have a good set of beliefs. If they do not, then a motivators problem is present. Value conflicts almost always escalate in intensity, they do not go away.

A person with a high respect for human life and who values people may still err in the treatment of others but when aware of their behavior, will apologize and make it right.

When you observe the negative side of behavior, you are seeing motivators conflict, or a person under enough stress to overextend their behavioral strengths to the point where those strengths become a weakness. **A person's behavioral style is totally neutral being made positive or negative based on their basic beliefs.**

Your motivators will identify the topics you enjoy discussing, and your behavior will indicate how you want to communicate about the topic.

DISC IS A SILENT LANGUAGE

People do not like to be labeled! The DISC language, when understood and used properly, is a silent language. People well trained show their knowledge of the language in the way they interact with others. **Read the following conversation:**

Person A: "Oh, you're a High I!"

Person B: "I'm a what?"

Person A: "A High I! There are four styles, D, I, S, and C. You're a High I—talkative, chatty, fun."

Person B: "Okay! I guess! Now, what are the others?"

Unfortunately, this type of conversation occurs much too often. **Several points must be made:**

1. A person's behavior is the sum of the intensity of all four factors (DISC) and should not be labeled as any of the four.

2. Person B had no knowledge of the language, much like hearing a foreign language. Little communication was taking place.

3. DISC only looks at observable behavior. People are much more complex than the DISC model shows.

This reference manual gives the language basics for you to learn the language. As the language is learned, it should not be discussed with those who don't know the language. In other words, do not have the above conversation with people who do not know the styles. **Do not openly refer to people as high or low D, I, S or C.**

TTI SI's assessments generate personal behavioral reports based on 384 different configurations of DISC.

DISC LANGUAGE RULES

RULE #1
Use and discuss the DISC language only with those who know the language.

RULE #2
Exhibit your knowledge of the language by knowing your behavioral style, silently recognizing other people's styles and then adapting for greater communication.

RULE #3
Teach others the language in a setting where appropriate time is available for understanding.

OBJECTIVES REVISITED

The DISC language does NOT measure:

- Emotional Intelligence
- Intelligence
- Motivators
- Education & Training
- Experiences
- Personal Skills (Competencies)
- Acumen

The DISC language DOES measure:

- BEHAVIOR

The DISC language IS:

- An Observable Language
- A Universal Language
- A Neutral Language
- A Silent Language

AUTHORS' NOTE:

To properly use the language and teach it, we must understand the parameters of what DISC IS and what DISC is NOT. By remaining within the confines of the language, the user will be free to see that we do not need to extend the model beyond its scope. It is incredibly powerful within its truthful parameters. In a manner of speaking, we have set the boundaries of the DISC "pond" that we can now swim in and explore. In training and education of the DISC language, people must be made aware of these boundaries to prevent overextension of the model. Now that the "pond" has been defined, freedom is given to explore the far reaches of correct application of the language. Its power, within its proper parameters, is astounding.

© 1993-2018 Target Training International, Ltd.

THE VALUE OF LEARNING THE DISC LANGUAGE

Chapter Objective

To provide solid, logical reasons for the necessity of learning the language and to assist in the understanding of why behavior may need to be modified.

Chapter Contents

- Benefits of Learning the DISC Language
- The Importance of Endorsement
- What is Endorsement?
- Elements that Impact Endorsement
- Prerequisites to Learning the Language
- Steps to Greater Endorsement
- Motivation Principles (Providing a Climate of Motivation)
- Objectives Revisited

"You must first make an investment before you can expect a return. Investment always precedes return. Always."

–Judy Suiter

© 1993-2018 Target Training International, Ltd.

BENEFITS OF LEARNING THE DISC LANGUAGE

"The most effective way to gain the commitment and cooperation of others is to "get into their world" and "blend" with their behavioral style."

1. GAINING COMMITMENT AND COOPERATION

People tend to trust and work well with those people who seem like themselves. **The most effective way to gain the commitment and co-operation of others is to "get into their world" and "blend" with their behavioral style.** Observe a person's body language, "how" they act and interact with others. Notice clues in their work or living area. By applying the DISC language, you will immediately be able to adapt to their style.

2. BUILDING EFFECTIVE TEAMS

People tend to be too hard on each other, continually judging behavior; therefore, team development tends to be slowed or halted due to people problems. An awareness of behavioral differences has an immediate impact on communication, conflict resolution and motivation for the team. Investment always precedes return. Investment in training the team on the DISC language gets an immediate return in team development. **According to specialists in team development,**

most teams never make it to high performance without training in a behavioral model and commitment to using it from the top management down.

3. RESOLVING AND PREVENTING CONFLICT

Understanding style similarities and differences will be the first step in resolving and preventing conflict. By meeting the person's behavioral needs, you will be able to diffuse many problems before they even happen. People prefer to be managed a certain way. Some like structure and some don't. Some like to work with people and some prefer to work alone. "Shot in the dark" management does not work in the 21st century. **The DISC language, combined with TTI Success Insights® Reports, will teach you more about a person in 10 minutes than you can learn in a year without DISC.**

4. GAINING ENDORSEMENT

Other words for endorsement are "credibility" or "influence." Every interaction you have with a person either increases or decreases your endorsement. Have you ever met a person who won't stop talking and relates his whole life story to you? When you see that person coming, do you dread the interaction? If so, it is because their behavior has caused them to lose endorsement with you, and, therefore, that person does not get the benefit of your time. Conversely, a person who you can't wait to see daily has gained your endorsement and, therefore, is deserving of your time. **The DISC language allows you to "stack the deck" in your favor.** By knowing a person's behavioral style, you can immediately adapt to their style and gain endorsement.

© 1993-2018 Target Training International, Ltd.

5. THE IMPORTANCE OF ENDORSEMENT

Through emails, texting, Internet surfing, reading and other media, our brains are being bombarded with increasing quantities of information. Overwhelmed by this scale, scope, and complexity of information, the masses depend on others for advice and support. As a result, more and more personal decisions are being made based on the perception and credibility of individuals, organizations, and countries. **In other words, most individuals rely on the words and actions of other people, organizations, and countries for help in making their decisions.** To stand above all others, leaders must have endorsement. To gain endorsement, you must understand the DISC language.

6. WHAT IS ENDORSEMENT?

Endorsement is "the approval, backing, or support of a person or thing by means of the pledging of one's own assets." Assets individuals can pledge can include their contacts, money, reputation, time and energy.

- If an individual has endorsement, they will always be provided the resources necessary to maintain or improve their own lifestyle.
- If an organization has endorsement, it will always be provided the resources necessary to maintain or improve its own growth.
- If a nation has endorsement, it will always be provided the resources necessary to maintain or improve its standard of living.

Gaining endorsement takes time. It starts with understanding the DISC language. **DISC is a prerequisite for learning who you are and, more importantly, how others see you.** Being seen as credible starts with using the DISC language. It is essential for your success.

"DISC is a prerequisite for learning who you are and, more importantly, how others see you."

ELEMENTS THAT IMPACT ENDORSEMENT

Five factors impact the ability of a person, an organization, or a country to gain endorsement.

1. **Competence (Technical, Systems, and People)**

   Technical competence goes beyond just demonstrating expertise in specific fields. Are you keeping up with changes in the way people communicate? Are you able to communicate using a variety of technologies? **Knowing what to do is an important ingredient in gaining endorsement, but adding personal qualities of reliability and resourcefulness is integral in creating a climate that encourages endorsement.** Systems competence is more than the ability to get priorities accomplished using protocols and approved systems within organizations. Systems competence anticipates future trends and recognizes obstacles to success.

   Competence in this area requires that you know how the work flows and how to measure and assure progress toward the goal. Trying to achieve a goal but not knowing how to gain the endorsement of others has derailed many potential leaders.

   People competence requires that you become an astute "people reader." **To accomplish objectives through high performance teams and understand the unwritten rules of the organizational politics, you must first recognize the behavioral styles, and motivations of others.** You must then adapt your own style for effective interaction with them.

2. Communication Skills (Verbal, Written, Multimedia)

Verbal communication is a catalyst in gaining endorsement. **Controlling how you come across as you speak and listen impacts the level at which you are invited to participate.** Communicating your message effectively requires an understanding of your tone, your pace, and the vocabulary you use. It is easy for some people to intimidate verbally when all they were trying to do was exude confidence. Others may speak too slowly, too loudly, or with too many details, losing endorsement despite possibly being the right person with the best solution at the right time.

Written communication still has a substantial impact on endorsement despite the emerging new vocabulary used when sending text messages. Despite a seemingly growing tolerance for typos, poorly constructed sentences, and even poor graphic design, how your communication looks to the reader impacts the attention they will give you. **First impressions do matter.** If you believe your message is worthy of serious consideration, present it in way that is a match to your reader.

Multimedia presentation skills have added a whole new dimension to communicating effectively. **Competence and comfort in the use of technology and the Internet is no longer an option, but a requirement, if you expect to be credible with your audiences.** Gaining endorsement in a world flooded with conflicting and abundant messages requires that every individual be adept in front of a camera, behind a microphone, and on a keyboard.

© 1993-2018 Target Training International, Ltd.

3. The Use of Feedback

Feedback is the giving, receiving, and acting upon various forms of information from others. The ability to observe, listen, and communicate effectively in today's world is undeniably an essential ingredient in gaining endorsement. Asking for feedback is viewed as a sign of intelligent and informed leadership. **People feel validated and included when their opinions are sought and heard.** Receiving feedback is a sign of maturity and strength. Openness to suggestions and information from others and the ability to take advice and receive guidance without defensive, self-justifying behavior is a gift that just keeps giving.

Processing feedback is the ability to evaluate information objectively and understand its implications. It's a highly sought-after skill in the Information Age.

Acting upon feedback is the ability to apply what you've heard and learned to bring about change and improvement. It's the ability to turn data into action, delivering a desired outcome based on relevant incoming data.

Reporting back is a fundamental ingredient in gaining endorsement. Endorsement is given when you acknowledge the value of feedback. **Even if specific feedback isn't adopted into the operational plan, specific acknowledgement completes the cycle.** You leave the door open for ongoing feedback when you report back sincerely.

4. Appearance

Appearance affects endorsement more than many people want to admit. People notice the way you dress, the way you shake hands, the way you make your contact, the way you walk. Anything a person "sees" can positively or negatively affect your endorsement. Your body language must agree with the words you speak. Your clothing choices can communicate a message of authority, equality, superiority, or disdain. Possessing the ability to conduct yourself with civility and poise is vital. Knowing which behavioral style supports a desired type of endorsement is more than just a "Dress for Success" mentality. Appropriateness of clothing, body language, and manners can make or break your ability to gain endorsement.

5. Relative Position

A person's title implies endorsement and status by default. A certain cachet and prestige is attached to people. Endorsement for most individuals with a title is a gift to be lost. Endorsement sometimes can be gained by just hanging out with the right people. Proximity and access to power is another sign of endorsement. Endorsement comes with the territory in most positional situations. However, acceptance isn't conferred by title or location; it must be granted. Position is therefore relative — others must bestow their own endorsement on you by agreeing to follow or recommend you; but as many a leader has learned, endorsement can be fleeting when the one who carries it is shown to be unworthy. Endorsement by position requires the responsibility to watch the company you keep.

© 1993-2018 Target Training International, Ltd.

STEPS TO GREATER ENDORSEMENT

To achieve greater endorsement, it is important to remember that endorsement is gained over time... but can be lost in a moment. In *First Break All the Rules,* authors Curt Coffman and Marcus Buckingham observed that self-aware people are the building blocks of great teams. Knowing and understanding yourself allows you to plot your goals and make appropriate course corrections, thereby avoiding an unintentional or un-anticipated loss of endorsement. **By understanding the DISC language and using TTI assessments, you can achieve the following:**

Know Yourself

Awareness of your own behavioral tendencies provides the basic foundation for increased communication. Each of us has certain inherent behavioral tendencies that make us unique, and to be aware of these provides us with the knowledge to modify our behavior. For example, some people interrupt when others are talking. If the interrupter is aware of this, they can consciously learn to listen more and wait before responding. The DISC language, with TTI Success Insights reports, provides you with basic information on your behavioral tendencies. Knowledge is power — if you apply it.

Control Yourself

Once you have developed a heightened awareness of your behavior, you can begin to consciously control your behavior. For example, if you like to verbalize and you meet a person who also likes to verbalize, you can consciously choose to listen more and ask questions knowing that the other person will enjoy the opportunity to verbalize even more.

Know Others

Know yourself first, and then learn to recognize behavioral differences in others. This heightened awareness allows you to take the third crucial step of application of the DISC language, creating more win/win situations.

Do Something for Others

Before you can appeal to a person's basic needs, you must know their needs. By knowing their basic needs, you can intentionally do something that will appeal to their basic needs, giving you greater endorsement. For example, if you know a person likes punctuality (behavioral trait), then you can make sure you are on time for his/her meetings. Another example, if you know a person likes to direct, you can put him/her in charge of a project.

All of these actions can help you to achieve endorsements in specific situations and retain it in others.

© 1993-2018 Target Training International, Ltd.

PROVIDING A CLIMATE OF MOTIVATION

THERE ARE THREE TYPES OF MOTIVATION:

The first is FEAR MOTIVATION, a "Do it, or else we can replace you" approach. Fear motivation in negotiating is basically the "take it or leave it" approach. Fear motivation is the easiest form of motivation; however, it is a motivation based on intimidation and power. The person in power, unable to effectively create a climate for other types of beneficial motivation, resorts to fear tactics. "Take it or leave it" often gets results because the person will do what's asked for fear of loss. Fear motivation always results in anger and resentment against the person using the fear tactics. Sometimes the threat of loss or punishment must be used, but should only be used when all other methods have failed. Fear motivation is the lowest form of motivation.

The second form of motivation is INCENTIVE MOTIVATION. Incentive motivation is the "carrot" held out that causes the person to want to run the race. "If you do this, then we will do this for you." Incentive motivation can be very powerful and should be a part of a compensation plan; however, it is not the strongest or highest form of motivation.

The third type, CAUSAL MOTIVATION, is the highest form of motivation. Causal motivation occurs when an environment is created that causes people to WANT to work and be the best they can be. As the title implies, causal motivation is working toward a "cause". People will work their hardest for something or someone they believe in. To develop causal motivation, there must first be a cause in which your team can believe, and then an environment must be created that will cause the team to want to work toward the vision or goal. People in a causally motivated environment are unafraid to answer the question, "What's in it for me?" People naturally want a return on their investment of time, talent, money, etc. To expect people to work for your cause and your shareholder's cause without concern for their dreams and goals, is blindness to the way we are. People do things for their reasons, not yours.

The DISC language is the door to more effective communication. To not learn it is to behaviorally "shoot in the dark." Remember: Performance is directly proportional to endorsement.

© 1993-2018 Target Training International, Ltd.

PREREQUISITES TO LEARNING THE DISC LANGUAGE

1. You must want to identify your strengths.

2. You must be willing to look at possible limitations in your behavior.

3. You must have a desire to bring out the best in others, to win through a people focus.

In other words:

"If you want to change others, you first must change yourself."

–Judy Suiter

You may not agree with these discussion statements, so take time to discuss them with others and get their viewpoint on each statement.

OBJECTIVES REVISITED

Benefits of learning the DISC language:

- Gain commitment and cooperation
- Resolve and prevent conflict
- Gain endorsement

"Why is it that so many companies invest millions in buildings and equipment, and yet invest so little in the development of their most important asset — people? It would seem we should take care of the people first and then they will take care of the company."

–Judy Suiter

© 1993-2018 Target Training International, Ltd.

HISTORY OF THE LANGUAGE

Chapter Objective

To provide a partial history of the DISC language and its major contributors, thus establishing its validity.

Chapter Contents

- History of the Language
- Emergence of Target Training International, Ltd.
- Objectives Revisited

"Nothing is so powerful as an insight into human nature... What compulsions drive a man, what instincts dominate his action... If you know these things about a man, you can touch him at the core of his being."

–William Bernbach

© 1993-2018 Target Training International, Ltd.

HISTORY OF THE LANGUAGE

The DISC language is based on observable behavior. **The objective of this chapter is to show that long, long ago people were watching people and noting observable behavioral differences.** Throughout history, scientists and researchers have observed basic behavioral similarities, and now these have been validated by companies such as Target Training International, Ltd. Instruments have been developed to assist people in maximizing their personal potential and the potential of their human resources. The lineage of the DISC language, although not then called DISC, takes us all the way back to Empedocles in 444 B.C.

EMPEDOCLES, 490 - 430 B.C. Empedocles was the founder of the school of medicine in Sicily. He stated that everything was made up of four "roots" or elements. These were: earth, air, fire and water. These four elements, he stated, can be combined in an infinite number of ways, just as painters can create a great many pigments with only four different colors.

HIPPOCRATES, 460 - 370 B.C. Hippocrates was an observer of people. He noticed the effect of the climate and the terrain on the individual. Defining four types of climates, he categorized behavior and appearance for each climate, even suggesting which people would conquer others in battle, based on the environmental conditions in which they were raised. **Hippocrates believed the climate and terrain affected behavior and appearance.**

1. **CLIMATE & TERRAIN:** Mountainous country. Rugged. Elevated and well watered. Changes of season are very great.
   PEOPLE: Savage and ferocious in nature. Many shapes. War-like disposition.

2. **CLIMATE & TERRAIN:** Low-lying places. Meadows. Uses warm waters. More hot winds than cold, ill-ventilated. Seasons are fine.
   PEOPLE: Not of large stature. Not well-proportioned. Broad and fleshy. Black-haired. Not courageous. Less phlegmatic and more bilious. Emotional. Not given to much labor. Short-fused.

3. **CLIMATE & TERRAIN:** High country. Level. Well-watered. Windy.
   PEOPLE: Of large stature. Like one another. Gentle and unmanly.

4. **CLIMATE & TERRAIN:** Thin, bare soils, ill-watered. Great changes of seasons. Not fenced. Blasted by the winter and scorched by the sun.
   PEOPLE: Hard. Well-braced. Blonde. Haughty and self-willed.

According to Hippocrates, a seldom-changing climate brings forth indolence whereas a climate with great changes causes the mind to labor, bringing forth courage. Frequent excitement of the mind induces "wildness, extinguishing sociableness and mildness of disposition." Current research validates Hippocrates' thinking, in the sense that environment can cause change in behavior.

NOTE The TTI Graph I is called "RESPONSE TO THE ENVIRONMENT." For more information on graphs refer to Chapter 5.

© 1993-2018 Target Training International, Ltd.

Hippocrates pursued his thinking further. After identifying four types of climate and terrain and their effect on behavior, he identified four temperaments (sanguine, melancholic, choleric, phlegmatic) and associated them with four bodily fluids (blood, black bile, bile, mucous). He then made this statement, "I think the inhabitants of Europe to be more courageous than those of Asia." In the history of conflict throughout the world, does history prove him to be correct?

- **SANGUINE**
- **MELANCHOLIC**
- **CHOLERIC**
- **PHLEGMATIC**

GALEN, 129 A.D. - 200 A.D.
Galen, of Rome, spoke of four body fluids and their effect on behavior and temperament. They were: blood, yellow bile, black bile and phlegm. He also stated that our bodies act upon and are acted upon by warm, cold, dry and moist.

CARL G. JUNG, 1875 - 1961.
In 1921, Jung published *Psychological Types* in Germany. He identified and described four "types". These four types are primarily oriented by the four psychological functions: thinking, feeling, sensation and intuition. These four are further divided into two divisions that Jung called "libido" or "energy." These two divisions are "extroverted" and "introverted." Jung believed the extroverted and introverted types were categories over and above the other four functions.

WILLIAM MOULTON MARSTON, 1893 - 1947.
The major developer of the DISC language is Dr. William Moulton Marston. Born in Cliftondale, Massachusetts, in 1893, Dr. Marston was educated at Harvard University. He received three degrees from that institution, an A.B. in 1915, and LL.B in 1918 and a Ph.D. in 1921.

Most of Dr. Marston's adult life was spent as a teaching and consulting psychologist. Some of his assignments included lecturing at The

American University, Tufts, Columbia and New York University. A prolific writer, Dr. Marston was a contributor to the *American Journal of Psychology*, the *Encyclopedia Britannica*, and the *Encyclopedia of Psychology* all while authoring and/or co-authoring five books.

Marston's most well-known contribution was his success in lie detection. His work was done at Harvard University, and in 1938 his book, *The Lie Detector,* was published. Lie detectors, including Dr. Marston's, have been used by law enforcement and crime detection officials in various countries for many years. **Here are some facts that you will find interesting:**

- Marston is acknowledged by most as the inventor of the lie detector.
- He invented (1915) the systolic blood pressure test for deception (first published in 1917).
- He interviewed 4200 criminals in Texas penitentiaries and found only three of them who believed themselves to be dishonest.
- A committee of prominent psychologists gave Marston's deception test a 97 percent reliable rating.
- Marston stated that when the lie detector has convinced a criminal (consciously or subconsciously) that he can no longer lie, it becomes easy to break down that criminal's habits of lying and build up, instead, mental habits of telling the truth.
- Marston stated the ultimate use of the lie detector was not for crime detection but for crime elimination by changing criminals into honest individuals.
- Marston worked on the Carl Jung Reaction Time Test and proved it was not reliable for determining deception. This proves that Marston was well aware of Carl Jung's work that is the foundation of the Myers-Briggs test. So the question remains, why Marston never mentioned Carl Jung's work in his book *Emotions of Normal People*.

© 1993-2018 Target Training International, Ltd.

- Marston said, "Only the truth can bring about a real emotional adjustment."
- The lie detector test offered a new tool to consulting psychologists in making personality adjustments.
- Marston wrote articles on how to apply the lie detector test to marital, social and personality adjustments.

Marston was ahead of the times, and his book *Emotions of Normal People* must have been written for professional psychologists, as his other writings are easy to read and understand. Perhaps he had so much knowledge that his profession was not ready for his ideas.

Every day TTI Value Added Associates are touching the lives of people in a way that was only a dream for Marston in 1915.

Marston continued his career as a consulting psychologist; but using the pen name of Charles Moulton, he spent most of his time during the last five years of his life as the originator, writer and producer of *Wonder Woman.* First published in book form, this endeavor turned out to be a most successful and enduring comic strip. After having been stricken with polio in 1944, Dr. Marston was partially paralyzed until his death at age 53 in 1947.

In 1928 he published a book, *Emotions of Normal People,* in which he described the theory we use today. **He viewed people as behaving along two axes with their actions tending to be active or passive depending upon the individual's perception of the environment as either antagonistic or favorable.**

Dr. Marston believed that people tend to learn a self-concept, which is basically in accord with one of the four factors. It is possible, therefore, using Marston's theory, to apply the powers of scientific observation to behavior and to be objective and descriptive rather than subjective and judgmental.

Marston did not invent the DISC behavioral measurement system, nor did he foresee the potential applications of his work. In the last 100 years since Marston published his research findings and observations, behavioral research has modified his ideas considerably. To the modern scientist, much of Marston's work may seem stilted and antiquated. Yet, the importance of his contribution in dividing human behavior into four distinct categories and using measurements of the strength of these responses as a means to predict human behavior remains undiminished.

By placing these axes at right angles, four quadrants were formed with each circumscribing a behavioral pattern.

1. **Dominance (D)**
   Produces activity in an antagonistic environment.

2. **Influence (I)**
   Produces activity in a favorable environment.

3. **Steadiness (S)**
   Produces passivity in a favorable environment.

4. **Compliance (C)**
   Produces passivity in an antagonistic environment.

© 1993-2018 Target Training International, Ltd.

Despite the contributions made to the field of behavioral research since Marston, the modern categories of DISC (Dominance, Influence, Steadiness and Compliance) owe much to his research. Thus it is helpful in understanding the working of the DISC system to keep Marston's categories and their original meaning in mind. The premise of the modern day DISC system is that all people demonstrate some behavior in each dimension. **The four dimensions used as the basis for the Style Insights instrument (and its various forms and applications) fall into the following categories:**

DOMINANCE - Problems and Challenges
How you approach and respond to problems and challenges and exercise power.

INFLUENCE - People and Contacts
How you interact with and attempt to influence others to your point of view.

STEADINESS - Pace and Consistency
How you respond to change, variation and pace of your environment.

COMPLIANCE - Procedure and Constraints
How you respond to rules and procedures set by others and to authority.

The DISC measurement system analyzes all of these factors and reveals one's strengths and weaknesses, one's actual behavior and tendencies toward certain behavior. Behavioral research suggests that the most effective people are those who understand themselves and others. The more one understands personal strengths and weaknesses coupled with the ability to identify and understand the strengths and weaknesses of others, the better one will be able to develop strategies to meet the demands of the environment. The result will be success on the job, at home or in society at large.

WALTER V. CLARKE, 1905 - 1978. Walter Clarke was the first person to build a psychological device based on the Marston theory. His instrument is called the "Activity Vector Analysis." Some of Clarke's original associates subsequently left his company, further refining the format as they created their own "adjective check-list forms."

The following individuals and companies have contributed to the DISC model:

1960s

- J.P. Cleaver
- Leo McManus

1970s

- Bill J. Bonnstetter
- John Geier

1980s

- Michael O'Conner
- Judy Suiter
- Target Training International, Ltd.

1990s

- Dr. David Warburton

THE EMERGENCE OF TARGET TRAINING INTERNATIONAL, LTD.

Target Training International, Ltd. (TTI), under the direction of Bill J. Bonnstetter, has staged a blistering pace in the innovation and development of the DISC language for over 30 years. Combined with continuing, intensive research validation, TTI has become the clear leader in product development and research in the area of behavior and motivators. **Listed below is the track record of TTI development:**

1980

- Validates a correlation between the appearance of a person's premises (personal or business) and their behavioral style.

1981

- Validates that salespeople tend to sell to styles similar to their own and buyers tend to buy from salespeople with a similar style to the buyer.
- Validates that if the salesperson adapts to the style of the buyer, sales will increase.
- Develops the "Buyer Profile Action Plan" to assist salespeople of all fields in recognizing and "blending" their styles.

1984

- First company to develop and introduce computerized and personalized reports on the DISC model.
- Identifies Graph III as not providing valid information when there is a significant disparity between Graphs I and II.
- Develops the most accurate validated truck driver selection program in the world. The program is based on the DISC model (see Page 341).

© 1993-2018 Target Training International, Ltd.

1985

- Introduces personalized software producing reports in sales and executive versions.

1986

- The reading level on the instrument is lowered to a ninth grade level.
- Introduces Sales Profile, Family Talk, Personal Insights, and Successful Career Planning reports.

1987

- Team Building version was introduced.

1988

- The introduction of Job Analysis and Interviewing Insights versions.

1990

- The introduction of the Behavioral Factor Indicator.
- Trademark granted for Managing for Success® software.

1991

- The introduction of the Graph Reader Program, Personal Interests, Attitudes and Values version.
- Clearly validates the universal application of the DISC language worldwide.
- Develops and introduces Customer Service version, the Work Environment Analysis and the Executive version.

1992

- Developed and patented the Success Performance Index, the first software on the market to merge behavior and motivators into one report.
- Funds an outside study by Dr. David Warburton and Judy Suiter to investigate the effects of Graph I and Graph II disparity on job satisfaction, mental health, stress and substance abuse.
- The introduction of Communicating with Style, Healthcare Insights, Time P.L.U.S., and education software for administrators, teachers and students.
- Creates 60-section, Success Insights Wheel®

1993

- Translates reports and assessments into Finnish, Swedish, German, Dutch, French, Italian, Spanish and Polish.
- First to design and introduce DISC software that allows you to select a multi-lingual response form and a multi-lingual report.

1994

- Mentoring program introduced.

1995

- Sales Strategy Index™ introduced to the marketplace.

1996

- New 10,000 square foot office building was built to accommodate corporate headquarters.
- Patent granted for the Employee Success Predictive System.

1998

- Research comparing US and German top sales performers using both behaviors and motivators.

1999

- Bill Bonnstetter authors *If I Knew Then What I Know Now,* published by Forbes.
- Internet Delivery Service® (IDS) created for sending and receiving assessments plus distributing the results; patent applied for.

2000

- Trademark granted for bicycle graphic depicting Success Insights Wheel®.

2001

- Introduced Interactive Reports and Blueprint for Success.
- Success Insights spun off as a separate, international division of TTI.

2002

- Introduction of Axiology.
- TriMetrix® System developed, coauthored with William Brooks.
- Created e-learning courses.

2003

- Drs. Peter Klassen and Russell Watson commissioned to perform validity studies on the new instruments.
- Validated that some of the words used on the questionnaire were no longer valid, and new words that were valid were added leading to new questionnaires: Style Insights® and Motivation Insights®.
- Updated logo and report layout.
- ODsurveys Plus® introduced.

2004

- IDS generates one report every 10.7 seconds.
- Developed new research software, TTI Success Insights Collection®.
- Instruments translated into 23 languages and sold in 50 countries.
- Celebrates 20th anniversary with a record attendance at the Winter Winners' Conference.
- Completed research study for predicting superior performance in a very specific job for a major employer, which showed the system to be 91% predictable classifying people into superior performer or inferior performer categories.

2005

- Study of financial planners completed.
- Additional office and warehouse facilities expanded to over 17,000 square feet.
- Talent Management Plus™ software developed for job matching.

2006

- New validity study re-validated behavior and motivators as well as the correlation between them.
- TQ® and the Personal Talent Skills Inventory® were introduced.

2007

- Patent granted for the Internet Delivery Service® (IDS).
- Major IDS update released.
- Patent granted for Performance DNA benchmarking process.
- Leadership Development Program revised for major distribution.

2008

- Managing Performance Priorities® (MPP) software released, enabling employees and managers to stay connected and perform well as a team.
- Performance DNA assessment reintroduced.
- Solutions 4 Hiring® becomes a division of TTI Performance Systems, Ltd.
- Offices are expanded with the purchase of a 20,000 square foot building.
- Released the TTI Emotional Quotient™ (EQ) assessment and report.

2009

- TTI University Online opened, offering online e-Learning courses in a unique module format.
- TTI University Training Center opened.
- Released a white paper on "Selecting Superior Performers Under the Law".
- Released engineering student study proving correlations between behavioral attributes, student success and student retention.
- TTI Metrics system created to measure ROI
- Distributor base grows to over 7,000 consultants, coaches and trainers.
- TTI grows to provide 30+ assessments, development and performance management tools in 30 languages and 75 countries.

2010

- TTI Strategic Business Services established, partnering with Value Added Associates by providing start-to-finish expertise and service to large clients.
- Serial entrepreneur research conducted to identify the attributes of successful entrepreneurs.
- Introduced the TTI Professional Development Series for boosting team communications.

- Social Media Guide book produced.
- Released an updated TTI Emotional Quotient™ assessment and report and correlations.
- Partnered with the Kern Family Foundation to conduct research aimed at developing more entrepreneurial-minded engineers and improving student retention.
- Created www.ttiassessments.com website.

2011

- Assessments interact with each other.
- Validated responding 1-2-3-4 is better than most/least.
- Acumen Report created.
- Re-normed behavioral and motivators assessments.
- Adverse impact study was completed on the behavioral instrument

2012

- Analyzed 1-2-3-4 responses on the behavioral assessment and confirmed those responses using EEG brain scans.
- Reprinted *Emotions of Normal People*.
- Debriefing guides and technical reports were published.
- Updated the manual for motivators.
- Updated TTI's Emotional Quotient assessment and report.
- Articles authored by Ron & Bill Bonnstetter appeared in several national publications: *The Harvard Business Review, Education Weekly, Washington Post, Fortune.*
- Nominated for the Edison Award.
- Research topics included student selection for residency program in surgery; environmental students.
- Behavior and motivators assessments combined to produce integrated report.
- Applied for patent for the process of validating ipsative assessments.
- *Acumen Capacity Index Manual* was written.

© 1993-2018 Target Training International, Ltd.

2013

- Reprinted *Types of Men.*
- Bill Bonnstetter and Ashley Bowers wrote *Talent Unknown.*
- Updated *The Universal Language DISC* reference manual.
- Lisa Aldisert's dissertation focused on leadership using TTI SI assessments.
- National Research Council's 21st century skills matched to TTI SI's DNA skills assessment.

2015

- U.S. Brain Patent awarded.

2016

- Canadian Brain Patent awarded.
- TTI Success Insights named "Best Place to Work."
- Bill J. Bonnstetter passed away.

TTI SUCCESS INSIGHTS IN THE FUTURE

TTI SI has done and will continue to do research on the correlations between behavior, motivators, personal skills, emotional quotient, acumen and the brain. To see past accomplishments and to follow our current research, visit www.ttisi.com. Concentration on research and validation of the assessments will keep TTI on the leading edge in its field.

OBJECTIVES REVISITED

Importance of the History:

- People have observed others as early as 444 B.C.
- DISC is based on observable behavior.
- Marston describes the theory we use today.
- Clarke was the first to develop an instrument.
- Bill J. Bonnstetter validated communication style.

AUTHORS' NOTE:

To record all the people who have made contributions to the field of human behavior would require volumes of research beyond the scope of this book. This chapter shows that as early as 400 B.C., people were being observed and similarities were being recorded. Those who have made contributions specifically to the DISC language have been mentioned. TTI is extensively chronicled due to their emergence in the field as the pacesetter. The reader should have a better appreciation of the history of DISC and those who have contributed to its development.

"To avoid criticism, do nothing, say nothing, be nothing."

–Elbert Hubbard

© 1993-2018 Target Training International, Ltd.

DEFINING & LEARNING THE LANGUAGE

Chapter Objective

To recognize the observable characteristics of the four pure behavioral styles, High D, I, S and C, and to provide the solid foundation for proper, effective usage of the language.

Chapter Contents

- Introduction
- Pure Behavioral Styles
- Research Proof
- The High D
- The High I
- The High S
- The High C
- Objectives Revisited

"In order to understand our relationships with other people, we must first understand ourselves."

–Bill J. Bonnstetter

© 1993-2018 Target Training International, Ltd.

INTRODUCTION

Albert Einstein stated, "Everything should be reduced to its simplest form, but not simpler." Such is the purpose of this chapter, to provide the reader with clear definitions of the DISC language, allowing you to "compartmentalize" four distinct behavioral styles in your mind:

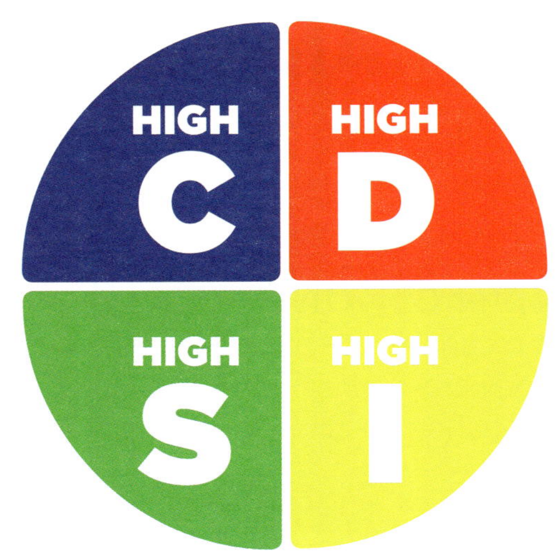

"All people exhibit all four behavioral factors in varying degrees of intensity."

-W.M. Marston

Once these four styles have been mastered, by opening your "behavioral eyes," you will begin to see others differently and appreciate those differences. **The ability to adapt your behavior to each of the styles will increase the effectiveness of communication allowing for greater understanding and appreciation of our similarities and differences.**

When discussing human behavior, the issue of "right" versus "wrong" is a non-issue. **The "D" is not better than the "I," nor is the "S" better than the "C."** Each behavioral style brings strengths and weaknesses to the situation. Each can be a winner, and the team needs all four styles to win. Right and wrong issues relate to ethics, which is not in the realm of the DISC language.

DISC is a NEUTRAL language!

PURE BEHAVIORAL STYLES

In this chapter, pure behavioral styles are being defined. Definition: **A style is "pure" if only one point is above the energy line.** For more information on graph reading refer to Chapter 5.

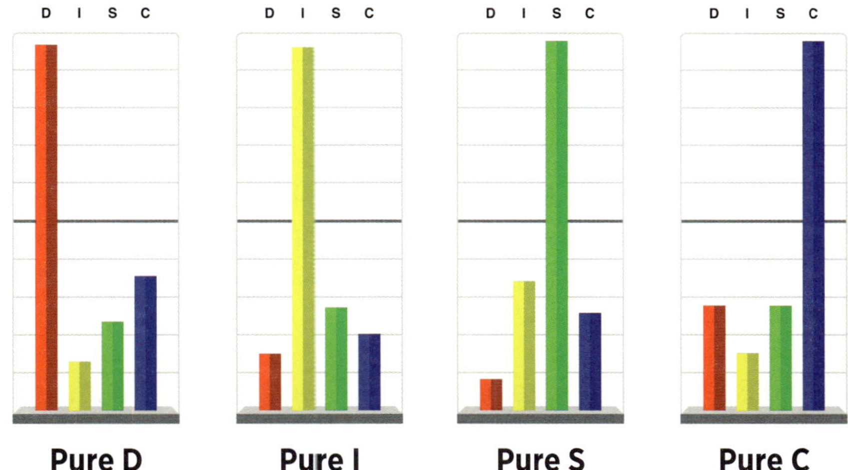

Pure D **Pure I** **Pure S** **Pure C**

© 1993-2018 Target Training International, Ltd.

Pure behavioral styles represent a very small percentage of the population, according to recent research by TTI.

- **Pure High D less than 1% of the population**
- **Pure High I about 2% of the population**
- **Pure High S about 0.5% of the population**
- **Pure High C about 0.25% of the population**

The behavior of most of the population is a combination of two or more styles; therefore, to refer to someone merely as a High D is useful in describing their core behavior only. **Definition: A "Core" style is the factor highest above the energy line.** The language should be mastered to see and understand the relationship of four factors. Step 1 of learning the DISC language is to learn the pure styles and be able to recognize a person's core behavior and adapt accordingly.

By learning the pure DISC language, you will have a strong foundation to build on to understand the interrelationships of the four factors of the language. **You are learning a new language of behavior, which, if learned properly, will open your "behavioral eyes" to a much greater understanding of those around you.**

Since 1984, TTI's software has analyzed both Graph I and II to generate a report. For each graph, the primary and secondary dimensions are identified. The primary is always the dimension farthest from the midline. The primary can be above or below the midline. The secondary is the next farthest from the midline and can be either above or below. Sometimes both the primary and secondary are above the midline. By using the printed percentages on the bottom of the graph, you can always mathematically determine the primary and secondary dimensions.

D
Demanding
Egocentric
Driving
Ambitious
Pioneering
Strong-Willed
Forceful
Determined
Aggressive
Competitive
Decisive
Venturesome
Inquisitive
Responsible

I
Effusive
Inspiring
Magnetic
Political
Enthusiastic
Demonstrative
Persuasive
Warm
Convincing
Polished
Poised
Optimistic
Trusting
Sociable

S
Phlegmatic
Relaxed
Resistant to Change
Nondemonstrative
Passive
Patient
Possessive
Predictable
Consistent
Deliberate
Steady
Stable

C
Evasive
Worrisome
Careful
Dependent
Cautious
Conventional
Exacting
Neat
Systemic
Diplomatic
Accurate
Tactful
Open-Minded
Balanced Judgment

© 1993-2018 Target Training International, Ltd.

The DISC language is based on OBSERVABLE behavior.
When we are observing a person, we can easily apply the DISC language if we know the characteristics of each of the four factors. Each person has one PRIMARY behavioral style. As we interact with people on a daily basis, without using an instrument, we can recognize the PRIMARY style and adapt accordingly. Advanced users of the language will be able to recognize the interrelationships of the four factors and greatly increase communication and understanding.

THE HIGH D

The dominant director, the driver, the D
Unconquerable, demanding, aggressive, free
Brave, decisive, competitive, tough
Up to the task, direct, sometimes rough!

Quick to the draw, flip with the lip
You'll get it direct, straight from the hip
They'll climb any mountain, nothing's too high
They aim to succeed, whatever they try!

Results is the focus, press on to new heights
Along the way, expect a few fights
Don't take it personal, they just speak their mind
So pick up the pace, or get left behind!

You may smirk a little when you hear them rant
Of all that they'll win if their wish you grant
Give them a challenge that's brave and bold
Stand back and watch as they "bring home
the gold"!

–Randy Widrick

© 1993-2018 Target Training International, Ltd.

THE HIGH D
DOMINANT, DRIVER, CHOLERIC

DESCRIPTORS

Direct	Domineering	Demanding
Daring	Aggressive	Impatient
Forceful	Strong Ego	Authoritative
Innovative	Strength	Adventuresome
Blunt	Goal-Oriented	Responsible
Decisive	Problem Solver	Risk-Taker
Competitive	Quick	Power
Strong-Willed	Challenge-Oriented	Self-Starter
Bold	Persistent	
Results-Oriented	Inquisitive	

FAMOUS HIGH D's

- Barbara Walters, TV news anchor
- Michael Jordan, former basketball player extraordinaire
- Cher, entertainer
- Hillary Clinton, Secretary of State
- Charles Barkley, former basketball player
- Madonna, entertainer
- John McEnroe, tennis player
- Fidel Castro
- Robert DeNiro, actor
- Donald Trump
- Henry Ford
- General Patton
- Mark Cuban
- Vince Lombardi
- Samantha Jones, character on *Sex in the City*
- David Letterman
- Captain Kirk, character on *Star Trek*

BARBARA WALTERS

When any celebrity agrees to do the interview with Barbara Walters, one thing is sure — the tough questions will get asked. Barbara Walters is unafraid of asking the hard personal questions. Her directness has taken her to the peak of her industry. Most celebrities consider it a career milestone to be featured on a Barbara Walters' special.

MICHAEL JORDAN

Is there any mountain in the annals of basketball history that Michael Jordan has not conquered? Anytime an opponent burned Air Jordan on one end of the court, you could easily predict that person would immediately see the bottom of Jordan's Nikes on the other end of the court, as the ball went smashing through the hoop. In an issue of *Time Magazine*, the press covered Michael Jordan's early retirement. Jordan said, "When I lose the sense of motivation and the sense to prove something as a basketball player, it's time to step down."

THE EMOTION OF THE D FACTOR: ANGER

Each of the four factors has an emotion linked to it. The emotion of the D factor is anger. A High D will tend to be quick to anger and have a short fuse. A person, whose D factor is low, will be slow to anger and have a long fuse. The higher the D, the shorter the fuse. By observing the intensity of the D's emotion of anger, the D factor can be quickly assessed as high or low when observing someone.

© 1993-2018 Target Training International, Ltd.

OUTSTANDING CHARACTERISTICS OF THE HIGH D

NEED TO DIRECT

High D's have an inherent need to direct. As extroverted people, High D's will usually give their opinion in clear, specific language. If the group or discussion is moving a little slowly, expect the High D to step up to the plate and push the group along. Given the authority and responsibility, High D's can take you to new heights that previously were considered impossible.

CHALLENGE

If a job loses challenge, expect the High D to become somewhat bored. High D's must have a continual challenge — a mountain to climb! If there is no challenge, the High D will create one. When basketball no longer offered a challenge to Michael Jordan, he left the game.

DESIRE TO WIN

Living is winning. The High D is driven to win, both in the corporate world, as well as on the golf course. Vince Lombardi's famous quote, "Winning isn't everything, it's the ONLY thing," is representative of the High D's approach to each situation. Other profiles desire to win but for different reasons. The High D's desire to win is related to being on top of the heap, proving it can be done.

DIRECT COMMUNICATION

In dealing with people, High D's will be direct and to the point. The flowery words will usually not be present as they say what they think. High D's may unintentionally come across as being too blunt to some other behavioral styles. High D's will take issue if they disagree, even heatedly, but will seldom hold a grudge. After they have spoken their mind, they tend to forget about it—no harm done. The High D is task-oriented, looking for results.

HIGH RISK

The thrill of victory; the agony of defeat. The High D can be a high risk-taker, perhaps not considering the consequences. Not intentionally trying to hurt others, the High D does not consider failure as an option. Because of the high risk factor, the D needs others to supply enough facts and data to make sure the jump is a relatively safe one. Often, the high risk factor allows the High D to take you "where no man has gone before."

The High D has the ability to juggle many balls at one time, but may lose interest in a project if the challenge ceases. Interested in the new, the unusual, and the adventurous, High D's will usually have a wide range of interests and be willing to try their hand at anything.

By utilizing the descriptors on Page 58, the famous examples and the outstanding characteristics, you should be beginning to develop a clear understanding of the High D behavioral style. The DISC language is based on observable behavior. By opening your "behavioral eyes," you will begin to notice the High D's around you.

© 1993-2018 Target Training International, Ltd.

PEOPLE READING: RECOGNIZING THE HIGH D

Understanding that the DISC language interprets how we act, behavioral observation has proven that the following attributes usually apply to the High D behavioral style. **Employ these cues to assist in quick recognition of the High D.**

QUICK HIGH D OBSERVABLE INDICATORS

Extroverted/Introverted:	Extroverted
People or Task-Oriented:	Task
More Direct or Indirect:	Direct
Overextensions:	Impatient
Geared to/Looking for:	Results/Efficiency
High D emotion:	Anger/Short fuse
Low D emotion:	Slow to anger/Long fuse

OBSERVABLE BEHAVIOR: HOW HIGH D's ACT

Buy:	Quick decision makers; new and unique products.
Change:	Love change.
Conflict response:	Fight back.
Drive:	Fast, always somewhere to get to in a hurry.

Decorate an office:	Status conscious, large desk, efficiency.
Email writing:	Direct, to the point. Results-oriented.
Gesture:	A lot of hand movement when talking, big gestures.
Goal setting:	Sets many goals, usually high risk and not written down.
Organization:	Efficient, not neat.
Read:	Executive book summaries.
Risk factor:	High risk-taker.
Rules:	May tend to break the rules. The end justifies the means.
Stand:	Forward leaning.
Stress relief:	Physical activity, preferably of a competitive nature.
Talk on the phone:	Little chitchat. To the point. Results.
Talk to others:	Direct. While others are talking may do other activities, as well as interrupt or jump to their next response.
Walk:	Fast, always going somewhere.

© 1993-2018 Target Training International, Ltd.

Refer often to these cues, until you have a clear picture of the High D style. Any one of these observable cues can instantly tell you that you are relating to a High D. **You must invest the time learning the language to use it effectively.**

NOTE **PURE STYLES are being described in this section! The High D style is definitely affected by the intensity of the I, S, and C response. Effective language learning will give you the skills to recognize the effect of the other factors and adapt accordingly.**

THE VALUE OF THE HIGH D TO THE TEAM

1. **Bottom-line Organizer**
2. **Self-starter**
3. **Forward Looking**
4. **Places High Value on Time**
5. **Challenge-oriented**
6. **Competitive**
7. **Initiates Activity**
8. **Challenges the Status Quo**
9. **Innovative**
10. **Tenacious**

1. **Bottom Line Organizer**

   High D's are results-oriented. If given the authority, they will cut through all the needless steps and get the job done. Many of the paper-pushing activities done in organizations add nothing to the value of the product turned out. Give the High D the job, set broad boundaries and watch it happen.

2. **Self-starter**

   Given the task, the responsibility and the authority, High D's will work long hours to show you they can make it happen. No need to push them to get them going.

3. **Forward Looking**

   High D's focus on the possibilities of what can happen. Obstacles represent a challenge to be overcome, not a reason to stop. Expect them to go for the GOLD.

4. **Places High Value on Time**

   High D's are driven for efficiency: quicker, faster, better. How much can be accomplished in the least amount of time. They will speed up others and the process, but expect other styles to resist the change and fast pace of High D's.

© 1993-2018 Target Training International, Ltd.

5. Challenge Oriented

A challenge is not an option for High D's. They MUST have a challenge. If there is a challenge, a High D will take it on. Regardless of how impossible, they will focus all their energies on making it happen. If the High D does not have a challenge they will create one.

6. Competitive

Winning is everything. A competitive situation, sales competition, family competition and sports competition all motivate the High D to perform even better.

7. Initiates Activity

The High D in sports is saying, "Give me the ball." Not one to sit around and discuss options, the High D wants to (and will) initiate activity to get desired results.

8. Challenges the Status Quo

Unconcerned with the "way we've always done it," the High D will reinvent the old way focusing on one goal — results. High D's will "rock the boat" in their quest for results and will find more efficient ways to get the job done.

9. Innovative

A fast mover, the High D's focus on efficiency causes them to be constantly looking for shortcuts to get the desired results.

10. Tenacious

Driven to results, challenges, and winning, the High D is forceful and direct. Anything other than winning is obviously losing, so the High D will be tenacious in overcoming obstacles to reach a goal.

EXAMPLE **Captain Kirk, on *Star Trek*, altered the Star Fleet computer program in the NO WIN SITUATION and became the only cadet to ever win the NO WIN. When asked why he altered the computer program he stated, "I don't believe in no win situations."**

It's very easy to see the value of High D's to the team. **Their fast pace, results-oriented approach is often misunderstood; but with the proper understanding and management, the High D is a tremendous person to have around.** Not having or wanting a High D on the team puts the team at a great disadvantage.

Based on the verbiage and descriptors given to this point, make a list of your associates who have a High D in their profile.

IDEAL ENVIRONMENT FOR THE HIGH D

- Freedom from controls, supervision and details.
- Evaluation based on results, not process or method.
- An innovative and futuristic-oriented environment.
- Non-routine work with challenge and opportunity.
- A forum for them to express their ideas and viewpoints.

COMMUNICATING WITH THE HIGH D

Be clear, specific and to the point.
Don't ramble on or waste their time.

Stick to business.
Don't try to build personal relationships or chitchat.

Come prepared with all requirements, objectives and support material in a well-organized package.
Don't forget or lose things, be unprepared, disorganized or messy.

Present the facts logically; plan your presentation efficiently.
Don't leave loopholes or cloudy issues if you don't want to be zapped!

Ask specific (preferably "What?") questions.
Don't ask rhetorical or useless questions.

Provide alternatives and choices for making their own decisions.
Don't come with the decision made or make it for them.

Provide facts and figures about probability of success or the effectiveness of options.
Don't speculate wildly or offer guarantees and assurances where there is a risk in meeting them.

If you disagree, take issue with the facts.
Don't take issue with the High D personally.

Provide a win/win opportunity.
Don't force the High D into a losing situation.

Motivate and persuade by referring to results.
Don't try to convince by personal means.

Support and maintain.
Don't direct or order.

ENGAGING THE HIGH D

THE HIGH D WANTS:

- To control their own destiny and the destiny of others.
- The power and authority to achieve results.
- Prestige, position and titles.
- An expensive vehicle, to obtain money, and material things that indicate success.
- An opportunity for rapid advancement.
- To maintain their focus on the bottom line.
- To follow communication tips listed above, always.
- Freedom from controls, supervision and details.
- Efficiency in people and equipment.
- New and varied experiences.
- Challenges with each task.
- A forum for verbalizing.

© 1993-2018 Target Training International, Ltd.

MANAGING THE HIGH D

- Clearly explain results expected.
- Negotiate commitments one-on-one.
- Define rules.
- Confront face-to-face in all disagreements.
- Provide challenging assignments.
- Show them the benefits of understanding and being easier on people.
- Assist them in learning to pace self and relax.
- Show them the benefits of understanding teamwork and participation.
- Show them the benefits of listening skills.
- Make sure their emotional intensity fits the situation.
- Plan advancement and a career path.

Refer to your list of those whom you believe to be High D's. Carefully examine your communication strategies and motivation techniques to determine if there are areas in which you are mismanaging the High D. High D's will always be High D's. **Your task is to bring out the best in them and to channel those energies to a win/win situation for all of the people involved.**

POSSIBLE LIMITATIONS OF THE HIGH D

The limitations listed for the High D are tendencies for the Pure High D, which represent a very small percentage of the population. Each of these tendencies are altered by the position of the I, S, and C factors and by the individual's motivators.

THE HIGH D MAY:

- Overstep authority.
- Be too direct.
- Be impatient with others.
- Be argumentative.
- Not listen well; be a one-way communicator.
- Take on too many tasks.
- Push people rather than lead them.
- Lack tact and diplomacy.
- Focus too heavily on task.

The possible limitations of the High D are the opportunities for growth. The very strengths of the D overused can become weaknesses. The task is to make the High D aware of his/her strengths and weaknesses and train him/her to cognitively make the correct choices needed for everyone to win.

© 1993-2018 Target Training International, Ltd.

HIGH D APPLICATION

To begin to use the language of the High D defined in this chapter, use the following steps:

1. Review the chapter for 15 minutes each day for 3 weeks cementing the High D characteristics in your mind.

2. Memorize the High D descriptors.

3. Apply the descriptors above and the High D characteristics in this chapter to those whom you contact regularly. Make a list of those whom you believe, by observation, to have a High D in their profile.

4. Refer often to Page 68 and adapt your style for better communication and understanding with the High D's you know.

5. As you meet new people, using the descriptors above, notice those who may be High D's and adapt your behavior for greater communication.

6. Stand back and watch the results! You'll be amazed at your effectiveness by using DISC, the Universal Language.

"If you invest the pennies from your pocket into your mind, your mind will fill your pocket!"

-Tom Hopkins

THE HIGH I

Influencer, expressive, sanguine, the I
Life's full of hope, the limit's the sky
Enthusiastic, fun, trusting, charming
Confident, optimistic, popular, disarming.

Words smooth as cream as they talk to you
Winning you over to their point of view
A sparkling eye, a smile that's bright
In the dark of night, the I sees the light.

A people person with a need to be liked
Inspiring the team to continue the fight
Talking a lot while getting work done
Don't worry a bit, work should be fun.

A joke or two, expect a high five
The High I adds humor, keeps things alive
Turn them loose and watch what's done.
The team is inspired to work as ONE.

–Randy Widrick

© 1993-2018 Target Training International, Ltd.

THE HIGH I
INFLUENCER, EXPRESSIVE, SANGUINE

DESCRIPTORS

Enthusiastic
Trusting
Charming
Popular
Gregarious
Influential
Confident
Open-Minded
Persuasive
Affable
Convincing
Inspiring
Spontaneous
Sociable
Effusive
Talkative
Emotional
Generous
Personable
Optimistic
Self-Promoting
Poised
Good Mixer

FAMOUS HIGH I's

- Arnold Palmer, professional golfer
- Former President Bill Clinton
- Comic characters of Steve Martin
- Eddie Murphy, actor comedian
- Andre Agassi, professional tennis player
- Will Smith, actor musician
- Will Farrell, actor comedian
- George Lopez, actor comedian
- Wayne Brady, actor
- Carrie Bradshaw, character from *Sex in the City*
- Jay Leno, comedian
- Ellen De Generes, comedienne
- Jim Carey, actor comedian

ARNOLD PALMER

Arnold Palmer is a people person. He values not only the recognition and friendship of other performers, but the adulation of an adoring public. His goal is not only to win tournaments, but also to win and maintain friendships. Palmer is a charger who can come from behind to win a tournament with several spectacular holes, or who can "stink up the course" if his game is off and his gambles don't pay off. Arnold Palmer's ability to inspire others and win them to his cause is the stuff of a great legend.

FORMER PRESIDENT BILL CLINTON

Could anyone watch President Clinton and NOT see that he is clearly a High I, behaviorally? Throughout the campaign in 1992, reporters continually commented on the way people energized then Governor Clinton. Verbally persuasive, optimistic, friendly and trusting, President Clinton, as leader of the United States, attempted to be very persuasive in his efforts to direct the country. President Clinton is clearly an extrovert, unafraid to show his emotion or express his concern. Even his foes state that he clearly cares about people, even if they disagree with his agenda.

© 1993-2018 Target Training International, Ltd.

THE EMOTION OF THE HIGH I: OPTIMISM

The higher the I plotting point on Graph II, the more optimistic the person will be. **High I's believe the impossible can be done and will hold incredible optimism as to the future.** This extreme optimism may not be grounded totally in data and facts. Conversely, a person with a Low I in their profile will tend to be pessimistic and more skeptical, requiring proof.

EXAMPLE **Statement made to a High I and a Low I:**
"If you invest with us, we can return 15% on your investment."

High I: "Really? That's a fantastic return."

Low I: "Yeah, Right! Prove it!"

OUTSTANDING CHARACTERISTICS OF THE HIGH I

NEED TO INTERACT

The High I has an inherent need to interact, loving opportunities to verbalize. The High I has a tendency to talk smoothly, readily and at length, using friendly contact and verbal persuasion as a way of promoting a team effort. They will consistently try to inspire you to their point of view.

NEED TO BE LIKED

Fundamentally, the High I wants to be liked and usually likes others, sometimes indiscriminately. Preferring not to be alone, the High I has a need for social affiliation and acceptance. Possessing a high level of trust in others, the High I may be taken advantage of by people.

Social rejection is the fear of the High I. "Praise in public and rebuke in private" is true for all people, but especially the High I. Incredibly optimistic, High I's will build on the good in others and see the positive side of a negative situation.

© 1993-2018 Target Training International, Ltd.

INVOLVEMENT

Expect the High I to be involved in just about everything. At their best, High I's promote trust and confidence and feel they can persuade people to the kind of behavior they desire. Usually, they perform very well in a situation where poise and smoothness are essential factors.

EMOTIONAL

Emotion is very difficult for High I's to contain. They do wear their "heart on their sleeve," and their face is very expressive of the emotions they are experiencing. This positive enthusiasm of the High I is very contagious, causing others to jump on whatever bandwagon the I is on.

Utilizing the descriptors on Page 74, the famous examples and the outstanding characteristics, you should be beginning to develop a clear understanding of the High I behavioral style. The DISC language is based on observable behavior. By opening your "behavioral eyes" you will begin to notice the High I's around you.

VALUE OF THE HIGH I: TRUST

The DISC language does not measure a person's motivators. However, an interesting value is integrated in the I profile. Research has shown that the higher the I plotting point, the greater tendency the person has to "trust" others. Conversely, the lower the I, the greater the tendency for distrust. When you meet optimistic people who seem to trust others, be assured they have a High I in their profile.

PEOPLE READING: RECOGNIZING THE HIGH I

Understanding that the DISC language interprets HOW we act, behavioral observation has proven that the following attributes usually apply to the High I behavioral style. **Employ these cues to assist in quick recognition of the High I.**

QUICK HIGH I OBSERVABLE INDICATORS

Extroverted/Introverted:	Extroverted
People or Task Oriented:	People
More Direct or Indirect:	Indirect
Overextensions:	Disorganization
Geared to/looking for:	Fun, the experience
High I emotion:	Optimism
Low I emotion:	Pessimism
High I value:	Trust*
Low I value:	Distrust*

*This is the only value that consistently correlates with behavior.

OBSERVABLE BEHAVIOR: HOW THE HIGH I's ACT

Buy:	Quick decision makers; showy products; impulse buyer.
Change:	May not notice change.

Conflict response:	Flight, run.
Drive:	Visual, looking around, radio on.
Decorate an office:	Contemporary, memorabilia of experiences.
Email writing:	More wordy letters, warm people focus.
Gesture:	A lot of big gestures and facial expressions when talking.
Goal setting:	Not good at setting goals. Intention is present, planning is not.
Organization:	Disorganized. A lot of piles.
Read:	Fiction, self-improvement books.
Risk factor:	Moderate risk-taker.
Rules:	May not be aware of rules and break them unintentionally.
Stand:	Feet spread.
Stress relief:	Interaction with people.
Talk on the phone:	Long conversations. A great deal of tone variation in voice.
Talk to others:	Verbal, at length. Personal with others. May have poor listening skills.
Walk:	Weave, people focus, may run into things.

© 1993-2018 Target Training International, Ltd.

Refer often to these cues, until you have a clear picture of the High I pure style. Any one of these observable cues instantly tells you that you are relating to a High I. **You must invest the time learning the language to use it effectively.**

NOTE **PURE STYLES are being described in this section! The High I style is definitely affected by the intensity of the D, S, and C response. Effective language learning will give you the skill to recognize the effect of the other factors and adapt accordingly.**

VALUE OF THE HIGH I TO THE TEAM

1. **Optimism & Enthusiasm**
2. **Creative Problem Solving**
3. **Motivates Others Toward Goals**
4. **Positive Sense of Humor**
5. **Team Player**
6. **Negotiates Conflict**
7. **Verbalizes with Articulateness**

1. **Optimism & Enthusiasm**

   The High I is the people person, possessing a great ability to motivate and get the team excited. When the going gets tough, the optimism and enthusiasm of the High I will keep the team together.

2. **Creative Problem Solving**

   High I's possess a very creative mind and if allowed, will be ingenious in their ability to come up with new, creative ideas and solutions to problems.

3. **Motivates Others Toward Goals**

   Leadership is the ability to move people toward a common goal. Although all four styles can do this, the High I motivates people through positive interaction and persuasion. This High I's ability causes others to want to work together as a team.

4. **Positive Sense of Humor**

   The High I adds fun to the team and to the task. Studies have proven that productivity is increased as the team begins to have fun. The High I adds that natural fun, humorous element to the team.

5. **Team Player**

   Needing much people interaction, the High I is a very good team player. Working together means having fun while getting the job done.

© 1993-2018 Target Training International, Ltd.

6. Negotiates Conflict

A natural mediator (not liking conflict), the High I can verbally persuade both sides to come to an agreement. Part of this is due to their ability to focus on the bright side of the issues. Also, if both parties know the High I mediator, both probably like him/her. People buy from people they like.

7. Verbalizes Articulately

If there is a presentation to be made, an argument to be won, someone who needs to be persuaded into something that is good for all, send in the High I's. In these situations they will paint an optimistic picture of the possibilities and have a greater chance of achieving the desired results, not to mention the fact that they will enjoy the opportunity of being energized by the chance to verbalize. However, make sure they have the necessary data.

The High I is a tremendous asset. **Their warm, friendly, fun demeanor adds an optimistic hope to the team.** When the hard times hit, as they always do, the High I can bring a light to the dark night.

Based on the verbiage and descriptors given to this point, make a list of your associates who have a High I in their profile.

IDEAL ENVIRONMENT FOR THE HIGH I

- Assignments with a high degree of people contact.
- Tasks involving motivating groups and establishing a network of contacts.
- Democratic supervisor with whom they can associate.
- Freedom from control and detail.
- Freedom of movement.
- Multi-changing work tasks.

© 1993-2018 Target Training International, Ltd.

COMMUNICATING WITH THE HIGH I

Plan interaction that supports their dreams and intentions.
Don't legislate or muffle.

Allow time for relating and socializing.
Don't be curt, cold or tight-lipped.

Talk about people and their goals.
Don't drive to facts, figures and alternatives.

Focus on people and action items. Put details in writing.
Don't leave decisions up in the air.

Ask for their opinion.
Don't be impersonal or task-oriented.

Provide ideas for implementing action.
Don't waste time in "dreaming."

Use enough time to be stimulating, fun, fast moving.
Don't cut the meeting short or be too businesslike.

Provide testimonials from people they see as important or prominent.
Don't talk down to them.

Offer special immediate and extra incentives for their willingness to take risks.
Don't take too much time. Get to action items.

ENGAGING THE HIGH I

THE HIGH I WANTS:

- An environment free from control data.
- Popularity and social recognition.
- Freedom of speech, people to talk to.
- Favorable working conditions.
- Group activities outside the job.
- Identification with the team.
- Public recognition of their ability.
- Monetary rewards.

© 1993-2018 Target Training International, Ltd.

MANAGING THE HIGH I

- Assist in setting realistic goals.
- Work with on-time management.
- Develop a friendship and make time for interaction daily.
- Maintain an open door policy for High I's to discuss any issues.
- Train on behavioral styles to increase effectiveness of people interactions.
- Station them in a people area where they can interact and get the job done.
- Allow them freedom of movement, without control.
- Set clear objectives of task to be accomplished.
- Look for opportunities for them to utilize their verbal skills.

Refer to your list of those whom you believe to be High I's. Carefully examine your communication strategies and motivation techniques to determine if there are areas in which you are mismanaging them. The High I will always be a High I. **Your task is to bring out the best in him/her and to channel those energies to win/win situations for all parties involved.**

POSSIBLE LIMITATIONS OF THE HIGH I

The limitations listed for the High I are tendencies for the pure High I, which represents a very small percentage of the population. Each of these tendencies may be negated by the position of the D, S, and C factor and/or the beliefs of the individual. DISC is a NEUTRAL language.

THE HIGH I MAY:

- Oversell.
- Act impulsively, heart over mind.
- Trust people indiscriminately.
- Be inattentive to detail.
- Have difficulty planning and controlling time.
- Overestimate their ability to motivate others or change behavior.
- Under instruct and over delegate.
- Tend to listen only situationally.
- Overuse hand motions and facial expressions when talking.
- Rely too heavily on verbal ability.

The possible limitations of the High I are the opportunities for training and growth. Managing is "getting things done through people." The task, then, is to make the High I aware of his/her strengths and weaknesses and train him/her to cognitively make the correct choices needed for everyone to win.

© 1993-2018 Target Training International, Ltd.

"Treat people as if they were what they ought to be and you help them to become what they are capable of being."

-Johann Wolfgang von Goethe

HIGH I APPLICATION

To effectively begin to use the language of the High I defined in this chapter, use the following steps:

1. Review the chapter for 15 minutes each day for 3 weeks cementing the High I characteristics in your mind.

2. Memorize the High I descriptors.

3. Apply the descriptors above and the High I characteristics in this chapter to those whom you contact regularly. Make a list of those whom you believe, by observation, to be High I's.

4. Refer often to Page 86 and adapt your style for better communication and understanding with the High I's you know.

5. As you meet new people, using the descriptors above, notice those who may be High I's and adapt your behavior for greater communication.

6. Stand back and watch the results! You'll be amazed at your newly found effectiveness by using The Universal Language, DISC.

THE HIGH S

The steady relater, amiable, High S
Mild, laid back, patient, no stress
Stable, sincere, passive, serene
Great listening skills, an "ace" on the team.

Hard at work behind the scenes
Helping to do what's best for the team
Others will tire, the S will finish
Determined to stay till the task has diminished.

Loyal, devoted, they'll be here awhile
Jumping around just isn't their style
Won't leave a job until it is over
Finish one first, you're not a rover.

Acutely aware of people's needs
Responding to personal hurts on the team
Although appearing slow in the jobs they do
When it comes to a team, the S is the "glue."

–Randy Widrick

© 1993-2018 Target Training International, Ltd.

THE HIGH S
STEADY, RELATER, AMIABLE, PHLEGMATIC

DESCRIPTORS

Passive	Mild	Sincere
Possessive	Inactive	Non-demonstra-tive
Amiable	Friendly	Team player
Steady	Systematic	Patient
Predictable	Serene	Stable
Understanding	Good listener	

FAMOUS HIGH S's

- Former First Lady Laura Bush
- Fred Rogers, children's TV host of *Mister Rogers' Neighborhood*
- Jimmy Carter
- Gandhi
- Tom Brokaw
- Charlie Brown
- Tonto from *The Lone Ranger*
- Charlotte York, character from *Sex in the City*

LAURA BUSH

Gentle, calm, relaxed, with a deep concern for others, Laura Bush is also a High S. Close ties to the family, she seems always willing to help others. She endears the hearts of America to her causes and added a distinction to her office as First Lady. America respects and loves the gentle, calm stability of Laura Bush.

EMOTION OF THE HIGH S: NON-EMOTIONAL

Read carefully to avoid misunderstanding. High S's are very emotional. So why are we saying non-emotional? High S's have an inherent ability to "mask" their emotions. Whether they are going through a terrible personal ordeal or have just won the lottery, you may not know. High S's do not express their emotions. If you play a game where bluffing is involved (we recommend you don't), you will experience the power of the "non-emotion" of the High S. The strong side of this trait is that the High S can build a great team while going through tough personal events. The weak side of this trait is that internalized emotion is not physically or mentally healthy. High S's will open up and share their concerns with people they trust.

Conversely, Low S's openly display their emotions wearing their "heart on their sleeve."

© 1993-2018 Target Training International, Ltd.

OUTSTANDING CHARACTERISTICS OF THE HIGH S

NEED TO SERVE

The High S has an inherent need to serve. Always the one to help out, the High S lends a hand to get the job done. Other styles may serve for differing reasons, but the High S has a natural tendency to serve. In other words, serving and helping energizes the High S.

LOYALTY

High S's do not switch jobs very often, preferring to remain in one company as long as possible. Also, the High S will tend to stay in a relationship a long time, be it business or personal for reasons of security and also harmony. With the goal of harmony, High S's become very adaptable to the situation, modifying their behavior to achieve a sense of stability and harmony.

PATIENT, RELAXED

Showing a cool, relaxed face, High S's are not easily triggered or explosive in nature. Although they are very active emotionally, they do not show their emotion. An introverted personality, they will hide their problems and not wear their "heart on their sleeve." High S's have been known to lead their teams to great heights, even while going through incredible personal struggles.

LONG-TERM RELATIONSHIPS

High S's will develop strong attachments to their work group, family, club or association. They operate very well as members of a team and coordinate their efforts with others easily. They will strive to maintain the status quo, since they do not want change that is unexpected or sudden.

CLOSURE

Closure is essential for the High S. In other words, they must be allowed to finish what they start. To start several jobs and leave them undone is stressful to the High S. In a task-oriented situation, they should be given a few tasks and allowed to complete them before moving on. Having to "juggle" many balls at once is also stressful to the High S. High S's tend to read one book before they start another. High S's have been observed to dislike watching a movie or TV program if they have missed the start.

High S's, once in an established groove or pattern, can follow it with unending patience. They have the ability to do routine work, at all skill levels, and develop good work habits. **Amiable, easygoing, and relaxed, the High S will build strong relationships with a few close people.** Sensibility, low risk, steadiness, and serenity mark the High S style.

Utilizing the descriptors on Page 92, the famous examples and the outstanding characteristics, you should be starting to develop a clear understanding of the High S behavioral style. The DISC language is based on observable behavior. By opening your "behavioral eyes," you will begin to notice the High S's around you.

© 1993-2018 Target Training International, Ltd.

PEOPLE READING: RECOGNIZING THE HIGH S

Understanding that the DISC language interprets HOW we act, behavioral observation has proven that the following attributes usually apply to the High S behavioral style. **Employ these cues to assist in quick recognition of the High S.**

QUICK HIGH S OBSERVABLE INDICATORS

Extroverted/Introverted:	Introverted
People or Task-oriented:	People
More Direct or Indirect:	Indirect
Overextensions:	Possessiveness
Geared to/Looking for:	Stability
Emotion of the High S:	Non-emotional
Emotion of the Low S:	Emotional

OBSERVABLE BEHAVIOR: HOW THE HIGH S's ACT

Buy:	Slow decision maker: traditional products
Change:	Does not like change. Needs much preparation.
Conflict response:	Tolerate, put up with it.
Drive:	Relaxed pace, no hurry.

Decorate an office:	Family snapshots, "homey" atmosphere.
Email writing:	Long letters giving lots of information.
Gesture:	Will gesture with hands, not large sweeping gestures.
Goal setting:	Goals are short-term, low risk. May use daily to-do lists.
Organization:	Usually some type of system. A little on the sloppy side.
Read:	People stories, fiction and nonfiction.
Risk factor:	Moderately low risk-taker.
Rules:	Will usually follow time-tested, proven rules.
Stand:	Leaning back, hand in pocket.
Stress relief:	Rest time/sleep. Hot baths.
Talk on the phone:	Warm conversationalist, friendly and concerned.
Talk to others:	Warm, not pushy. Will listen before talking.
Walk:	Steady, easy pace.

© 1993-2018 Target Training International, Ltd.

Refer often to the behavioral cues until you have a clear picture of the High S's pure style. Any one of these observable cues can instantly tell you that you are relating to a High S. **You must invest the time learning the language to use it effectively.**

NOTE **PURE STYLES are being described in this section! The High S style is definitely affected by the intensity of the D, I, and C response. Effective language learning will give you the skill to recognize the effect of the other factors and adapt accordingly.**

VALUE OF THE HIGH S TO THE TEAM

1. **Dependable Team Worker**
2. **Work Hard for a Leader & Cause**
3. **Great Listener**
4. **Patient & Empathetic**
5. **Good at Reconciling Factions, Calming & Stabilizing**
6. **Logical & Step-wise Thinker**
7. **Will Finish Tasks**
8. **Loyal, Long-term Relationships**

1. **Dependable Team Worker**

   Always willing to help out, the High S will be a great team player. Usually stays in a situation a long time, the High S loyalty has a stabilizing effect on the team.

2. **Work Hard for a Leader & Cause**

   If the High S believes in the leader and the cause, they will work extremely hard to make it happen (other styles will also work hard, but for different reasons). High S's will be quick to assist others in areas in which they are familiar. When the High S accepts the task, expect them to be around for a while and to logically move toward completion.

3. **Great Listener**

   Listening skills are natural behavior for High S's. Even when interrupted, they will stop and look you in the eye and listen. Great listening ability makes them natural at helping people work through problems. Combined with their logical thinking, they become great assets to have on the team.

4. **Patient & Empathetic**

   Combined with great listening skills, High S's are very patient. Really trying to understand the situation the other person is in, they sometimes can become too adapting. Usually they will give the other person the benefit of the doubt and may stay in a situation or relationship too long, hoping against hope that it will get better.

© 1993-2018 Target Training International, Ltd.

5. **Good at Reconciling Factions, Calming & Stabilizing**

   Driven by a desire for harmony and peace, High S's can be a great asset in stabilizing a conflict situation. Again, their patience, listening ability, and logical approach can bring the situation back into harmony and focus.

6. **Logical & Step-wise Thinker**

   Involved in the planning process, High S's are a great asset. Oftentimes goals are set and the plans to get there are never thought out. High S's can bring lofty ideas back to the realm of the real world and point out gaps and flaws in the plan, due to their logical thinking process.

7. **Will Finish Tasks**

   Closure is of utmost importance to High S's. They can, but do not enjoy juggling a lot of balls. A task that is started must be finished. The High S will finish the first task and then move on to the next. Also having the ability to organize effectively, the High S will develop a system to get the job done.

8. **Loyal, Long-term Relationships**

   High S's on the team will form loyal, long-term relationships with whom they associate. When the going gets tough, the High S may be able to hold the team together because of the close relationships they have nurtured and developed.

High S's bring some incredible strength to the team. **Their loyalty and ability to form close relationships has a cementing effect on the people around them, pulling everyone together for a common goal.**

Based on the descriptors and verbiage to this point, make a list of your associates who have a High S in their profile.

IDEAL ENVIRONMENT FOR THE HIGH S

- Jobs for which standards and methods are established.
- Environment where long standing relationships can be or are developed.
- Personal attention and recognition for tasks completed and well done.
- Stable and predictable environment.
- Environment that allows time for change.
- Environment where people can be dealt with on a personal, intimate basis.

© 1993-2018 Target Training International, Ltd.

COMMUNICATING WITH THE HIGH S

Start with personal comments. Break the ice.
Don't rush headlong into business or the agenda.

Show sincere interest in them as people.
Don't stick coldly or harshly to business.

Patiently draw out their personal goals and ideas. Listen and be responsive.
Don't force a quick response to your objectives.

Present your case logically, softly, non-threateningly.
Don't threaten with positional power or be demanding.

Ask specific (preferably "How?") questions.
Don't interrupt as they speak. Listen carefully.

Move casually, informally.
Don't be abrupt and rapid.

If the situation impacts them personally, look for hurt feelings.
Don't mistake their willingness to go along for satisfaction.

Provide personal assurances and guarantees.
Don't promise something you can't deliver.

If a decision is required of them, allow them time to think.
Don't force a quick decision; provide information.

ENGAGING THE HIGH S

THE HIGH S WANTS:

- Logical reasons for change.
- Identification with team members.
- Harmony. A happy home and work life.
- Procedures that have been proven.
- A road map to follow.
- Closure on tasks.
- Time to adjust to change.
- Appreciation.
- Recognition for loyalty and service.
- To know you care.
- To work with a small group of people, develop relationships.

© 1993-2018 Target Training International, Ltd.

MANAGING THE HIGH S

- Clearly explain upcoming changes in order to prepare them.
- Make an effort to get to know them and their needs.
- Allow them the opportunity to finish the tasks started.
- Assign them fewer, larger projects.
- Encourage their contribution in meetings.
- Involve them in the long-term planning.
- Work to stretch them carefully to new heights.
- Create a non-threatening environment, allowing disagreement.
- Reward them for good work habits.
- Clearly define parameters and requirements of the task.
- Assign them to work with a small group of people.
- Do not switch them from team to team.
- Praise in public, rebuke gently in private.

Refer to your list of those you believe to be High S's. Carefully examine your communication strategies, motivation techniques and see if there are areas in which you are mismanaging him/her. The High S will always be a High S. **Your task is to bring out the best in them, and to channel those energies to win/win situations for all parties involved.**

POSSIBLE LIMITATIONS OF THE HIGH S

The limitations listed for the High S are tendencies for the Pure High S, which represent a very small percentage of the population. Each of these tendencies may be negated by the position of the D, I, and C factor or the motivators of the individual.

THE HIGH S MAY:

- Take criticism of work as a personal affront.
- Resist change just for change sake.
- Need help getting started on new assignments.
- Have difficulty establishing priorities.
- Internalize feelings when they should be discussed.
- Wait for orders before acting.
- Give false sense of compliance.
- Be too hard on themselves.
- May stay involved in a situation too long.
- Not project a sense of urgency.

Studies have shown that when persons focus on overcoming their weaknesses, they also diminish their strengths. The most effective people are those who understand themselves and surround themselves with people who are lovingly honest. All people have strengths and weaknesses.

> **"Our task is to build on the strengths, 'two heads are better than one,' 'many hands make light work' and 'a strand of three is not easily broken'."**

© 1993-2018 Target Training International, Ltd.

CHAPTER APPLICATION

To begin to use the language of the High S defined in this chapter, use the following steps:

"I have yet to find the person, however exalted his station, who did not do better work and put forth greater effort under a spirit of approval than under a spirit of criticism."

–Charles Schwab

1. Review the chapter for 15 minutes each day for 3 weeks cementing the High S characteristics in your mind.

2. Memorize the High S descriptors.

3. Apply the descriptors above and the High S characteristics in this chapter to those whom you contact regularly. Make a list of those whom you believe, by observation, to be High S's.

4. Refer often to Page 102 and adapt your style for better communication and understanding with the High S's you know.

5. As you meet new people, using the descriptors above, notice those who may be High S's and adapt your behavior for greater communication.

6. Stand back and watch the results! You'll be amazed at your newly found effectiveness by using DISC, the Universal Language.

THE HIGH C

Compliant, analytical, melancholic, the C
Methodical, courteous, complete accuracy,
restrained, diplomatic, mature and precise
Accurate, systematic, those standards are nice.

Planning and organizing done to perfection
The smallest detail is no exception
Consistently clear and objective thinking
Gives the team top-notch results without blinking.

And when it comes time to make a decision
You'd best have the facts to accomplish the mission
The C at your side with all the correct facts
Will assure the return on your investment won't lack.

Go by the book, follow the rules
Procedures are written, use the right tools
Standards are crucial, both now and later
In God we trust, all others use DATA!

–Randy Widrick

© 1993-2018 Target Training International, Ltd.

THE HIGH C
COMPLIANCE, ANALYTICAL, MELANCHOLIC

DESCRIPTORS

Perfectionist	Fact-finder	Systematic
Courteous	Restrained	Analytical
Mature	Precise	Methodical
Accurate	Diplomatic	Conventional
Conscientious	High standards	Sensitive
Evasive	Patient	Exacting

FAMOUS HIGH C's

- Former Vice President Al Gore
- Diane Sawyer, TV anchor
- Spike Lee, actor director
- Mr. Spock on *Star Trek*
- Jack Nicklaus
- Kevin Costner, actor
- Allen Greenspan
- Isaac Newton
- Sherlock Holmes
- Miranda Hobbes, character on *Sex and the City*

VICE PRESIDENT AL GORE

With an analytical approach, former Vice President Gore laid out the facts and figures of government waste, focusing on systems and procedures of how things are handled (or mis-handled). Whether one agrees with his thinking or not, former Vice President Gore is well thought out and analytical in his approach to the environment as well as government. *Time Magazine* gave an account of Gore's success in a debate with Ross Perot over NAFTA (North American Free Trade Agreement). Gore was urged by his advisors to play to his strength — to be "wooden," not animated. Typical of a High C, he spent many hours studying alone. He analyzed all of Perot's claims, looking for flaws. Then he had a group of aides fire questions at him for over two hours and additionally held a mock debate. Gore took control of tactics and strategy. Gore told his team that he wanted to hammer Perot with facts. On all accounts, former Vice President Al "Wooden" Gore won the debate.

EMOTION OF THE HIGH C: FEAR

The emotion of the C factor is fear. The higher the C factor the more the individual will be low risk, following procedures and going "by the book." Research by TTI in this area has proven conclusively that a person with a High C in their profile is a better driver than a person with a Low C in their profile. Also observed is the fact that parents who are High C's tend to be more protective of their children, due also to the emotion of fear. Conversely, the lower the C factor, the more the person will be high risk and tend to break rules and procedures.

© 1993-2018 Target Training International, Ltd.

OUTSTANDING CHARACTERISTICS OF THE HIGH C

NEED FOR PROCEDURES

High C's strive for a stable and orderly life and tend to follow procedures in both their personal and business lives. Dependent upon procedures, they will usually stick to methods that have brought success in the past.

BY THE BOOK

"Going by the book" is the first rule of conduct for High C's. They are very aware of and sensitive to the dangers of mistakes and errors, preferring a professional disciplined approach to problem solving. They are often the "quality" people who will write proven procedures to ensure the proper outcome.

PERFECTIONIST

Preferring to compete with themselves, the High C is constantly striving toward better ways of doing things. There is a right way to do things and a wrong way. High C's have the desire to be right, which usually means that they will come down on the safe side of a problem where there is less risk. They would rather be cautious than brash, conventional than bold. The lower the I the higher the tendency toward being a perfectionist.

PRECISE AND ATTENTIVE TO DETAIL

High C's are data gatherers and will gather all possible facts (maybe too many) related to a specific problem. They are systematic thinkers, precise and attentive to detail. When called upon by other styles, the C will tend to ask questions to clarify the data and go to the heart of the issue. The High C is very careful in thought and deed.

PROOF AND EVIDENCE

A statement made with little or no proof will not fly with the High C. "Prove it" is the calling card of the High C.

"In God we trust, all others use data," depicts the High C very well. This drive for proof and facts can save a company a great deal of money that would have been wasted in inconclusive speculation.

High C's tend to be loyal and dedicated, doing whatever is expected of them to the best of their ability. They are more tacticians than strategists.

Utilizing the descriptors on Page 108, the famous examples and the outstanding characteristics, you should be beginning to develop a clear understanding of the High C behavioral style. The DISC language is based on observable behavior. By opening your "behavioral eyes" you will begin to notice the High C's around you.

© 1993-2018 Target Training International, Ltd.

PEOPLE READING: RECOGNIZING THE HIGH C

Understanding the DISC language interprets HOW we act. Behavioral observation has proven that the following attributes usually apply to the High C behavioral style. Employ these cues to assist in quick recognition of the High C.

QUICK HIGH C OBSERVABLE INDICATORS

Extroverted/Introverted:	Introverted
People or Task-Oriented:	Task
More Direct or Indirect:	Direct
Overextensions:	Critical
Geared to/looking for:	Procedures/information
Emotion of the High C:	Fear
Emotion of the Low C:	No Fear

OBSERVABLE BEHAVIOR: HOW THE HIGH C's ACT

Buy:	Very slow buyers, proven products.
Change:	Concerned about the effects of change.
Conflict response:	Avoidance.
Drive:	Careful, follow rules. Best drivers.

Decorate an office:	Graphs, charts, functional.
Email writing:	Direct, to the point, with appropriate data.
Gesture:	Very reserved, little or no gestures.
Goal settings:	Good at setting safe goals, probably in many areas. Goals may be safe with little risk or reach.
Organization:	Everything in its place. Perfectly organized.
Read:	Nonfiction, technical journals.
Risk factor:	Very low.
Rules:	"By the book." Knows and follows rules.
Stand:	Arms folded one hand on chin.
Stress relief:	Alone time.
Talk on the phone:	Little chitchat. To the point. May be short or long depending on data needed.
Talk to others:	Direct. Questioning, clarifying.
Walk:	Straight line

© 1993-2018 Target Training International, Ltd.

Refer often to these cues until you have a clear picture of the High C style. Any one of these observable cues can instantly tell you that you are relating to a High C. **You must invest the time learning the language to use it effectively.**

NOTE **PURE STYLES are being described in this section! The High C style is definitely affected by the intensity of the D, I, and S response. Effective language learning will give you the skill to recognize the effect of the other factors and adapt accordingly.**

VALUE OF THE HIGH C TO THE TEAM

1. **Objective Thinker**
2. **Conscientious**
3. **Maintains High Standards**
4. **Defines, Clarifies, Gets Information, Criticizes & Tests**
5. **Task-oriented**
6. **Asks the Right Questions**
7. **Diplomatic**
8. **Pays Attention to Small Details**

1. **Objective Thinker**

   When dialoguing with High C's, the real world is the arena. They deal in the area of objective fact and will make you prove your case. The High C brings a reality to plans, analyzing and testing the data for accuracy.

2. **Conscientious**

   High C's take their work personally, almost as an extension of their being. The finished task is a reflection of their attention to small details. They are usually very loyal and will go the extra mile to get the job done.

3. **Maintains High Standards**

   In a book called *The Wisdom of Teams* (Katzenbach & Smith, 1994), one characteristic was found on all high performance work teams: they were committed to the highest standards. The High C will even assist in writing the standards. With a quality focus, the High C assists the team in consistency of standards and operation, adding order to the scenario.

4. **Defines, Clarifies, Gets Information, Criticizes & Tests**

   A great objective thinker, the High C will blow holes in plans that are not thought out. Their skeptical nature looks at all possibilities before they buy into the plan. Utilized in this way, the High C can be a great asset to any team. Oh, and don't argue with a C unless you are sure you have your "ducks in a row." Collectors of data, the High C is a walking computer, always analyzing, testing, and clarifying.

© 1993-2018 Target Training International, Ltd.

5. **Task-oriented**

   The world is not all touchy-feely. The High C places importance on accuracy when completing tasks. They have made significant contributions to such events as going to the moon. In contrast, the High I would still be planning the party for the arrival.

6. **Asks the Right Questions**

   One of the most significant contributions the High C's make to any organization is asking the rough questions. This talent often leads to destruction of a shallow plan.

7. **Diplomatic**

   If given the opportunity, High C's will be very diplomatic in sharing the data to support their conclusions. They prefer discussions void of emotional appeal.

8. **Pays Attention to Small Details**

   Many projects would be a total disaster if it weren't for the High C's attention to detail. Every organization needs a C on their team for those projects where the little things make a big difference.

In summary, the High C sets the standards for the team and maintains them. **In a world of fast pace and change, the High C keeps us closer to reality with their objective thinking processes. High C's, with their questioning, analyzing and clarifying style do not allow us to get away with "sloppy thinking."** Sometimes misunderstood, they can take ideas that are too "lofty" and bring them back to a state of realism. Based on the verbiage and descriptors given to this point, make a list of your associates who you believe to have a High C in their profile.

IDEAL ENVIRONMENT FOR THE HIGH C

- Where critical thinking is needed and rewarded
- Assignments will be completed according to process, procedure and constraints.
- Technical, task-oriented work, specialized area
- Noise and people are at a minimum
- Close relationship with small group of people
- Environment where quality and/or standards are important

© 1993-2018 Target Training International, Ltd.

COMMUNICATING WITH THE HIGH C

Prepare your case in advance.
Don't be disorganized or messy.

Approach them in a straightforward, direct way.
Don't be casual, informal or personal.

Use a thoughtful approach. Build credibility by looking at all sides of each issue.
Don't force a quick decision.

Present specifics, and do what you say you can do.
Don't be vague about expectations or fail to follow through.

Draw up an "Action Plan" with scheduled dates and milestones.
Don't overpromise results, be conservative.

Take your time, but be persistent.
Don't be abrupt and rapid.

If you disagree, prove it with data and facts or testimonials from respected people.
Don't appeal to opinion or feelings as evidence.

Provide them with the information and the time they need to make a decision.
Don't use closes, use incentives to get the decision.

Allow them their space.
Don't touch them.

ENGAGING THE HIGH C

THE HIGH C WANTS:

- Operating procedures in writing.
- Safety procedures.
- To be part of a quality-oriented team.
- No sudden or abrupt changes.
- Reassurance that the job is being done correctly.
- Information and data available.
- Time to think.
- Objective, tough problems to solve.
- Manager who follows company policy.

© 1993-2018 Target Training International, Ltd.

MANAGING THE HIGH C

- Involve them in defining standards that are undefined.
- Involve them in implementation of the standards.
- Clearly define requirements of the job and expectations.
- Allow them the opportunity to finish the tasks started.
- Set goals that have "reach" in them.
- Encourage their contribution in meetings.
- Involve them in the long-term planning.
- Train them in people skills and negotiating.
- Respect their personal nature.
- Allow them to work with a small group of people, in a less active area.
- Do not criticize their work unless you can prove a better way.

Refer to your list of those you believe to be High C's. Carefully examine your communication strategies and motivation techniques to see if there are areas requiring change and be willing to be the one who has to adapt.

POSSIBLE LIMITATIONS OF THE HIGH C

The limitations listed for the High C are tendencies for the pure HIGH C, which represent a very small percentage of the population. Each of these tendencies may be negated by the position of the D, I, and S factor.

THE HIGH C MAY:

- Hesitate to act without precedent.
- Overanalyze: analysis paralysis.
- Be too critical of others.
- Get bogged down in details.
- Not verbalize feelings, but internalize them.
- Be defensive when criticized.
- Yield position to avoid controversy.
- Select people much like themselves.
- Be too hard on themselves.
- Tell ideas as opposed to sell ideas.

As stated, the intensity of the D, I, and S factors can offset the limitations of the C factor. As with all styles, their very strengths are the cause of their weaknesses. The challenge, knowing you need the strengths of all four styles on your team, is to grow and learn to bring out the best in each style, maximizing strengths and minimizing the weaknesses of each style.

© 1993-2018 Target Training International, Ltd.

HIGH C APPLICATION

To begin to use the language of the High C defined in this chapter, use the following steps:

1. Review the chapter for 15 minutes each day for 3 weeks cementing the High C characteristics in your mind.

2. Memorize the High C descriptors.

3. Apply the descriptors above and the High C characteristics in this chapter to those whom you contact regularly. Make a list of those whom you believe, by observation, to be High C's.

4. Refer often to Page 118 and adapt your style for better communication and understanding with the High C's you know.

5. As you meet new people, using the descriptors above, notice those who may be High C's and adapt your behavior for greater communication.

6. Stand back and watch the results! You'll be amazed at your newly found effectiveness by using DISC, the Universal Language.

"People rarely get fired for incompetence. It's not getting along that is almost always the underlying reason for dismissal."

–Stuart Margulies, Industrial Psychologist

OBJECTIVES REVISITED

Once this chapter has been learned, you should be at the following stage:

A. Definition & Learning

Having properly reviewed each segment of this chapter, you will have four distinctly different "compartments" in your memory. **Each compartment will have:**

1. Visual pictures of famous examples.
2. Visual pictures of people you know.
3. Descriptors of the "compartment style" (DISC).
4. Behavioral style indicators.

B. Observation

By observing and opening your "behavioral eyes," you will see how people act. Now that the language is "compartmentalized," you will be able to identify the "core" behavioral style as you observe people. Then by referring to the communication sections in this chapter, you will be able to increase your effectiveness immediately.

© 1993-2018 Target Training International, Ltd.

READING THE DISC LANGUAGE

Chapter Objective

To provide you with information and instructions to become proficient in graph reading using the Style Insights® Instrument.

Chapter Contents

- The Style Insights Instrument
- Scoring Method
- Understanding Graph I
- Understanding Graph II
- The Energy Line
- Graph Reading
- Four-step Plan
- Unusual Graphs
- TTI's Success Insights Wheel®
- Objectives Revisited

"He who knows others is learned, he who knows himself is wise."

–Lao Tse

© 1993-2018 Target Training International, Ltd.

THE INSTRUMENT: STYLE INSIGHTS®

This assessment is made up of 24 frames. Each frame has four sets of words. The individual ranks the items from one to four, one being most like them, and four being least like them. 2 and 3 are also scored somewhat like me and less like me respectively. **Based on the individual's responses to the 24 item questionnaire, over 20,000 different graphs can be plotted for either Graph I or Graph II.** The magnitude of those numbers results in thousands of individualized computer-generated reports.

The Style Insights® instrument is far more sophisticated than instruments that only measure one factor against another in each question. The Style Insights assessment asks you similar types of questions 24 times. Consistent repetition in assessments assures accuracy and provides a better outcome in the report. Specifically, this is an example of how we achieve reliability in an assessment by asking that same question over and over again.

TTI continually performs a factor analysis on every adjective used in the Style Insights questionnaire and replaces them as statistics indicate they no longer measure what they were designed to measure.

TAKING THE STYLE INSIGHTS INSTRUMENT

To ensure highest accuracy, the following instructions should be given to the individual taking the instrument:

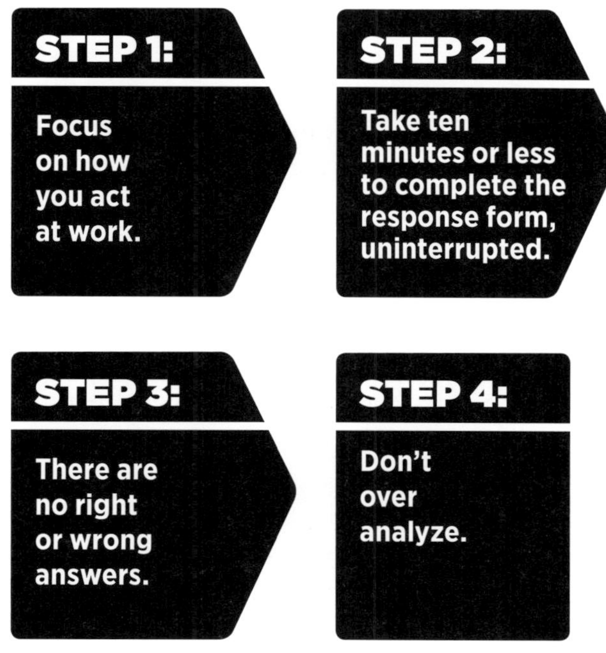

© 1993-2018 Target Training International, Ltd.

Rank the items in each list. Number them from 1 to 4, with 1 as the MOST like you. Continue to rank until you have ordered all the phrases from MOST (1) to LEAST (4). Repeat the process until complete.

1.
- ____ Enthusiastic
- ____ Contented, satisfied
- ____ Positive, confident
- ____ Peaceful, tranquil

2.
- ____ Careful, calculating
- ____ Bold, daring
- ____ Supportive
- ____ Charming, delightful

3.
- ____ Expressive
- ____ Daring, risk-taker
- ____ Diplomatic, tactful
- ____ Satisfied, content

4.
- ____ Respectful, shows respect
- ____ Pioneering, exploring, enterprising
- ____ Optimistic
- ____ Accommodating, willing to please, ready to help

5.
- ____ Willing, agreeable
- ____ Eager, impatient
- ____ Methodical
- ____ High-spirited, lively, enthusiastic

6.
- ____ Logical
- ____ Obedient, will do as told, dutiful
- ____ Unconquerable, determined
- ____ Playful, frisky, full of fun

7.
- ____ Adventurous, willing to take chances
- ____ Analytical
- ____ Cordial, warm, friendly
- ____ Moderate, avoids extremes

8.
- ____ Good mixer, likes being with others
- ____ Structured
- ____ Vigorous, energetic
- ____ Lenient, tolerant of others' actions

9.
- ____ Competitive, seeking to win
- ____ Considerate, caring, thoughtful
- ____ Outgoing, fun-loving, socially striving
- ____ Harmonious, agreeable

10.
- ____ Aggressive, challenger, takes action
- ____ Life of the party, outgoing, entertaining
- ____ Easy mark, easily taken advantage of
- ____ Fearful, afraid

11.
- ____ Stimulating
- ____ Sympathetic, compassionate, understanding
- ____ Tolerant
- ____ Aggressive

12.
- ____ Talkative, chatty
- ____ Controlled, restrained
- ____ Conventional, doing it the usual way, customary
- ____ Decisive, certain, firm in making a decision

SAMPLE

Rank the items in each list. Number them from 1 to 4, with 1 as the MOST like you. Continue to rank until you have ordered all the phrases from MOST (1) to LEAST (4). Repeat the process until complete.

13.
_____ Well-disciplined, self-controlled
_____ Generous, willing to share
_____ Animated, uses gestures for expression
_____ Persistent, unrelenting, refuses to quit

14.
_____ Sociable, enjoys the company of others
_____ Patient, steady, deliberate
_____ Self-reliant, independent
_____ Soft-spoken, mild, reserved

15.
_____ Gentle, kindly
_____ Persuasive, convincing
_____ Humble, reserved, modest
_____ Magnetic, attracts others

16.
_____ Captivating
_____ Kind, willing to give or help
_____ Resigned, gives in
_____ Force of character, powerful

17.
_____ Companionable, easy to be with
_____ Easygoing
_____ Outspoken, speaks freely and boldly
_____ Restrained, reserved, controlled

18.
_____ Factual
_____ Obliging, helpful
_____ Willpower, strong-willed
_____ Cheerful, joyful

19.
_____ Attractive, charming, attracts others
_____ Systematic
_____ Stubborn, unyielding
_____ Pleasing

20.
_____ Restless, unable to rest or relax
_____ Neighborly, friendly
_____ Popular, liked by many or most people
_____ Orderly, neat

21.
_____ Challenging, assertive
_____ Critical thinker
_____ Casual, laid-back
_____ Light-hearted, carefree

22.
_____ Brave, unafraid, courageous
_____ Inspiring, motivating
_____ Avoid confrontation
_____ Quiet, composed

23.
_____ Cautious, wary, careful
_____ Determined, decided, unwavering, stand firm
_____ Convincing, assuring
_____ Good-natured, pleasant

24.
_____ Jovial, joking
_____ Organized
_____ Nervy, gutsy, brazen
_____ Even-tempered, calm, not easily excited

SAMPLE

© 1993-2018 Target Training International, Ltd.

UNDERSTANDING GRAPH I

Graph I is our "MASK" graph. A mask indicates we are putting on something to cover our true identity. We tend to adapt our behavior to survive or succeed in a specific environment. **Graph I is the behavior we allow others to see, even though it may not be our true behavior.** The responses used in Graph I identify a person's responses to their environment. In other words, the behavior a person feels he/she needs to exhibit to survive and succeed at the job.

Graph I is the MOST CHANGEABLE. We adapt our behavior to the environment. Graph I shows this adaptation. Graph I will change depending on the environment we focus on. For example, a person transferring from an accounting position to a sales position may need to utilize more people skills to succeed in the new environment. Adaptation of their behavior would appear in Graph I.

UNDERSTANDING GRAPH II

Graph II is our basic or natural behavior. Poetically speaking, "Graph II is you." **Graph II identifies a person's NATURAL behavior, the real you.** By reading this graph, we can learn what you are like under pressure or when you are totally at ease. When you are under stress or pressure, the mask comes off, and we see Graph II behavior. When things are going good, and you can "let your hair hang down," we see Graph II behavior.

Graph II is the LEAST CHANGEABLE. Because Graph II is the real you, it is of utmost importance in understanding yourself. If you were a people person in high school, you will probably be a people person when in your rocking chair. Graph II will seldom change significantly.

Graph II can change when you experience a significant emotional event. At times, when a person has taken a Style Insights Instrument in the past, they may say their Graph II is totally different. When questioned, we inevitably discover that the person has been through an emotional event such as marriage, the birth of a child, surgery, car accident, death of a loved one, or some event that caused them to change. **Otherwise, Graph II will remain fairly consistent throughout a person's lifetime.**

© 1993-2018 Target Training International, Ltd.

THE ENERGY LINE

The Energy Line is the center line of the graphs, the foundation from which intensity levels can be determined. When we discuss the DISC language, often we refer to a person as a High D, High I, High S, or High C. Simply stated, High D means that the D plotting point is furthest up from the Energy Line. High C would mean the C factor is the highest plotting point above the Energy Line and so on. A low D would indicate that the D factor is the lowest plotting point below the Energy Line.

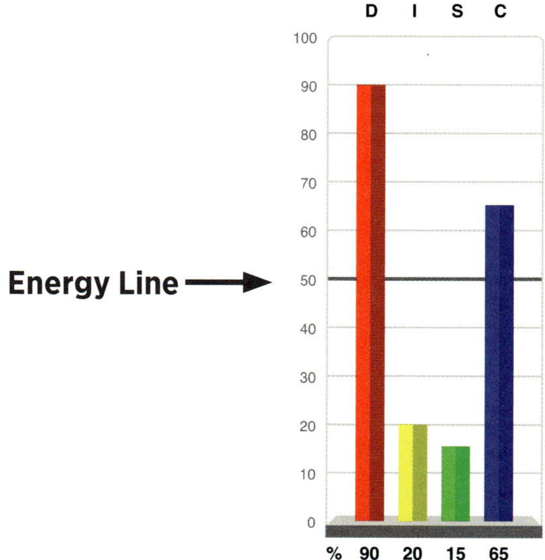

In the above example, the individual would be understood to be a High D because the D factor is the farthest plotting point away from the Energy Line.

However, to understand the behavior of the whole person, we would not only look at the characteristics of the High D, but also the intensity of the I, S, and C factors and their relationship, high or low, to the Energy Line and to each other.

At the end of this chapter you will be able to read any graph without reading the computer report.

GRAPH READING

A Four-Step Plan to Greater Behavioral Understanding

STEP 1: Determine core behavioral style and factor relationships for Graph II.

STEP 2: Give feedback.

STEP 3: Check for disparity between Graph I (Adapted) and Graph II (Natural).

STEP 4: Repeat process for Graph I.

The graph reading process begins first with Graph II, the NATURAL RESPONSE. After the behavior of Graph II has been analyzed, the same process can be applied to Graph I.

STEP 1: DETERMINE CORE (ABOVE LINE) BEHAVIORAL STYLE AND FACTOR RELATIONSHIPS OF GRAPH II

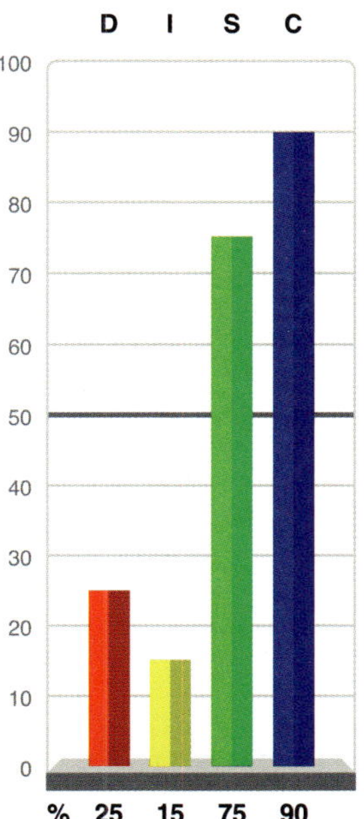

The core behavioral style is the highest plotting point above the Energy Line. In the example DISC graph on the left, the Core behavioral style is a High C.

CORE C		
Factor Relationships	Spread	Tendency
C/I	75	Strong
C/D	65	Strong
C/S	15	Moderate
S/I	60	Strong
S/D	50	Strong
D/I	10	Moderate

© 1993-2018 Target Training International, Ltd.

Now that we know the Point Spread for each relationship, we can identify the tendency. The tendency is the statement's probability of accuracy and can be Strong, Moderate, or Weak depending on the point spread.

Strong, Moderate and Weak Tendencies
The rule to follow for identifying Strong, Moderate and Weak tendencies is as follows:

POINT SPREAD

STRONG tendency: Point spread greater than or equal to 20, associated verbiage will tend to be highly accurate; the absolute truth.

MODERATE tendency: Point spread of 10 - 19, associated verbiage will explain a tendency toward a certain behavior.

WEAK tendency: Point spread of 9 or less, verbiage may not be accurate; too close to call.

STEP 2: GIVING FEEDBACK

C is the Core Style so give feedback based on High C. Refer to the previous Example for details.

C Feedback		Factor Relationship Feedback
C/I	**Strong:**	Precise, accurate, perfectionist.
C/D	**Strong:**	Adaptable, dependable, and soft spoken.
C/S	**Moderate:**	Alert and ready to adapt to systems, but cautious.
S/I	**Strong:**	Concentrating on details, reflective, intense.
S/D	**Strong:**	Patient, nonchalant, lackadaisical, resigned.
D/I	**Moderate:**	Incisive, argumentative, direct, analytical, and creative.

Arnold Palmer - High I

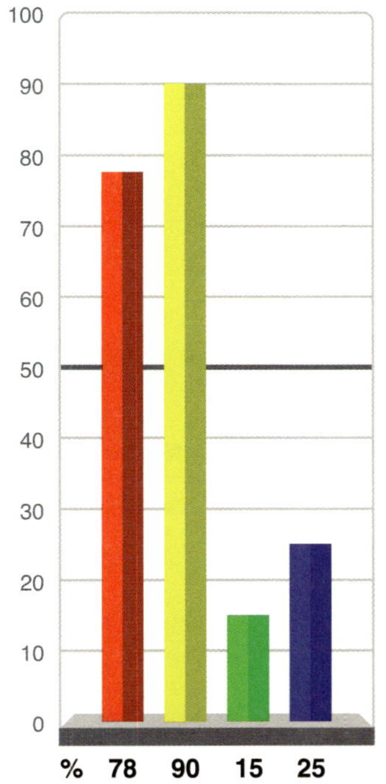

Jack Nicklaus - High C

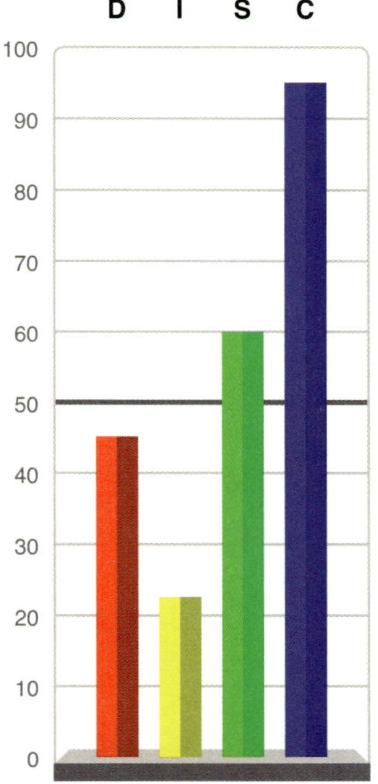

I Optimistic, trusting

I/S Sociable, contact ability

I/C Projects self-confidence

I/D Amiable, friendly

D/S Results-oriented, sense of urgency

D/C Decisive, risk-taker, pioneering

C/S Spontaneous and unconventional; expressive and opinionated

C Compliance

C/I Precise, perfectionist

C/D Adaptable, dependable, soft-spoken

C/S Alert and sensitive to problems, controls, rules, mistakes

S/I Concentrating on details, reflective, intense

S/D Patient, nonchalant

D/I Gentle, unobtrusive, complacent

BOTH WIN THEIR OWN UNIQUE WAY!

Repeat Step 2 on the following Famous People's Graphs:

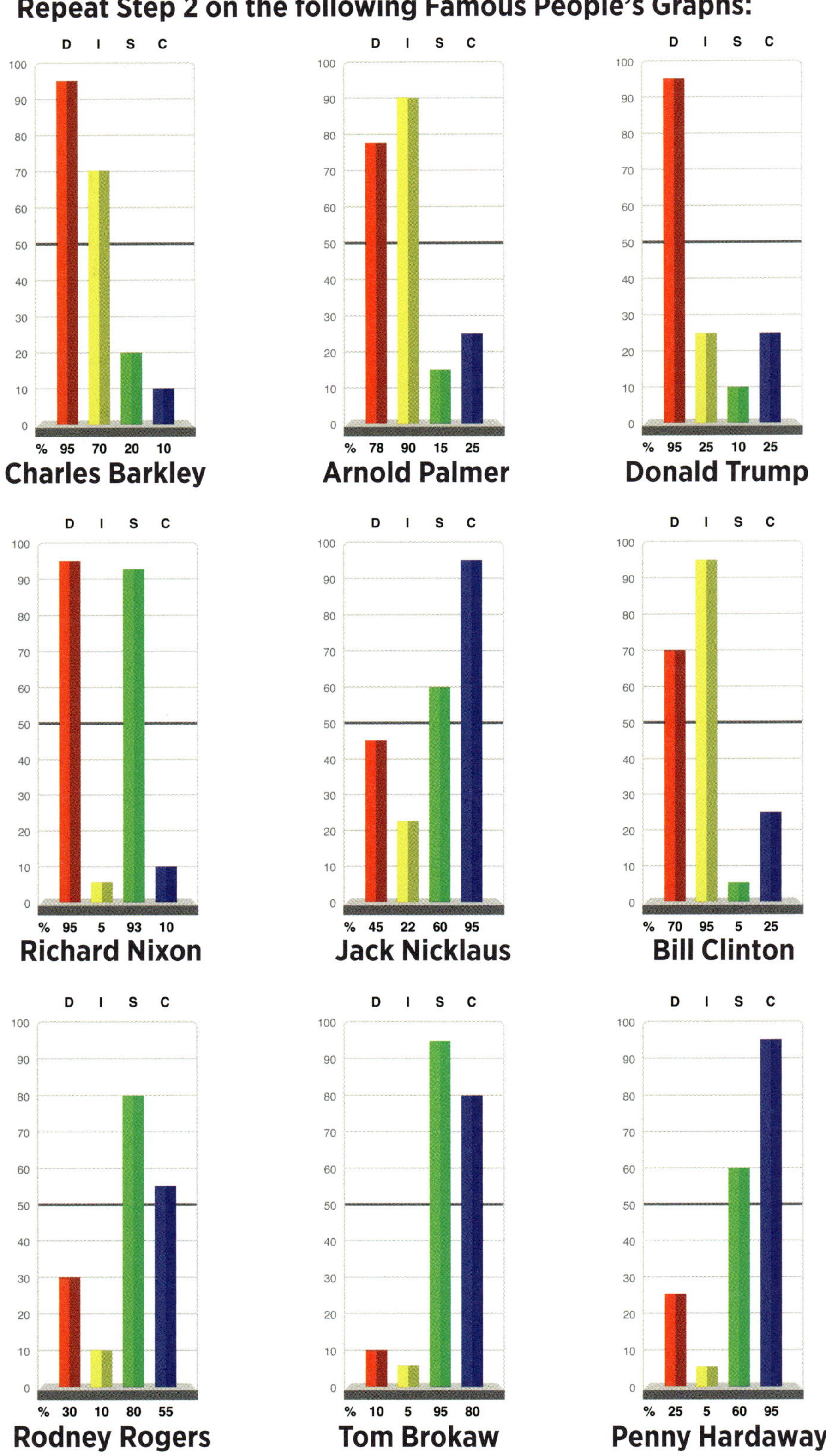

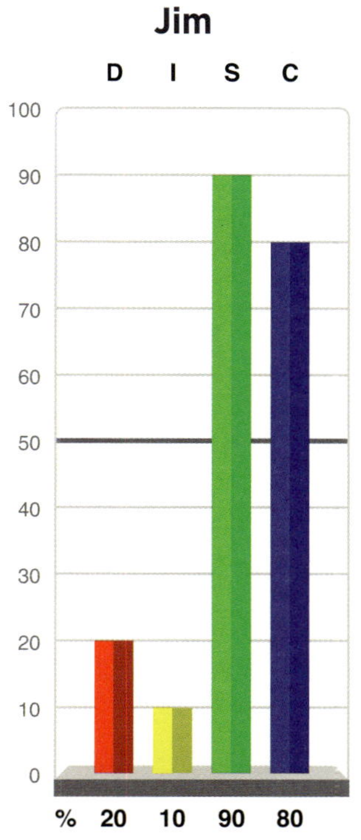

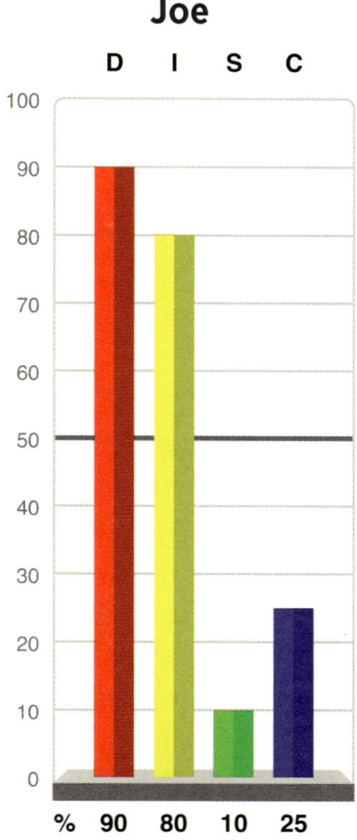

How will Jim communicate with Joe?

How will Joe feel about Jim's natural communication style?

How will Joe communicate with Jim?

How will Jim feel about Joe's natural communication style?

Communication is the key to managing, motivating, leading, parenting, etc. Use this process to demonstrate to both parties the power of TTI's assessments.

The following pages include the information needed to learn how to read all possible graphs.

© 1993-2018 Target Training International, Ltd.

HIGH D: DOMINANT

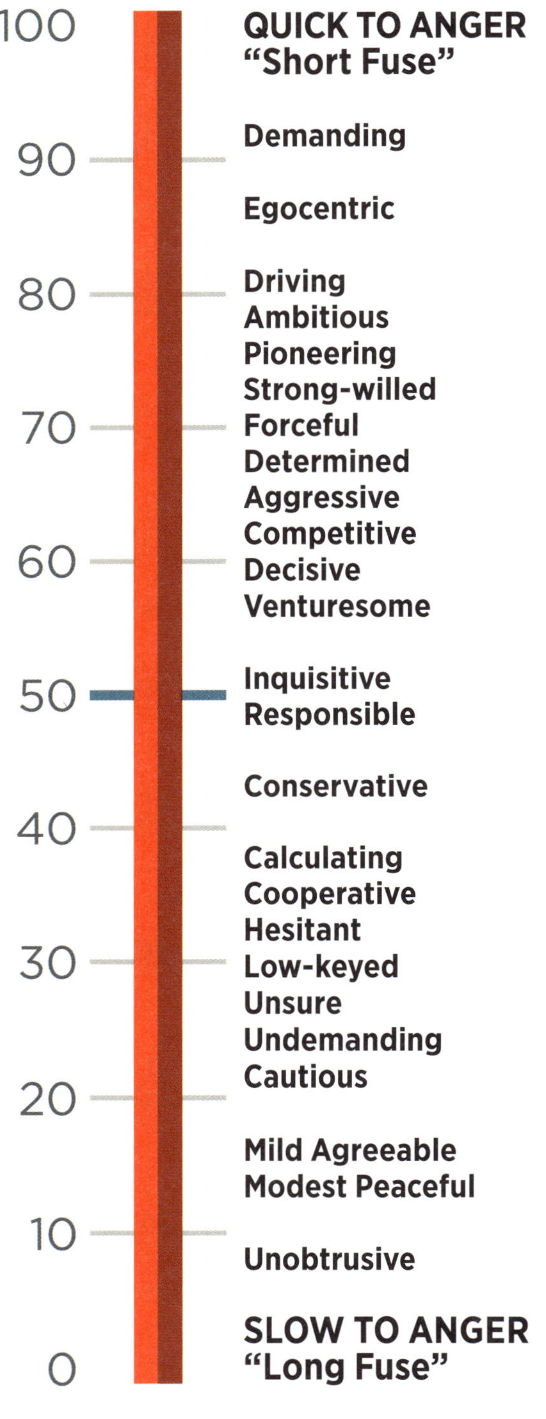

PROBABLE STRENGTHS*

- Ego
- Problem-solver
- Likes challenging assignments
- Drives for results
- Positive
- Likes confrontation
- Comfortable with power and authority
- Motivated by direct answers

POSSIBLE LIMITATIONS*

- Oversteps authority
- Uses fear as a motivator
- Poor listener
- Lacks tact and diplomacy
- Dislikes routine work
- Over delegates, under instructs

*Probable/Possible because we are only discussing one factor — statements may change based on intensity of the other three factors.

TOP FACTOR D STYLE COMBINATIONS

	DESCRIPTORS	VERBIAGE
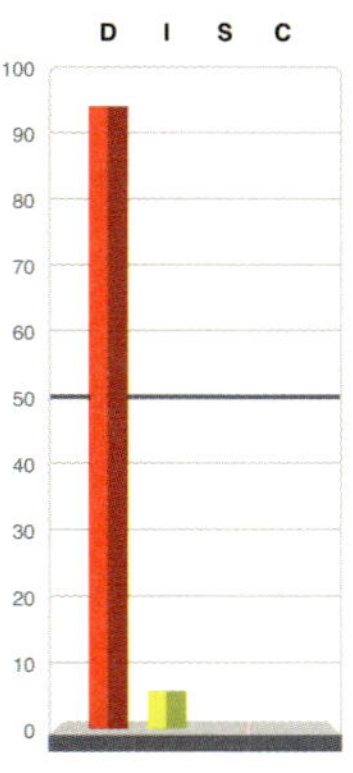	**D1. D/I** Incisive, argumentative, direct, analytical, creative and/or innovative, straight-forward.	Seeks and solves problems in an independent direct manner. Any situation can be faced and dealt with given time and technique.
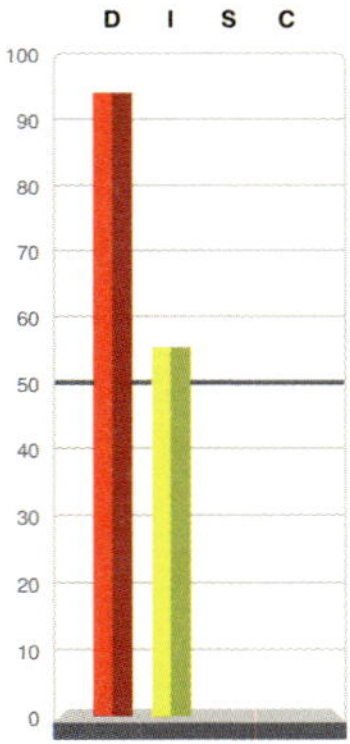	**D2. D/I** **Both above line** Incisive, argumentative, direct, creative and/or innovative, straight-forward.	Seeks and solves problems persuasively with the support of people. How to understand others and solicit their help represents an appealing challenge.
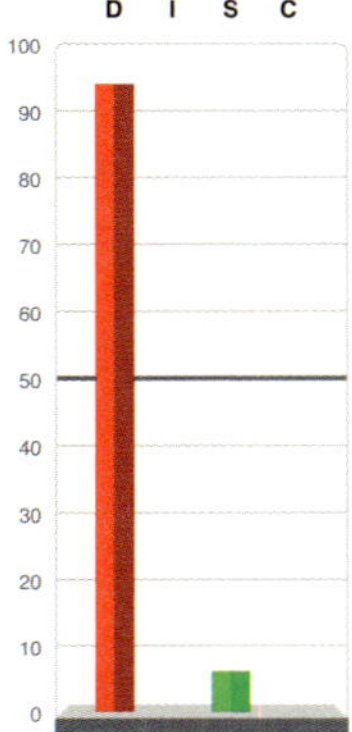	**D3. D/S** Results-oriented, urgent, driving, deadline conscious, self-starter, wide scope of activities.	Anxiously impatient to overcome obstacles and competition in the most expedient way from the many choices of action available. Driven to succeed.

© 1993-2018 Target Training International, Ltd.

	DESCRIPTORS	VERBIAGE
	**D4. D/S** **Both above line** Results-oriented, urgent, driving, deadline conscious, self-starter.	Prefers limited daily activities. Actively goal-oriented. Chooses to go after solutions to problems rather than wait to see how they come out.
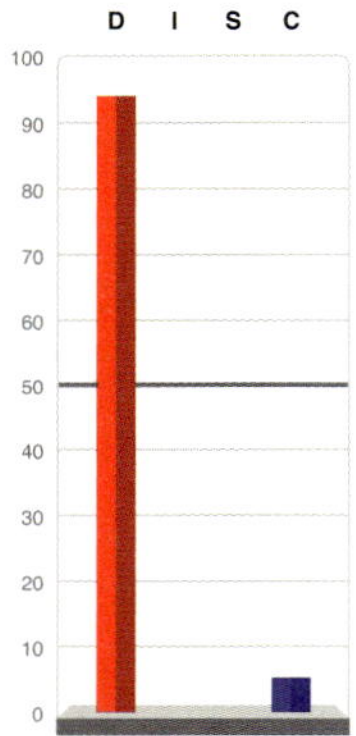	**D5. D/C** Decisive individualist, daring, bold, gutsy, risk-taker, venturesome, pioneering.	Aggressively and independently tackles problems with little regard for possible drawbacks in choice of solutions.
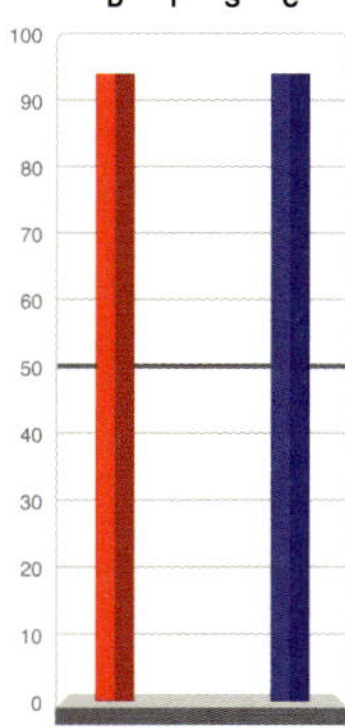	**D6. D/C** **Both above line** Demanding, vacillating, temperamental, Get it done — do it right.	Driving for results, paying close attention to detail and quality.

DESCRIPTORS	VERBIAGE
D7. D/I **Both below line** Internal heat, emotions internalized.	Inner intensity felt, but not displayed to others, magnified if standards aren't met.

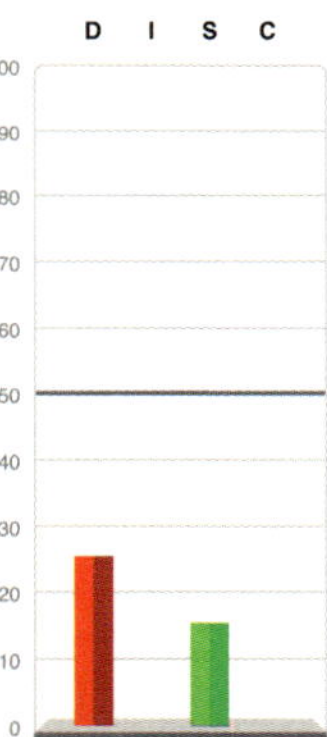

DESCRIPTORS	VERBIAGE
D8. D/S **Both below line** Cautious, cooperative and flexible; eager yet low-key.	Has a reflective approach to problems. Prefers a variety of activities. Can be impatient, but appears to be undemanding.

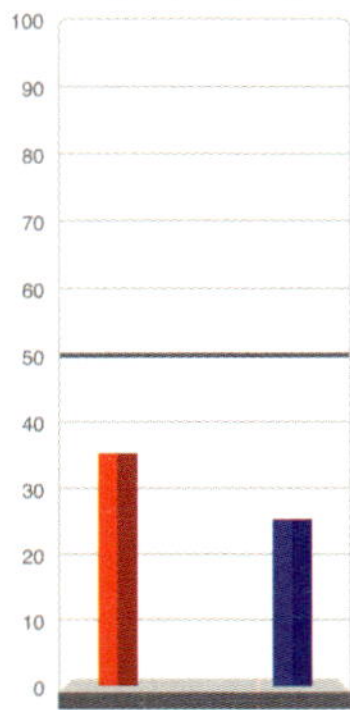

DESCRIPTORS	VERBIAGE
D9. D/C **Both below line** Independent yet cooperative, low-key, change-agent.	Make decisions outside of set policies. Low-key yet questions the current process and procedures.

© 1993-2018 Target Training International, Ltd.

HIGH I: INFLUENCER

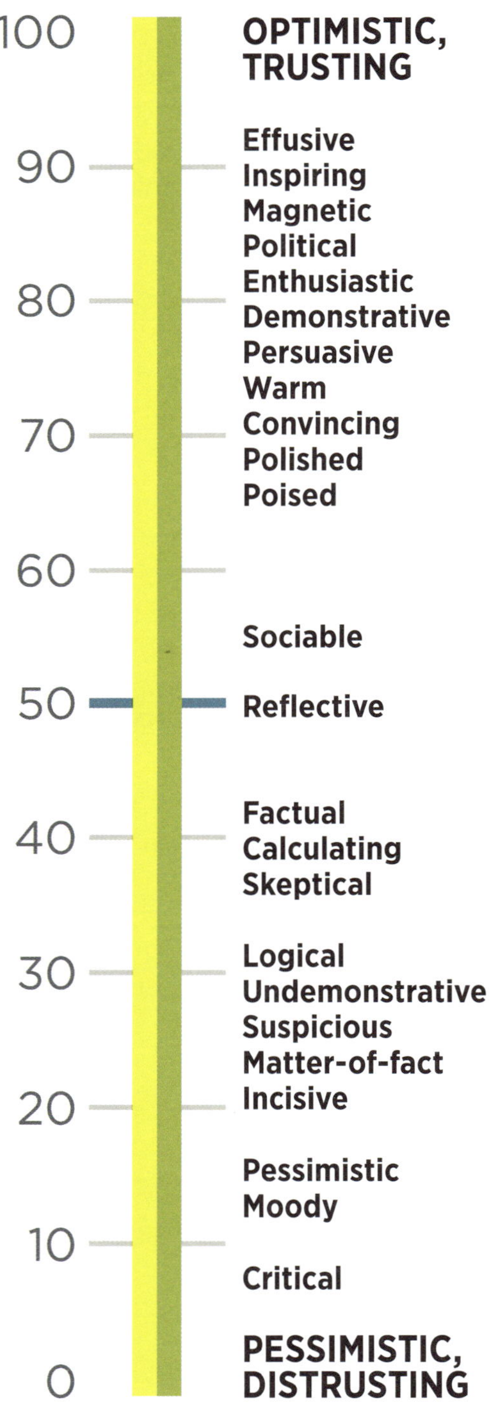

PROBABLE STRENGTHS*

- Socially and verbally aggressive
- Very optimistic
- Good at persuading people
- Can see the "big dream" and communicate it
- People-oriented
- Team-oriented
- Motivated by praise and strokes

POSSIBLE LIMITATIONS*

- Acts impulsively — heart over mind
- Unrealistic in appraising people
- Inattentive to detail
- Situational listener
- Disorganized

*Probable/Possible because we are only discussing one factor — statements may change based on intensity of the other three factors.

TOP FACTOR I STYLE COMBINATIONS

	DESCRIPTORS	VERBIAGE
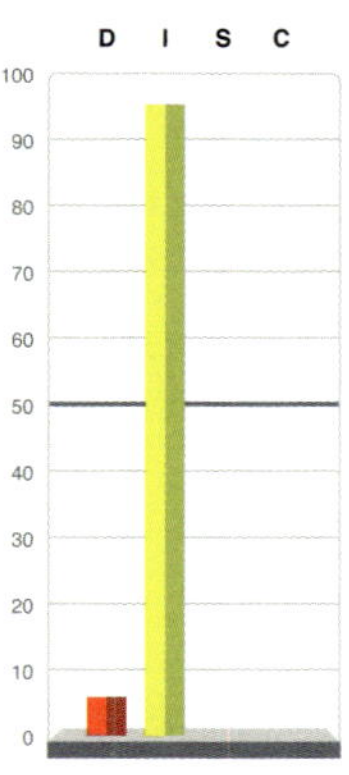	**I1. I/D** Obliging, conciseness, accommodating.	Persuasively and emotionally looks to people for support and inner satisfaction more than as a way to help reach personal goals.
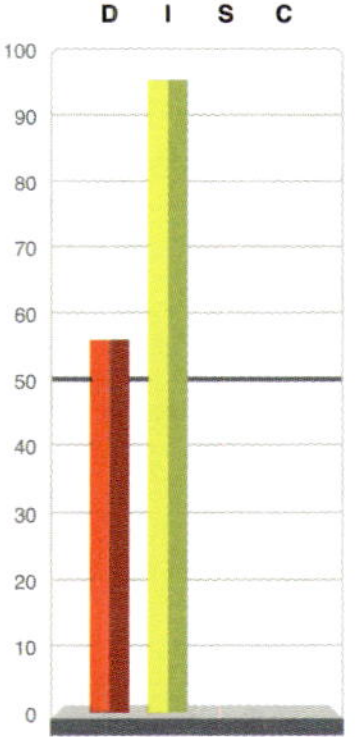	**I2. I/D** **Both above line** Amiable, friendly, affable.	Cordially enterprising. Enjoys communicating with people, with awareness for the supportive strength they provide to succeed. Convinces and promotes in a friendly, talkative manner to achieve goals.
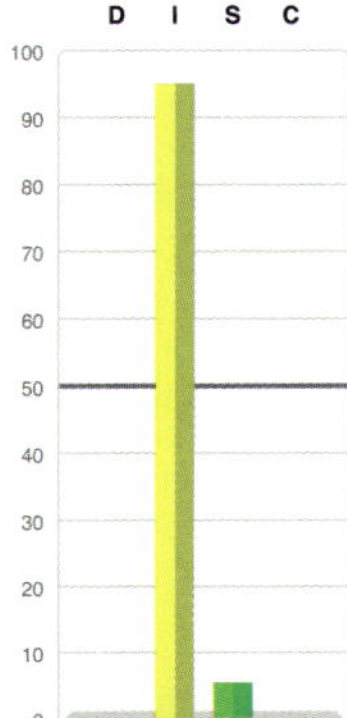	**I3. I/S** Sociable, contact ability, good mixer.	Actively seeks communications and relationships with a variety of people. Extroverted in demeanor.

© 1993-2018 Target Training International, Ltd.

	DESCRIPTORS	VERBIAGE
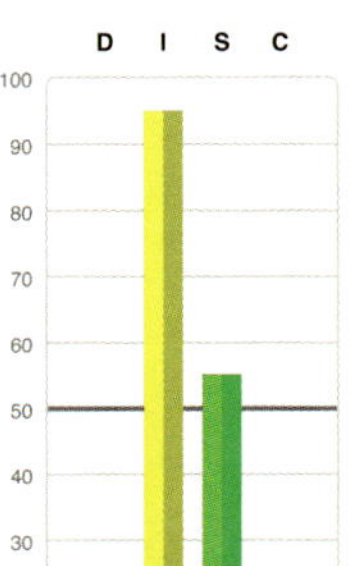	**14. I/S** **Both above line** Contact ability, good mixer, gregarious and sociable	Openly friendly with others in many situations, but primarily with groups of established friends and associates. Sociable and enjoys the uniqueness of each human being.
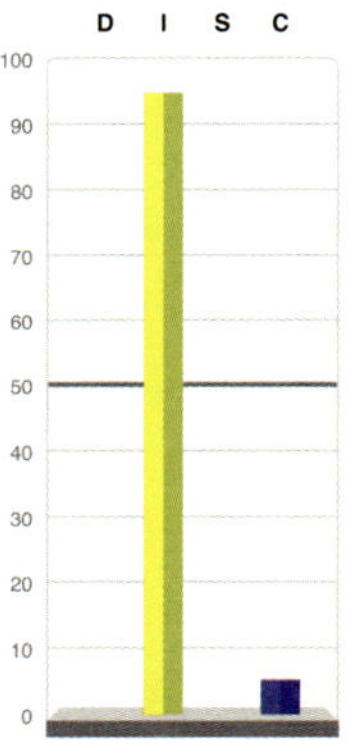	**15. I/C** Projects well, self-assured, self-confident	Confident and relaxed with others, even in social situations that may seem risky and uncertain. Sees people for their qualities rather than as a threat.
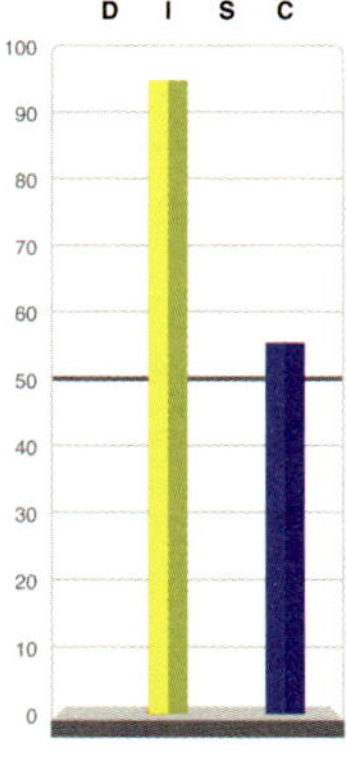	**16. I/C** **Both above line** Diplomatic, quality social relations	Interacts with people in an assured and poised manner.

	DESCRIPTORS	VERBIAGE
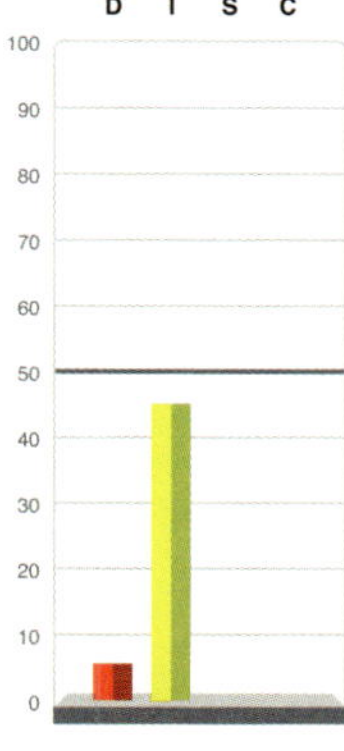	**17. I/D** **Both Below Line** Gentle, shy, meek, timid, unobtrusive, reticent, complacent	Inner intensity of each situation felt but not displayed to others. Magnified if standards are not met.
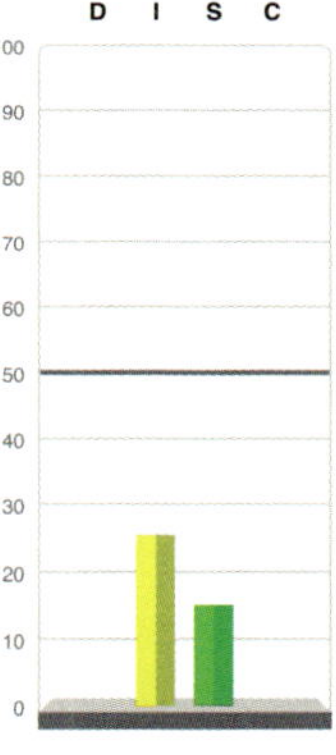	**18. I/S** **Both Below Line** Logical and matter-of-fact; flexible and variety-oriented.	Involved in more activity but with less communication. Enjoys a faster-paced, autonomous environment.
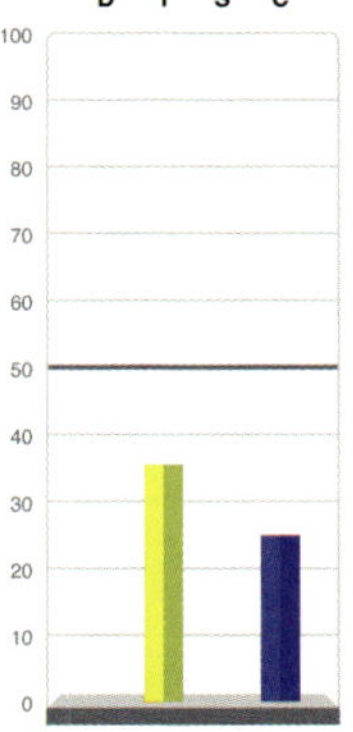	**19. I/C** **Both Below Line** Opinionated, unsystematic; independent and logical.	Able to rationalize why they bend the rules and push the boundaries.

© 1993-2018 Target Training International, Ltd.

HIGH S: STEADINESS

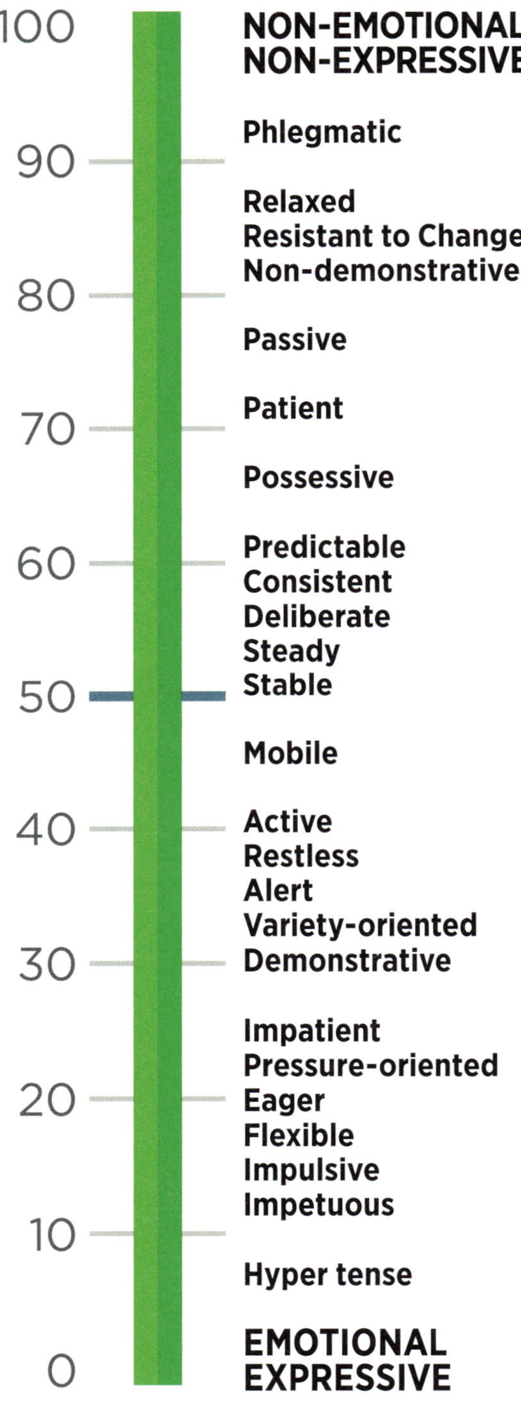

PROBABLE STRENGTHS*
- Loyal to those they identify with
- Good listener
- Patient and empathetic
- Likes to have team environment
- Long service is deemed important
- Oriented toward family activities
- Motivated toward traditional procedures

POSSIBLE LIMITATIONS*
- Tends to get in a rut,
- Maintains status quo
- Resists change
- Holds grudges
- Lacks projected sense of urgency
- Slow to act without precedent
- Hesitates to move
- Rather than delegate, may do work themselves

*Probable/Possible because we are only discussing one factor — statements may change based on intensity of the other three factors.

TOP FACTOR S STYLE COMBINATIONS

	DESCRIPTORS	VERBIAGE
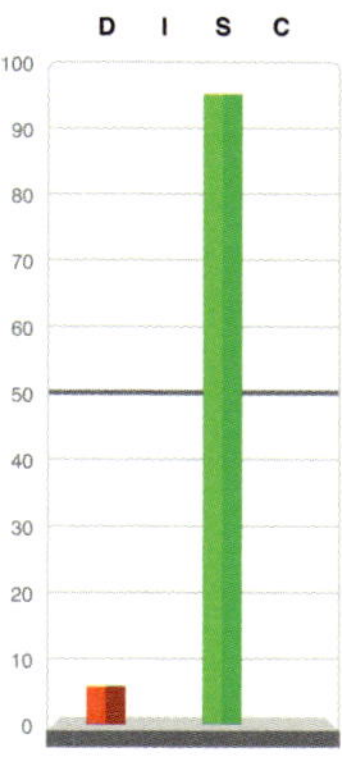	**S1. S/D** Patient, nonchalant, lackadaisical, resigned; uses humor to avoid confrontation	Patient and stable under pressure. Prefers to wait out problems and difficult encounters rather than confront them.
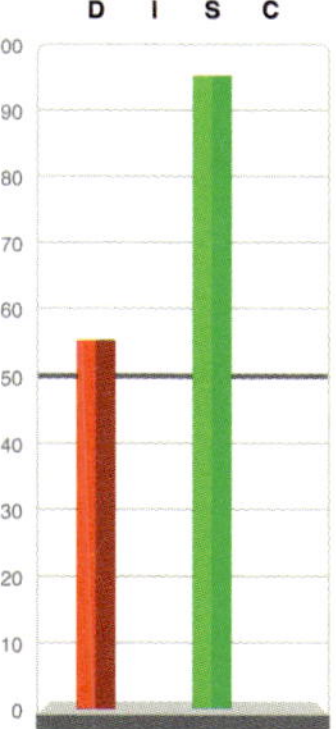	**S2. S/D** **Both above line** Patient, nonchalant, lackadaisical, resigned; can become stubborn	Tolerates difficulty and relies on situations to eventually change for the better in most cases.

© 1993-2018 Target Training International, Ltd.

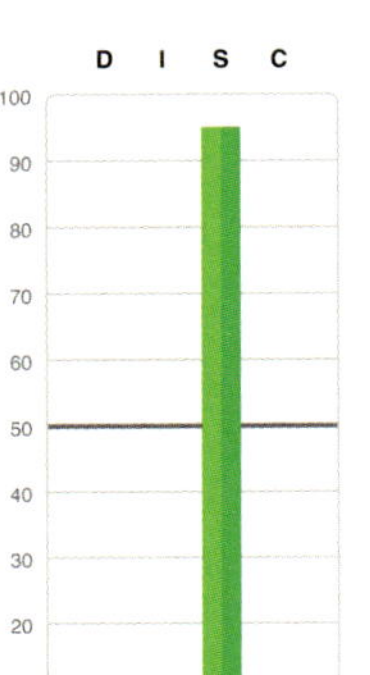

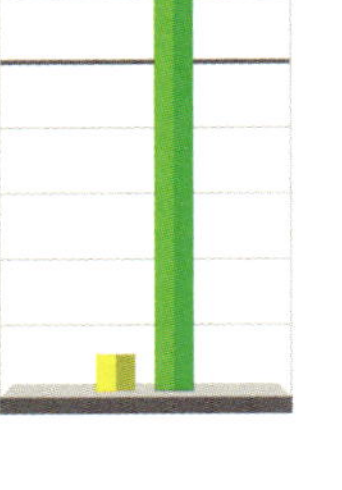

DESCRIPTORS

S3. S/I

Concentrating on details; reflective, intense, low trust.

VERBIAGE

Able to focus and not be distracted for long periods of time. Will logically and systematically center all attention on current needs, with little concern for personal loneliness or being liked by others.

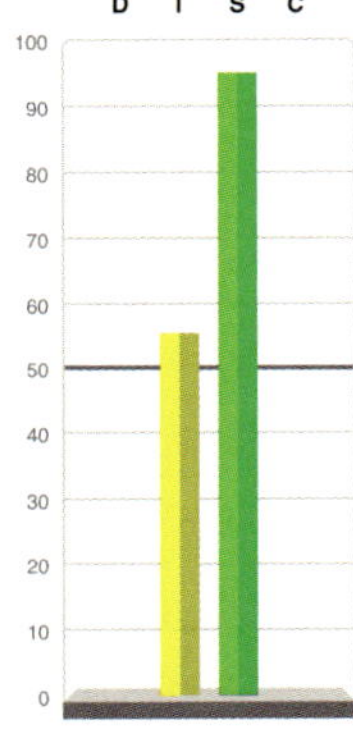

DESCRIPTORS

S4. S/I

Both above line

Concentrating on details; reflective, intense.

Is intent and reflective, but friendly. Accepts and depends on the support of selected individuals.

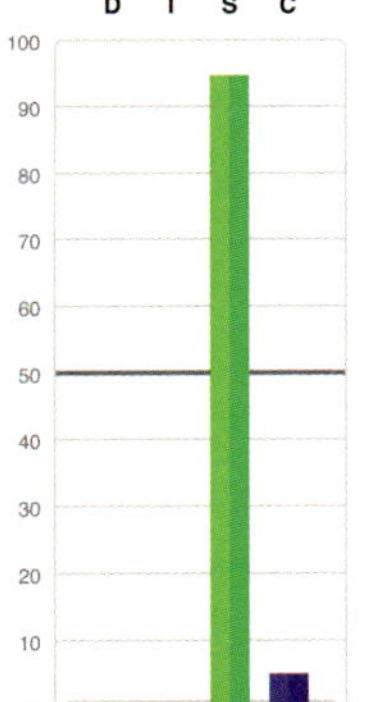

S5. S/C

Persistent, persevering; may display some independence.

Persistently holds to views, even when they are contrary to the opinions of others. May be dogmatic in nature and extremely resistant to change in approaches to problems and people.

	DESCRIPTORS	VERBIAGE
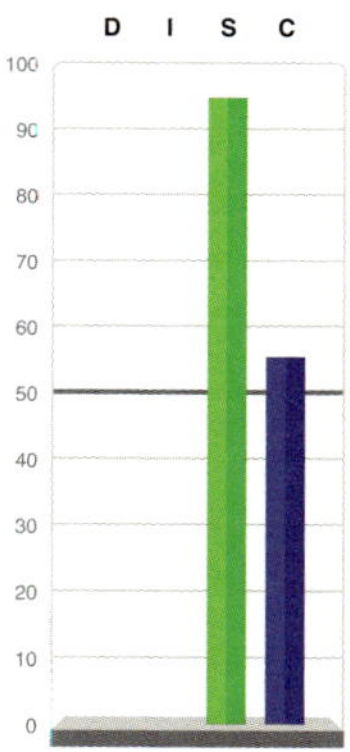	**S6. S/C** **Both above line** Persistent, persevering.	Determined to be on course with past procedures, but not at the expense of quality or with no regard for the expectations of others.
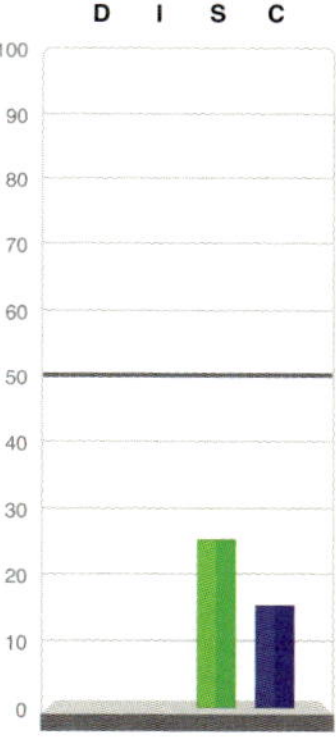	**S7. S/C** **Both below line** Spontaneous and unconventional; expressive and opinionated.	Will engage quickly to push the pace, fostering out-of-the-box thinking.

© 1993-2018 Target Training International, Ltd.

HIGH C: COMPLIANCE

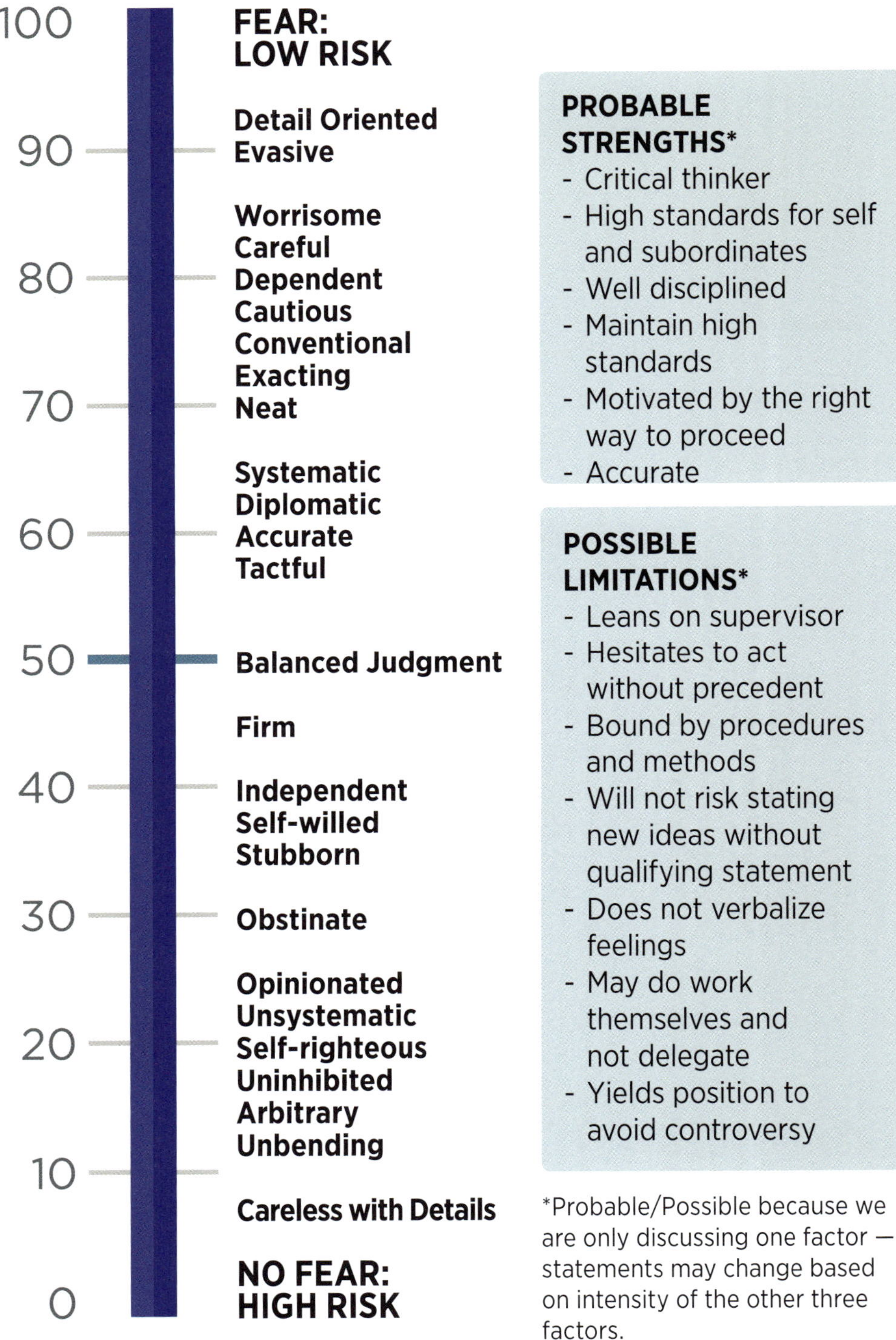

PROBABLE STRENGTHS*

- Critical thinker
- High standards for self and subordinates
- Well disciplined
- Maintain high standards
- Motivated by the right way to proceed
- Accurate

POSSIBLE LIMITATIONS*

- Leans on supervisor
- Hesitates to act without precedent
- Bound by procedures and methods
- Will not risk stating new ideas without qualifying statement
- Does not verbalize feelings
- May do work themselves and not delegate
- Yields position to avoid controversy

*Probable/Possible because we are only discussing one factor — statements may change based on intensity of the other three factors.

TOP FACTOR C STYLE COMBINATIONS

	DESCRIPTORS	VERBIAGE
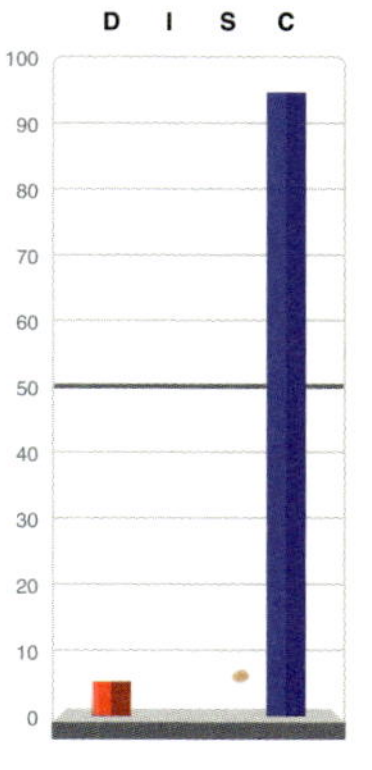	**C1. C/D** Adaptable, dependable, soft-spoken. Uses humor to avoid confrontation.	Willing to adapt rather than risk confrontation. Behaves according to established and respected systems and procedures.
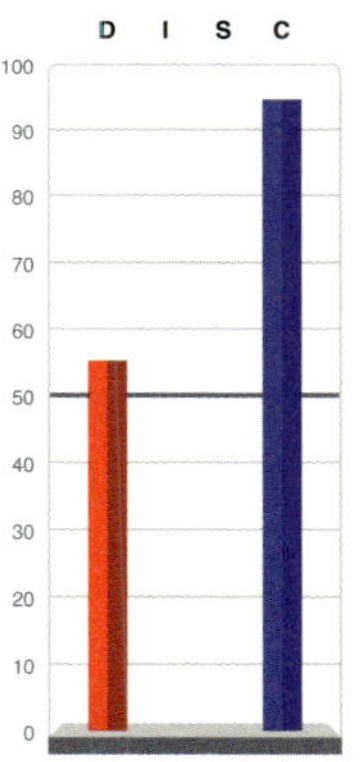	**C2. C/D** **Both above line** Adaptable, dependable, soft-spoken; will confront when pushed.	Diplomatic and concerned with the approval of others, especially of supervisors and key associates. Probably will push quite hard to find correct, acceptable answers.

© 1993-2018 Target Training International, Ltd.

	DESCRIPTORS	VERBIAGE
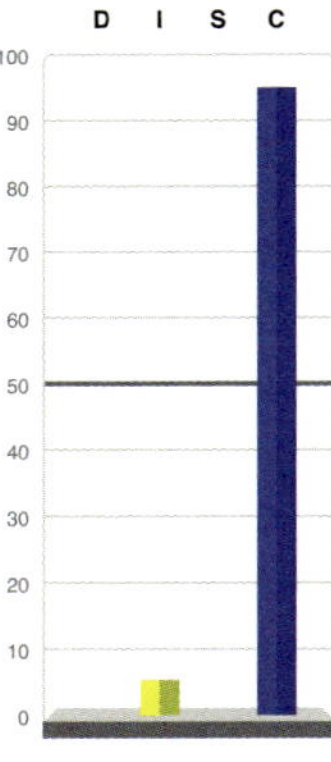	**C3. C/I** Precise, accurate, perfectionist; careful with details.	A stickler for quality, system and order. Precise, with utmost concern for quality. Analytical rather than persuasive in efforts to achieve correctness.
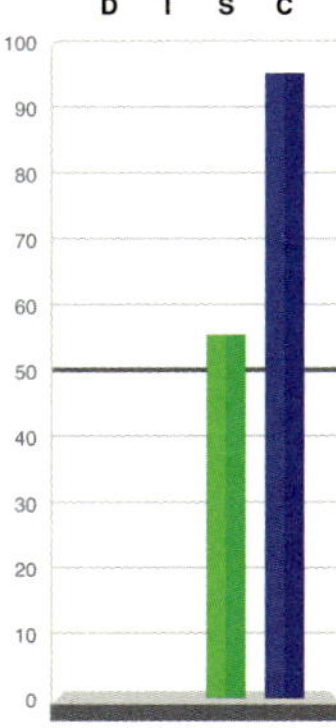	**C4. C/S** **Both above line** Precise, accurate, perfectionist; careful with details; stickler for quality, system and order; situational with application of descriptors.	Alert and ready to adapt to respected systems and procedures, but cautious and takes time to assess possible consequences. Especially wary of making change, which may damage long-standing relationships and/or is contrary to deeply ingrained techniques and procedures.

DESCRIPTORS	VERBIAGE
C5. C/S Alert and sensitive to: problems, controls, dangers, mistakes, errors, rules, regulations, procedures; aware of social, economic and political implications of one's decisions.	Very sensitive to changes in the social and work environment, willing to adapt accordingly. Complying with what seems correct at the moment may result in being impulsive in actions.

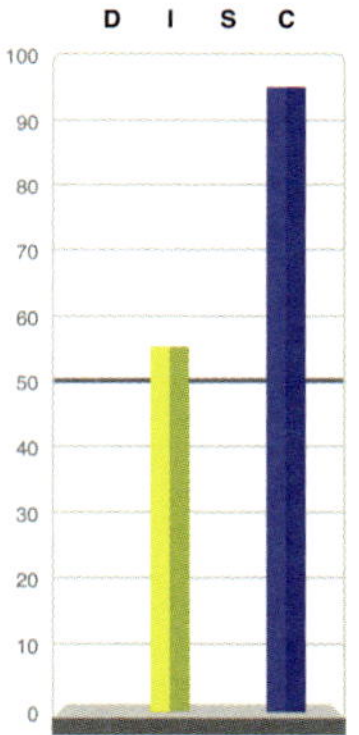

DESCRIPTORS	VERBIAGE
C6. C/I **Both above line** Alert and sensitive to: problems, controls, dangers, mistakes, errors, rules, regulations, procedures, disciplines.	Organized, even in relationships. Polite and cooperative with people. Appreciates company of people with similar ideas and views as theirs who are organized and quality conscious.

© 1993-2018 Target Training International, Ltd.

EMOTIONS OF THE FOUR DIMENSIONS

D EMOTION: ANGER

The higher the plotting point, the more the person will tend to have a short fuse, or be impatient. This does not mean they will "blow up." They may be able to control the anger, but they definitely will become impatient and anger quickly.

The lower the D plotting point, the more the person will tend to be patient and slow to anger.

I EMOTION: OPTIMISM/TRUST

The higher the I plotting point the more the person will look on the bright side of things and exhibit a high trust level.

The lower the I plotting point, the more the person will tend to be pessimistic and exhibit a low level of trust.

S EMOTION: NON-EMOTIONAL

The S has feelings. However, the higher the plotting point of the S, the more the person will not demonstrate or show their emotion, because they do not want to burden you with their problems. The person will internalize the emotion and tell you everything is all right when it isn't.

The lower the S factor, the more you will hear and see the emotion the person is going through.

C EMOTION: FEAR

The higher the C factor, the more the person will follow the rules due to a fear of making mistakes or errors. A C factor above the midline will tend to go by the book. The fear factor may be hidden and not shown.

The lower the C factor the more the person is likely to be a high risk-taker, showing little fear; may believe rules are just guidelines and will break them, if necessary.

GRAPH READING

STEP 3: CHECK GRAPH I & GRAPH II DISPARITY

Research has shown that adapting behavior in Graph I that is significantly different from Graph II can cause stress, mental health problems and job dissatisfaction. The larger the movement, the more significant the correlation. **An example of disparity can be demonstrated by the following graphs:**

Graph I - Adapted

Graph II - Natural

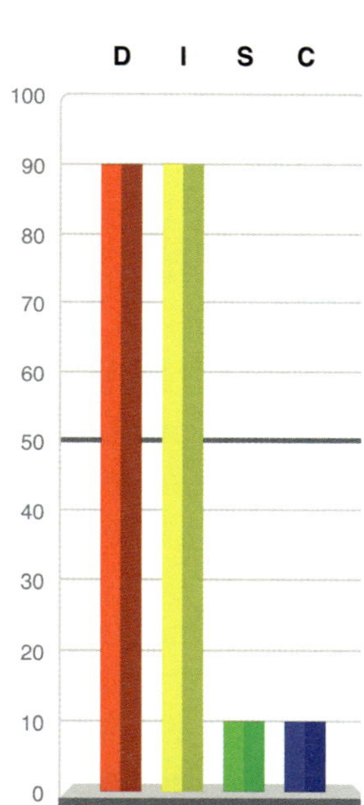

When a High D, High I, Low S or Low C goes to church, the environment calls for the person to adapt their behavior to Low D, Low I, High S, High C. A person can tolerate this type of change for a period of time. The time expands if the person's passion, beliefs and value needs are being met. The same person experiences the same adapted behavior when they work on doing their tax returns. Excessive time spent in an activity that a person sees of little or no value can cause stress. This is the reason many salespeople have resisted call reporting systems.

© 1993-2018 Target Training International, Ltd.

Adapting: Is the change between Graph I (Adapted) and Graph II (Natural) job related? By this we mean: Is Graph I mirroring the Workplace Behaviors Graph? If the answer is "yes," then the adapted behavior will enhance performance on the job.

If Graph I is significantly different from the Workplace Behaviors Graph, we must do a little detective work. **The person could be adapting behavior for any of the following reasons:**

- **Trying to survive.**
- **Guarding themselves from consequence or because of fear.**
- **Don't understand the behavior needed to be successful on the job.**
- **Searching to discover who they really are.**

Any movement in a factor from Graph II to Graph I indicates you are adapting your behavior to meet the demands of your current environment. Always look at the direction of the movement from the intensity of each factor in Graph II.

The following information will provide insights into typically what the movement means. However, until you analyze the environment, we can only give you some ideas as to what typical movement means. **Why a person is adapting their style is important to discover.** A person may adapt their behavior in Graph I to survive or succeed. Care should be taken to discover the true motive behind the change. If it is job related, the person is adapting to succeed. If the change is not job related, then security may be an issue.

WHAT ADAPTING MEANS

EXAMPLE ONE: (Up or down movement based on change from Graph II)

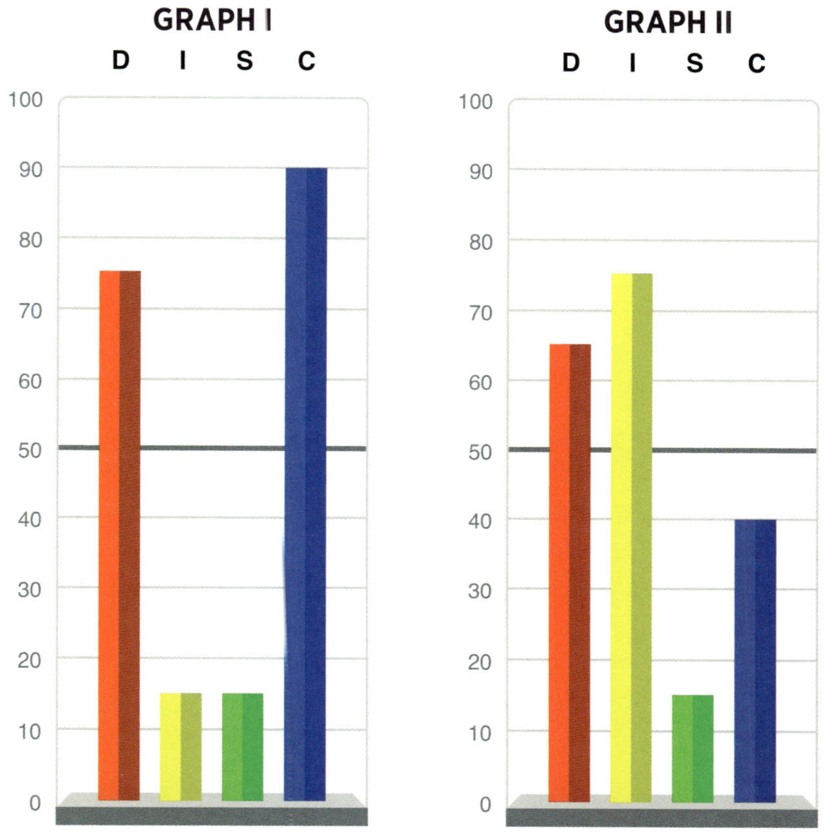

D Not significant movement.

I Moves down.

S Not significant movement.

C Moves up.

© 1993-2018 Target Training International, Ltd.

POSSIBLE INTERPRETATION

I Lowering trust level.

C Responding to procedures (security, concerns).

Typically when we see this type of situation, the person has been hurt in a relationship or laid off from a job. They are lowering their I factor to guard from being hurt by being too trusting. This experience has led them to meet their security needs by following procedures or not taking risks.

WHAT ADAPTING TYPICALLY MEANS

Direction of factor movement is determined from Graph II to Graph I.	
D goes up	Become more assertive and challenge-oriented.
D goes down	Become less assertive.
I goes up	Become more outgoing and people-oriented.
I goes down	Become less trusting, guard what you share.
S goes up	Slow the world down.
S goes down	Increase activity level and pace.
C goes up	Respond to procedures, lower risk taking or protects security.
C goes down	Become more independent, be your own person.

Graph disparity should be a concern to all when the change is significant. An open discussion will usually lead to discovery of the real reason for adapting new behavior.

NOTE **Many or most unemployed people raise their C factor in Graph I. This is a response to society's rules. When unemployed, you must call, write, interview, etc.**

Currently, many employees who were fortunate enough not to get a pink slip or be fired raise their C factor. They are adapting behavior so they are not the next person out the door. This is their response to their security needs.

© 1993-2018 Target Training International, Ltd.

DISPARITY & CORRELATION

EXAMPLE TWO:

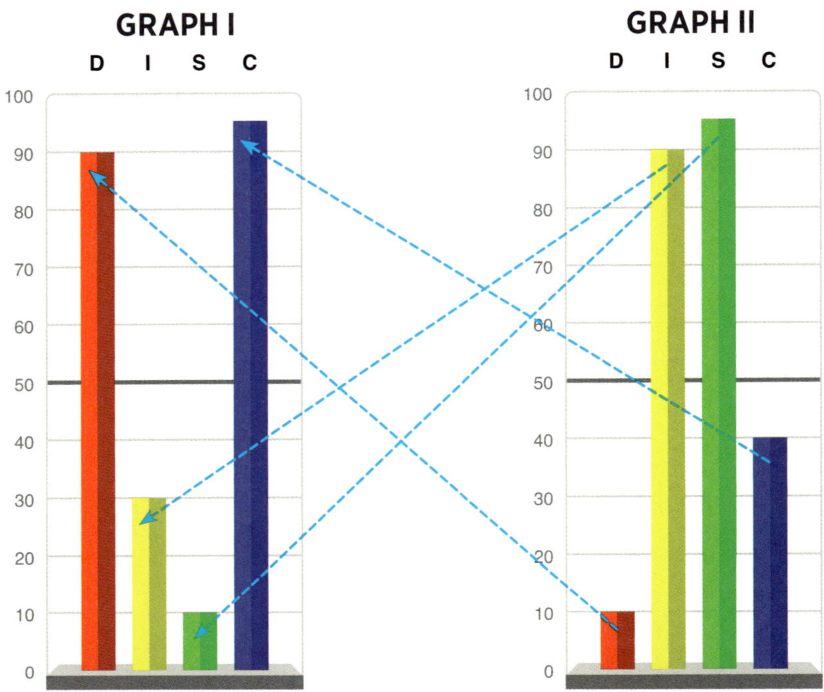

Research conducted by Dr. David Warburton and Judy Suiter indicates that the disparity between Graph I and Graph II has a correlation with job satisfaction, health problems and stress. Although further research needs to be completed, the initial finding shows that when there is disparity between Graphs I and II, job satisfaction goes down over a period of time and health problems increase. Common sense also tells us that an introverted person would probably not be very happy as an outside salesperson and an extroverted person would not fit into an accounting profession handling data all day long. The person in Example 2 masks their true behavior to succeed in their environment (Graph I). This person is expending a great amount of energy to maintain the mask and admitted to being under a great deal of stress.

EXAMPLE THREE:

GRAPH I – ADAPTED

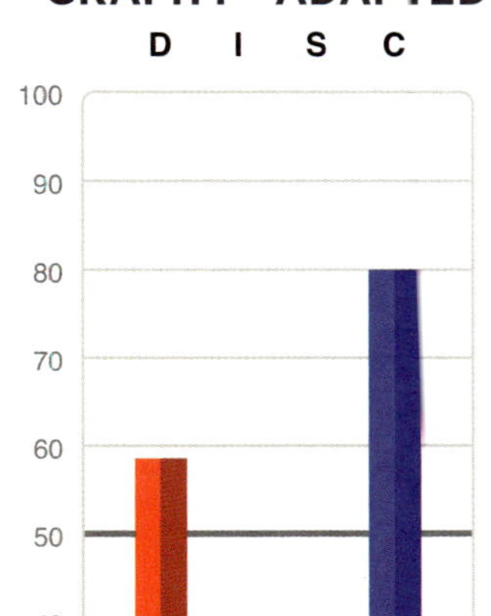

GRAPH II – NATURAL

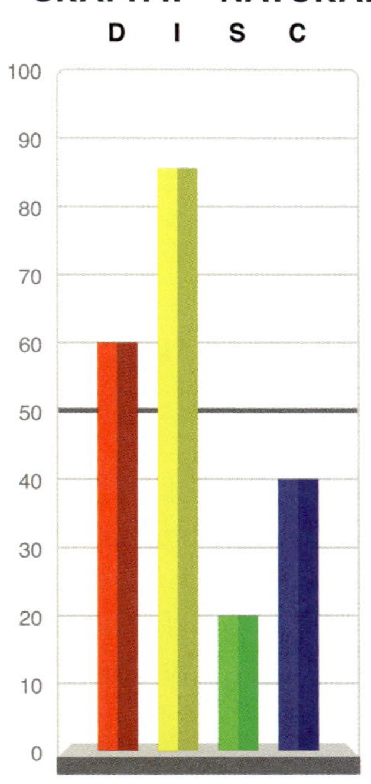

No Disparity:

D The plotting point of the D factor in both graphs is about the same.

S The plotting point of the S factor in both graphs is about the same.

Disparity:

I Note the High I in Graph II is a Low I in Graph I. Emotionally, this person normally displays a great deal of optimism and trust (Graph II), but in his work environment (Graph I) is displaying pessimism and distrust. Why? This question should be asked, and dialogue can resolve the difference.

© 1993-2018 Target Training International, Ltd.

C Note the C movement from just below the Energy Line in Graph II to a very high intensity of Graph I. Naturally, this person tends to follow rules depending on the situation. However, in the work environment, this person is totally following established rules and procedures. Emotionally, the person is displaying in Graph I a high degree of compliance. Why? Again, the question should be asked and dialogued.

NOTE **It has been validated that when a person is afraid of losing his/her job, the C factor will rise to a high intensity in Graph I.**

More research needs to be done on the effect masking has on mental and emotional health and well being. Graph I and Graph II disparity has a definite effect on stress, mental ill health, and job satisfaction, as shown by research of Dr. David Warburton and Judy Suiter.

STEP 4: REPEAT THE PROCESS FOR GRAPH I (ADAPTED)

Use this four-step process in conjunction with Style Insights Instrument Graph I for greater behavioral understanding of their adapted behavior. TTI reads the graphs in a similar manner analyzing both the high and low intensity levels in Graphs I and II.

UNUSUAL GRAPHS

Although the Style Insights Instrument is designed to measure NORMAL BEHAVIOR, there are two graphs that can occur which indicate unusual behavior. The Style Insights Instrument is not a clinical instrument; however, it is used by many professionals as a tool to assist people in understanding their behavior. The two unusual patterns must be approached based on their occurrence in either Graph I or Graph II.

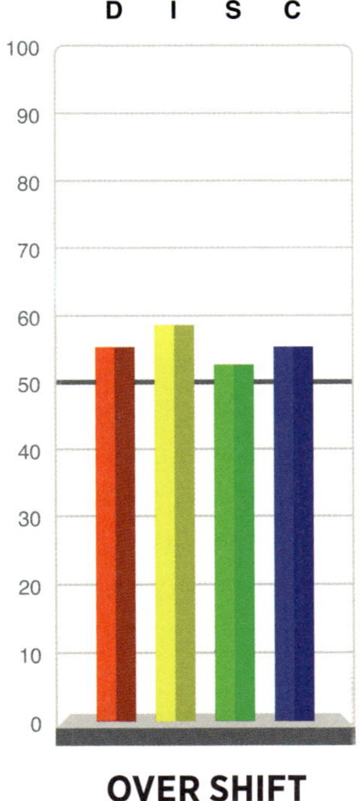

OVER SHIFT
All plotting points above the energy line.

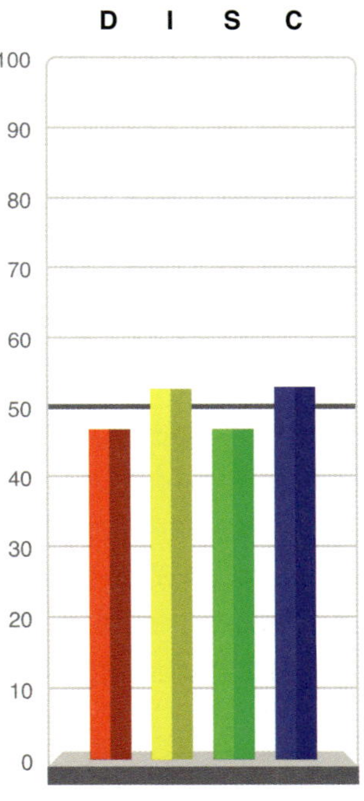

TIGHT
All plotting points near the energy line (45 to 55 percent).

© 1993-2018 Target Training International, Ltd.

Unusual graphs (Over shift, Tight) in Graph I may be caused by the following reasons:

1. Attempting to outsmart the instrument.
2. Trying to be an overachiever.
3. Over-analyzing by taking too long to respond.
4. Being new to the job and not understanding the behavior required to be successful.
5. Transition from one environment to another.
6. Inability to understand the adjectives.

Unusual patterns in Graph I are usually temporary. Having the person respond to the instrument again with a proper focus will usually produce the proper graph. Also, a person new to the job needs to wait a few weeks before responding to the second instrument, so they have the opportunity to determine the correct work behavior. Use the Workplace Behaviors Instrument to discover the behavior needed by the job and then discuss the results. **(Refer to Chapter 7)**

Unusual graphs (Over shift, Tight) in Graph II can be caused by a person who is:

1. Attempting to outsmart the instrument.
2. Over-analyzing by taking too long to respond.
3. Experiencing a significant emotional event or a personal trauma (Tight graph only).
4. Under pressure to "be all things to all people" (Over shift graph only).
5. Inability to understand the adjectives.

When an unusual pattern appears in Graph II, ask questions to determine if the person understood the questionnaire and had an ideal setting to take the questionnaire. If the person was interrupted or had trouble completing the questionnaire, ask the person to retake the assessment. Then if the same pattern appears, it should be taken seriously. This person is experiencing discomfort and the result will have a direct effect on performance. Many times professional help is needed for this person to discover who he/she really is, or what factors are influencing his/her graph results.

© 1993-2018 Target Training International, Ltd.

TTI'S SUCCESS INSIGHTS WHEEL®

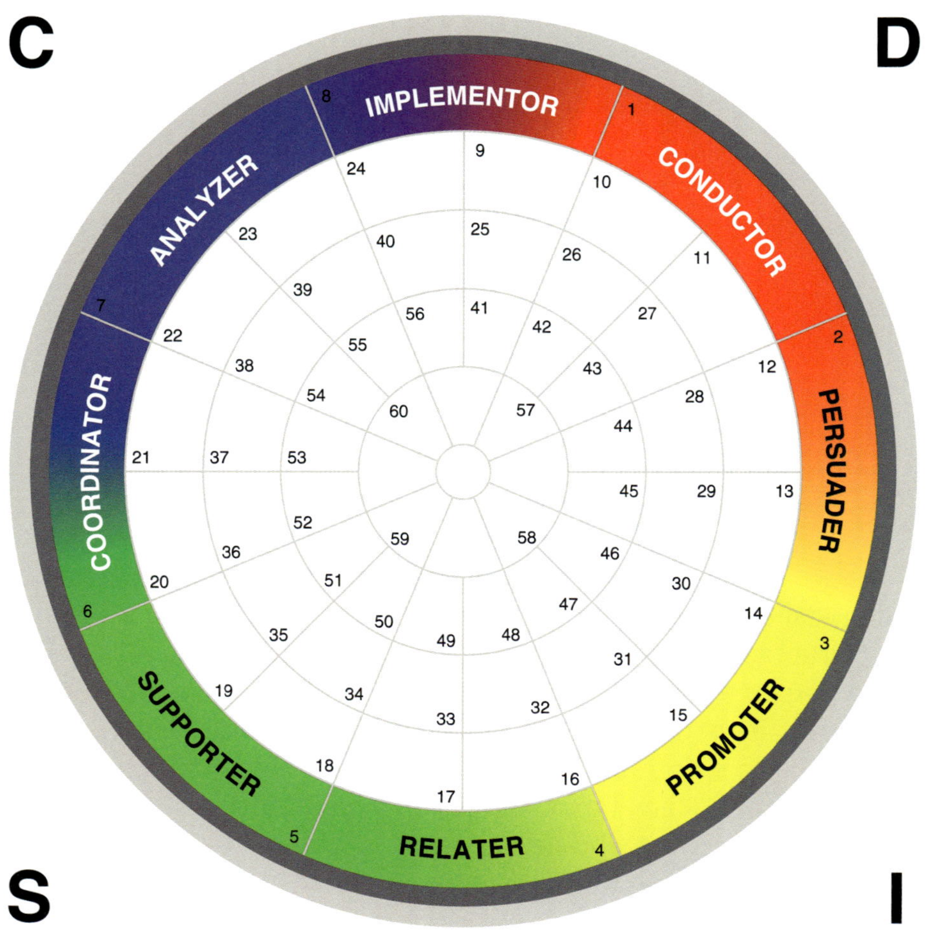

The Success Insights Wheel was added to reports to visually enhance the understanding of one's behavior both naturally and in the work environment. TTI is the first behavioral assessment company to use a wheel page to plot behavior. The Success Insights Wheel has proven its value by increasing the overall understanding of TTI reports, decreasing the time needed to train, and eliminating the need for clients to be able to read graphs.

Why was the Success Insights Wheel developed? TTI believes that visual aids are an important component in learning. People especially benefit from learning the DISC concept and language through a visual model that is easily understood, such as the Success Insights Wheel. The Wheel provides a visual format for plotting the data obtained from the Style Insights response form. We believe the Wheel model is an easier method of introducing DISC.

The Wheel can be used to demonstrate the behavioral differences between a person's Natural Style, Adapted Style and Workplace Behaviors®. In addition, the DISC professional can plot an entire team's behavioral composition and identify potential conflicts at a glance.

TTI is the first behavioral assessment company to use a wheel page to explain behavior. The Success Insights Wheel was first used by TTI's Success Insight's European Distributors. It has proven its value by eliminating the need for your clients to have graph reading skills.

© 1993-2018 Target Training International, Ltd.

HOW TO INTERPRET THE SUCCESS INSIGHTS WHEEL

The Success Insights Wheel uses the 60 most common graphs. The Wheel model is comprised of 48 basic graphs with 12 exceptions. A person's high factor determines the quadrant in which the graph will appear. The TTI Success Insights reports are generated based on 384 graphs, which represent 324 more individualized graph interpretations.

The SUCCESS INSIGHTS WHEEL is made up of eight different spokes, which are:	
Relater	I,S
Supporter	S
Coordinator	S,C
Analyzer	C
Implementer	D,C
Conductor	D
Persuader	D,I
Promoter	I

TTI SUCCESS INSIGHTS WHEEL® APPLICATIONS

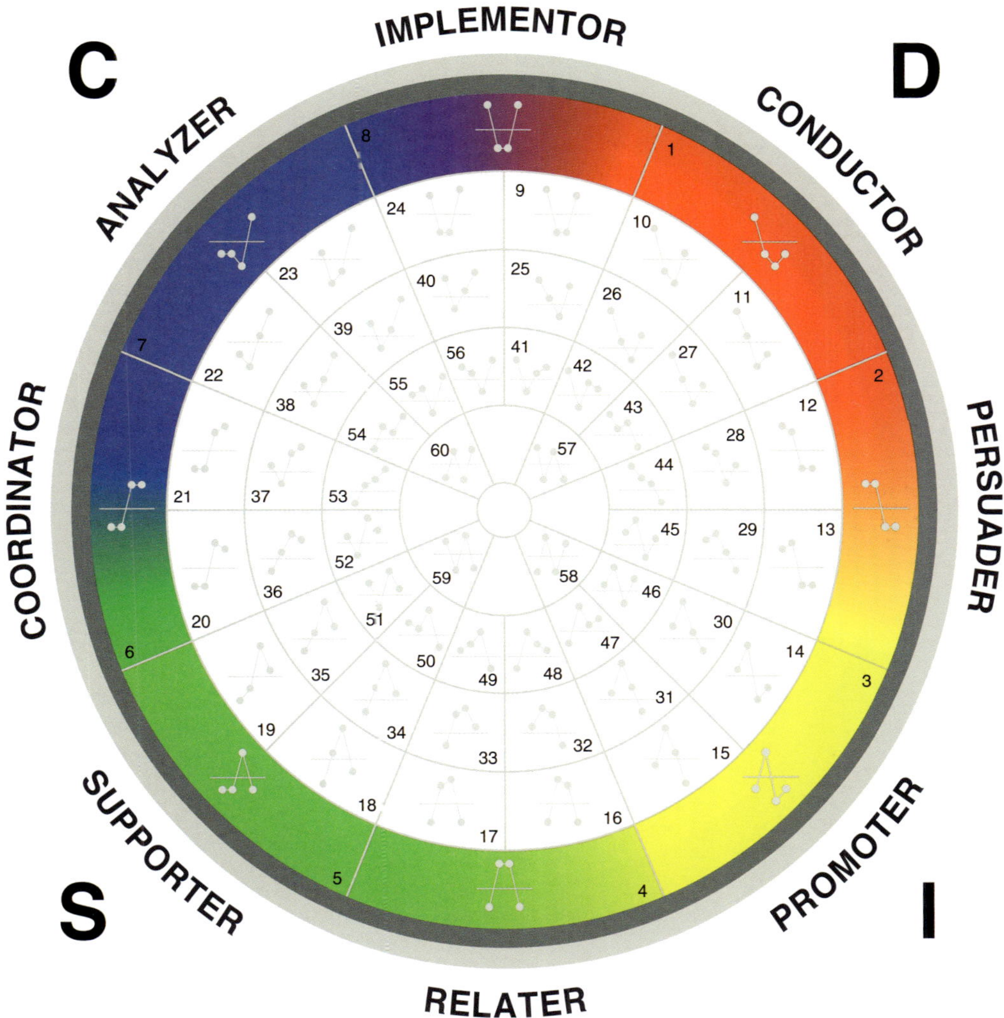

© 1993-2018 Target Training International, Ltd.

How is this person adapting?

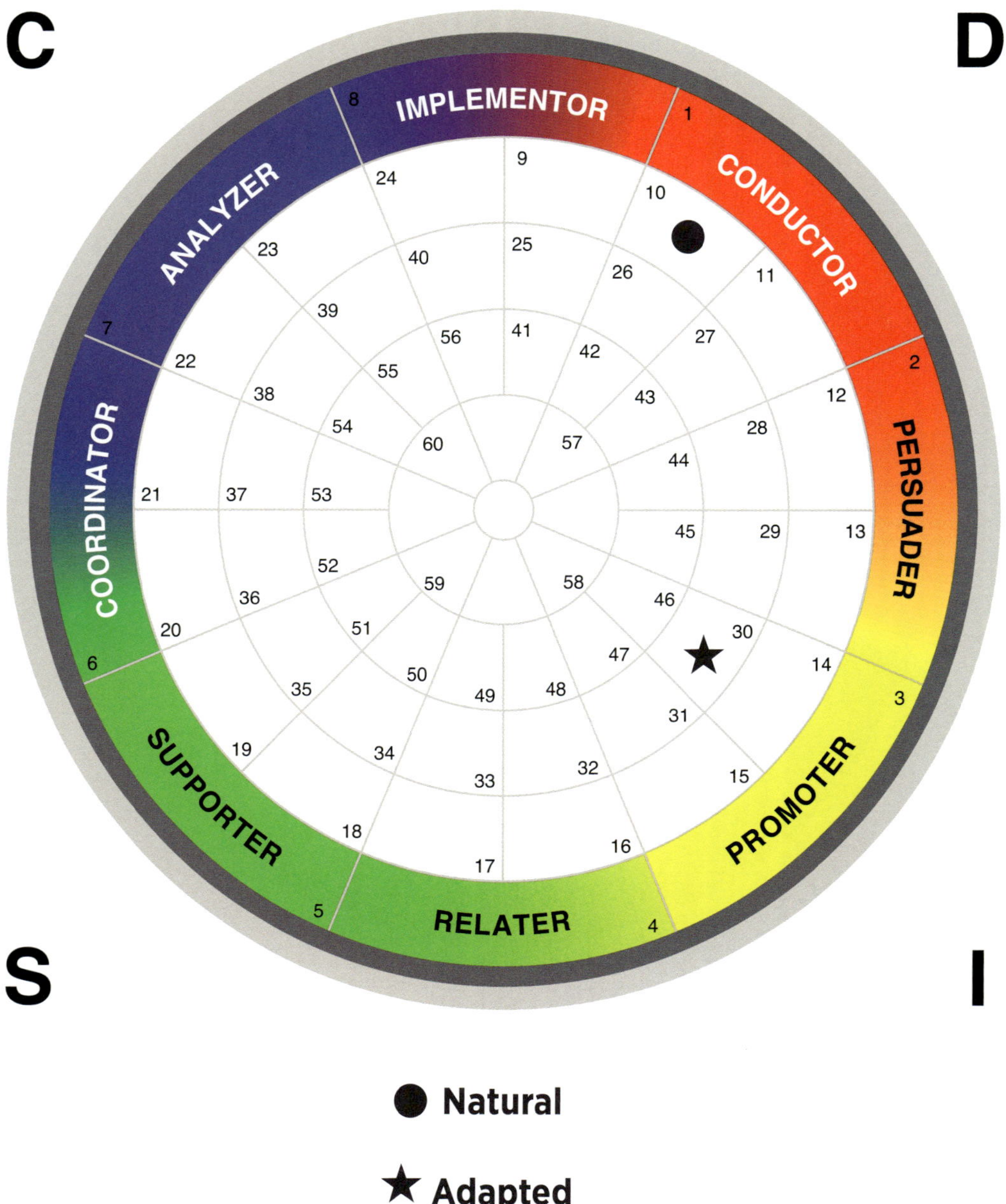

How will Person A and Person B get along?

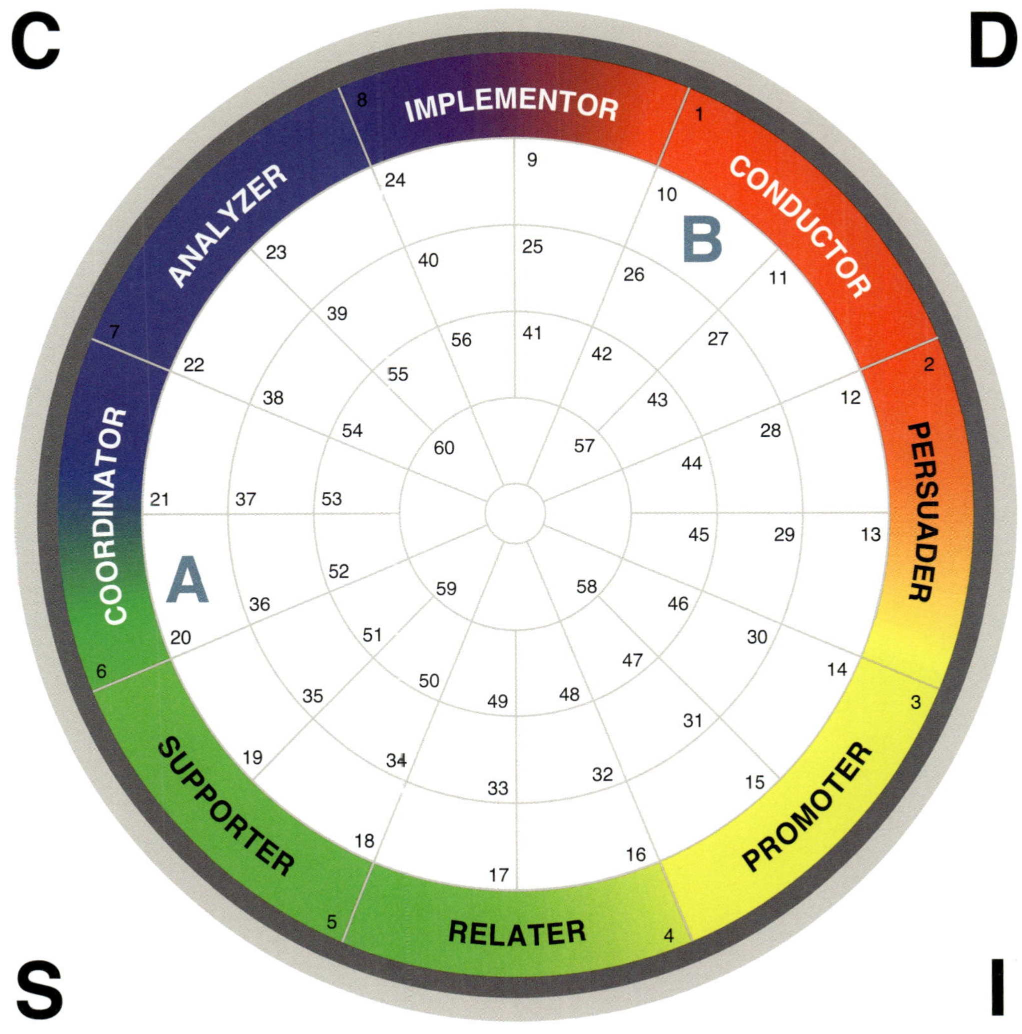

© 1993-2018 Target Training International, Ltd.

A person adapting behavior due to job-related issues:

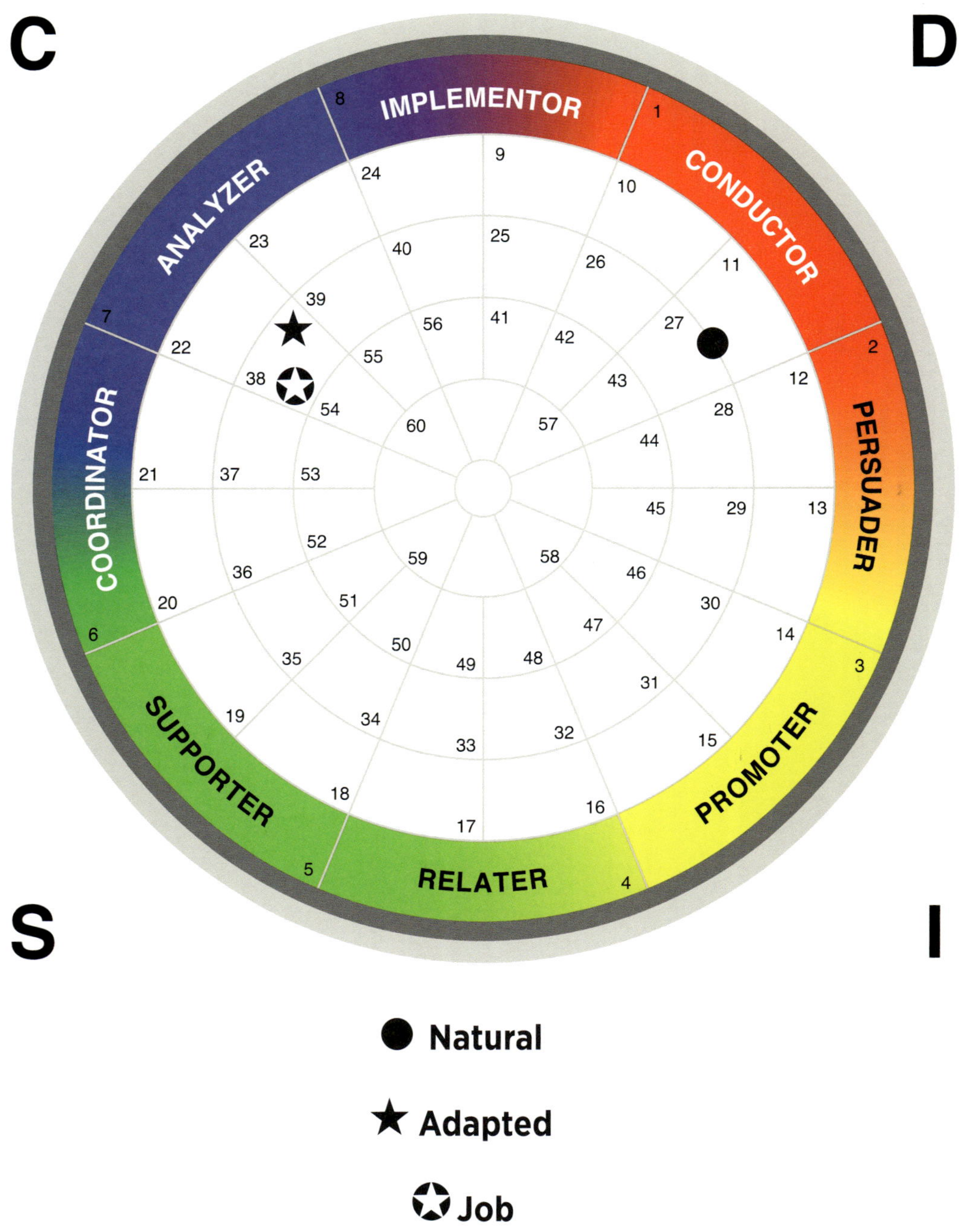

OBJECTIVES REVISITED

Our research proves that the mastering of these objectives is directly related to your success.

© 1993-2018 Target Training International, Ltd.

BLENDING THE LANGUAGE

Chapter Objective

To move from basic to more advanced knowledge and application of the language by examining compatibility and blending of the different styles therefore enhancing communication and team performance.

Chapter Contents

- Introduction
- Blending the Language: Style Combinations
- High D blending
- High I blending
- High S blending
- High C blending
- Objectives Revisited

"I didn't say that I didn't say it. I said that I didn't say that I said it. I want to make that perfectly clear."

–George Romney

© 1993-2018 Target Training International, Ltd.

INTRODUCTION

PEOPLE GENERALLY MAKE THE MISTAKE OF ASSUMING THAT OTHERS INTERACT AND THINK IN THE SAME WAY THEY DO.

One of the biggest challenges to effective interaction is to recognize that people may have a behavioral style different from our own. Much interaction breaks down immediately because of a lack of awareness of behavioral differences. All people do not communicate the same way.

Effective communicators will first:

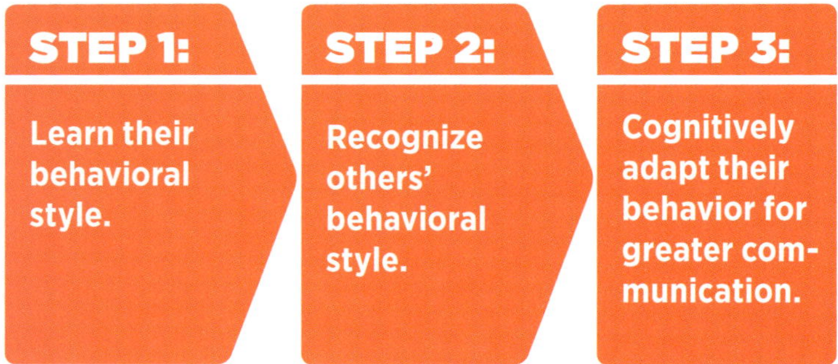

One of the most important skills to acquire is the ability to interact effectively with people at all levels of the organization. **Over 80% of the people who move up in corporations are promoted because of their people skills, NOT technical ability.**

Most people already adapt their behavior to the environment. The DISC language provides the knowledge to be able to adapt more quickly to the person by observing behavioral cues.

BLENDING THE LANGUAGE: STYLE COMBINATIONS

Understanding how the different styles "blend" will allow for a more thorough understanding of the DISC language and its powerful impact on interpersonal relationships and work interactions.

The DISC model interprets HOW we act. Most relational problems, either work, social, or personal are based on conflicting beliefs (values). DISC does not measure an individual's values. Many people who have conflicting behavioral styles (DISC) have had long, successful relationships. Why? Understanding and adapting.

NOTE **An individual whose highest plotting point in Graph II is the D factor is referred to as a High D in this chapter (likewise with the I, S, and C factors). Please remember, "how" a person acts is determined by the intensity of all four factors, high and low.**

Behavioral Style Match (BSM)

This rating of either good or fair, indicates how well styles will initially blend and how much a person must adapt to effectively communicate. It is followed by a graphic showing the "comfort zone" and the "discomfort zone" of the interaction.

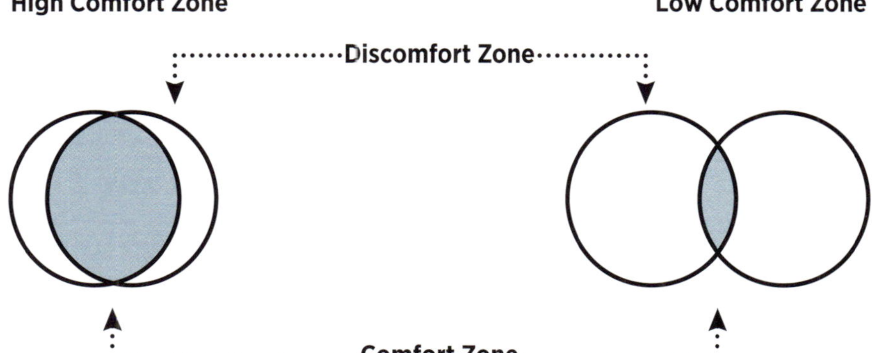

© 1993-2018 Target Training International, Ltd.

FIRST IMPRESSIONS & SOCIAL INTERACTIONS

How Your Style May Initially React with Various Styles

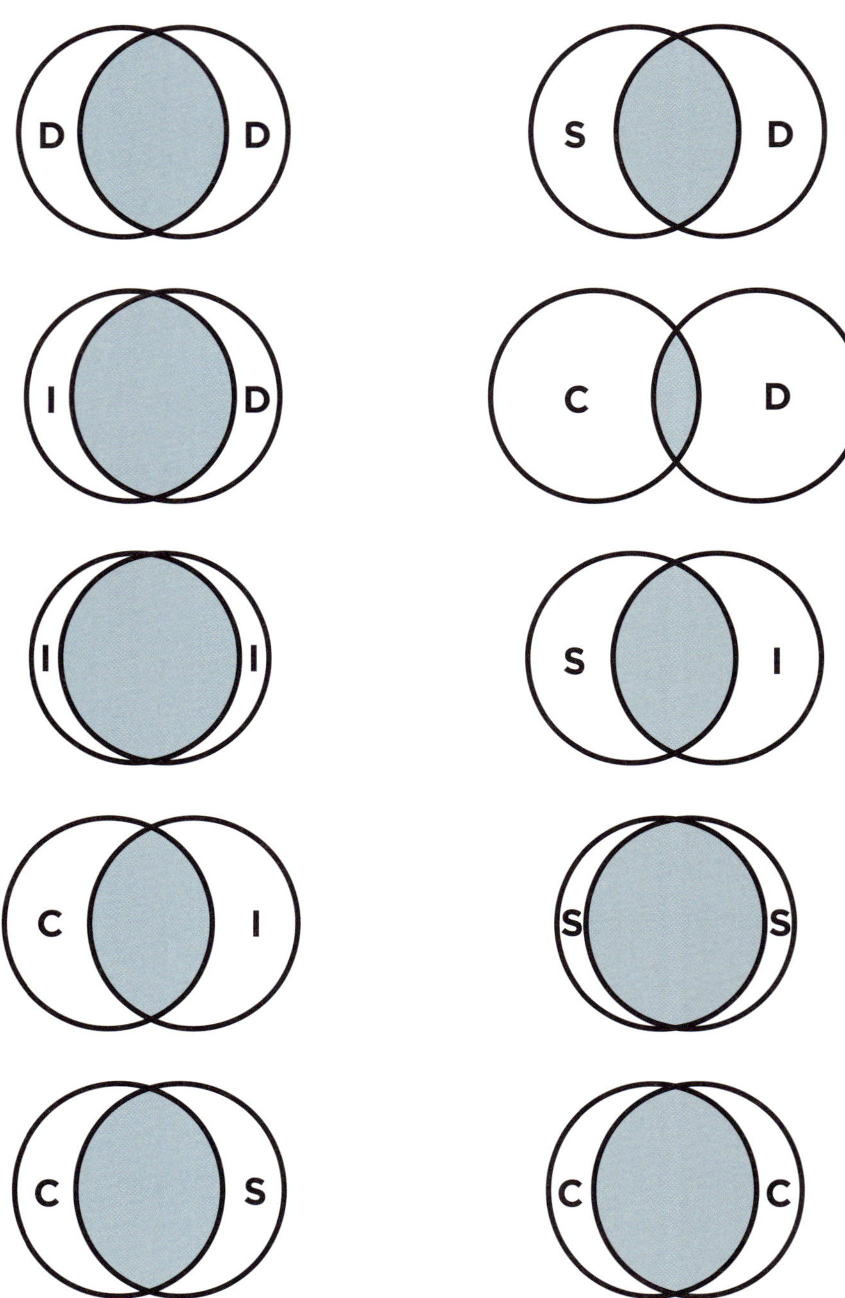

HIGH D BLENDING

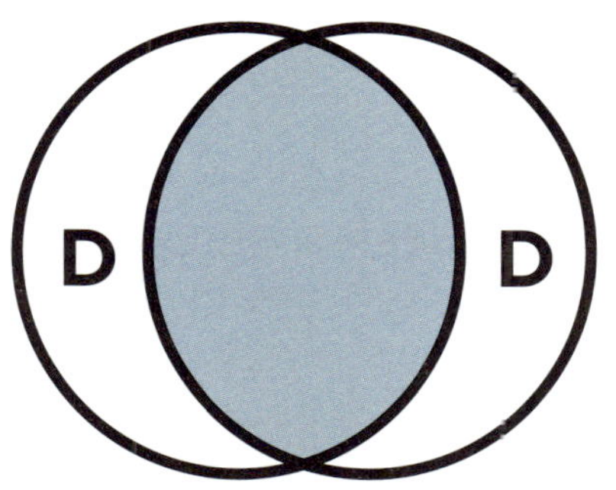

HIGH D / HIGH D
High D communicating with a High D

BSM: Good

High D's are competitive, direct and self-reliant. Two High D's will understand each other's drive for action. Both need a challenge and both need to direct. Expect the discussion between the two to be lively, as both are unafraid of conflict. If a vision and purpose is clearly painted, the High D's can work together well to get it done. Both are high risk-takers and may need to slow down to look at the facts. Because of their tendency to be task-oriented, each will need to heighten their awareness of the other and cognitively take time to listen before acting.

High D is looking for: RESULTS/EFFICIENCY

© 1993-2018 Target Training International, Ltd.

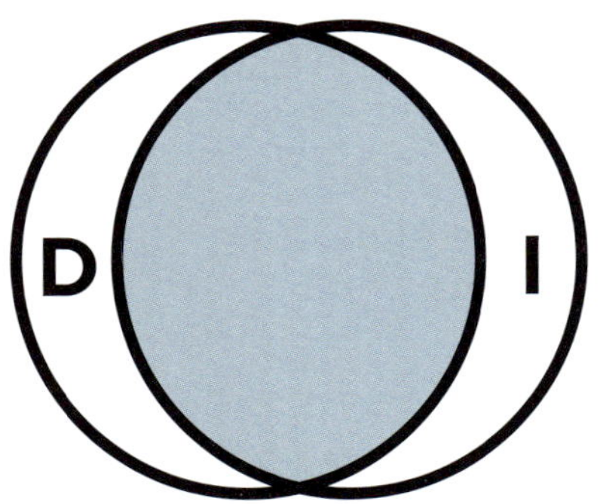

HIGH D / HIGH I
High D communicating with a High I

BSM: Good

The High D and High I are both risk-takers and desire to change their environment and the world, for better or worse (depending on their values). Both extroverted, they differ in the way they approach people. The High I will use verbal ability to win others to their argument, whereas the High D will be very direct and to the point. Working well together, the High D will need to add a little fun to the task and slow down just a bit, knowing that interaction and fun are motivating to the High I. The High D must allow the High I to verbalize and also must allow a bit more time for the decisions to be made.

High I is looking for: The EXPERIENCE

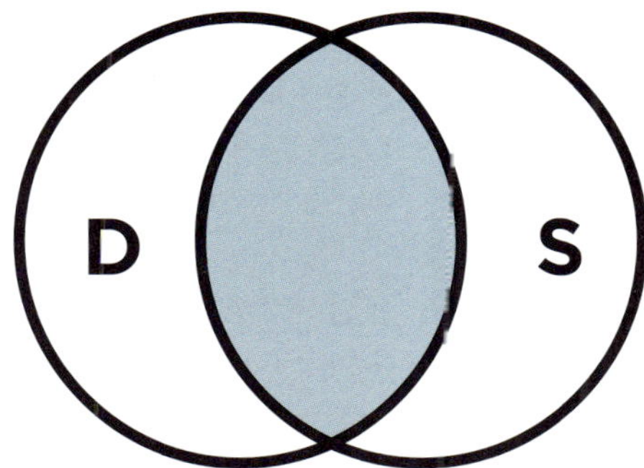

HIGH D / HIGH S
High D communicating with a High S

BSM: Fair
The High D will have a tendency to overpower the High S because of the High D's sense of urgency and high risk. The High D will need to slow down significantly, making sure the High S has the time to process the information given. The High S is a moderately low risk taker, requiring time to think. Desiring harmony, the High S may have a tendency to go along, even though disagreeing with the High D. Non-emotional by nature, the High S will not show emotion. Lack of emotional display must not be confused with agreement. The High D must work hard to develop a trust relationship that allows the High S the comfort to verbalize concerns. This means the High D will need to work hard at listening.

High S is looking for: SECURITY

© 1993-2018 Target Training International, Ltd.

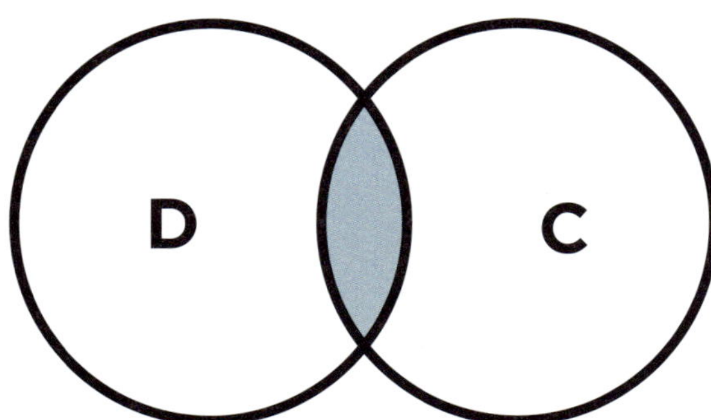

HIGH D / HIGH C
High D communicating with a High C

BSM: Fair
Fast mover to a slow mover. High risk to low risk. Little need for data compared to a great need for data. Quick decision-maker to a slow decision-maker. The High D will need to adapt extremely to increase the communication with the High C. The greatest challenge for the High D is to slow down and get the facts. The High D needs to give more information than normal but not talk personally with the High C or be too pushy. Both the High D and High C share a need to use time wisely and to control their environment.

High C is looking for: INFORMATION

HIGH I BLENDING

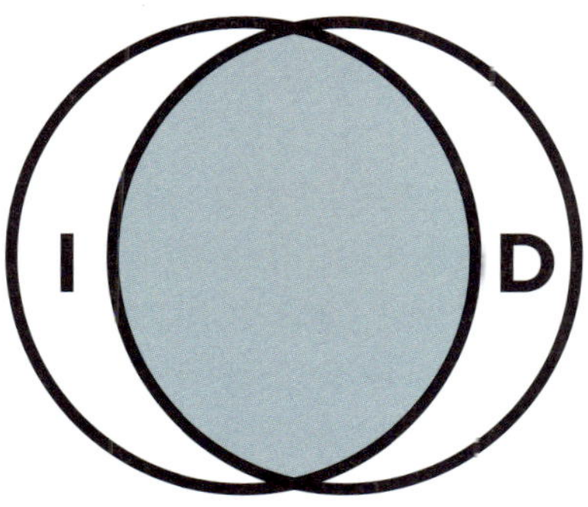

HIGH I / HIGH D
High I communicating with a High D

BSM: Good

High I's tend to be very verbal in their efforts to persuade someone to their point of view. A good behavioral match, as both styles are extroverted and see the big picture. The High I will need to be more direct with the High D and not beat around the bush in the discussion. Also, the High I will need to allow the High D to carry the conversation and work on asking more questions instead of telling the answers. The boldness and directness of the High D may be somewhat intimidating to the High I, causing the High I to give ground when ground should not be given. Being aware of the fact that the High D likes a battle, the High I can maintain their position without fear of loss.

High D is looking for: RESULTS/EFFICIENCY

© 1993-2018 Target Training International, Ltd.

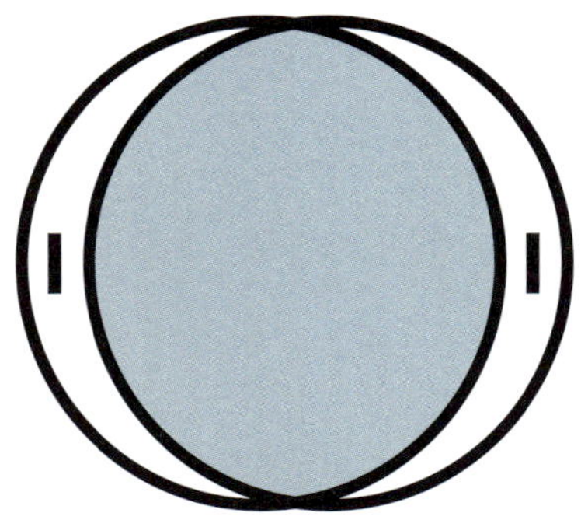

HIGH I / HIGH I
High I communicating with a High I

BSM: Good

High I's have creative, high-risk ideas but often need other styles to help keep their feet on the ground. Two High Is together will have a tremendous amount of fun. Make sure that the task completion and accomplishment is there, as the people-focus can easily cause them to get off track. Set strict schedules and deadlines, as the time management could be a possible problem.

High I is looking for: The EXPERIENCE

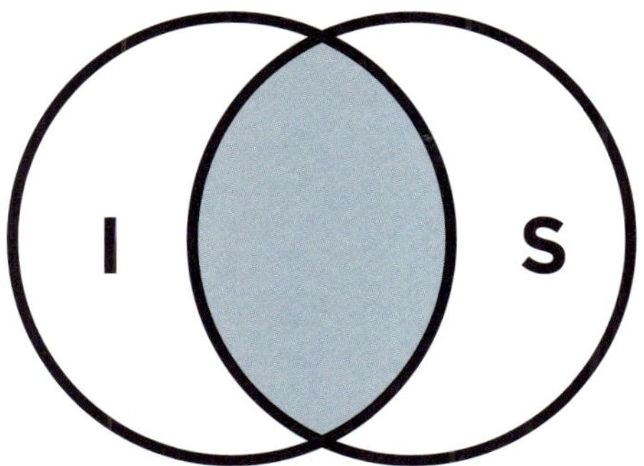

HIGH I / HIGH S
High I communicating with a High S

BSM: Good

The High I will definitely enjoy a commonality with the High S in the area of people orientation. Both styles share the need for warmth and interaction on a personal level. The High I will need to tone down their approach, as it will be viewed by the High S as overly enthusiastic or perhaps insincere and pushy. The High I also has a greater sense of urgency and a higher risk factor than that of the High S. So the adaptation for the High I is to tone down, slow down and encourage the High S to interact. Again, don't assume that the non-emotional nature of the High S is an indication of agreement. You will probably not know what the High S is thinking unless you are told. Therefore, the High I must talk less and ask more questions hoping to build a trust relationship.

High S is looking for: SECURITY

© 1993-2018 Target Training International, Ltd.

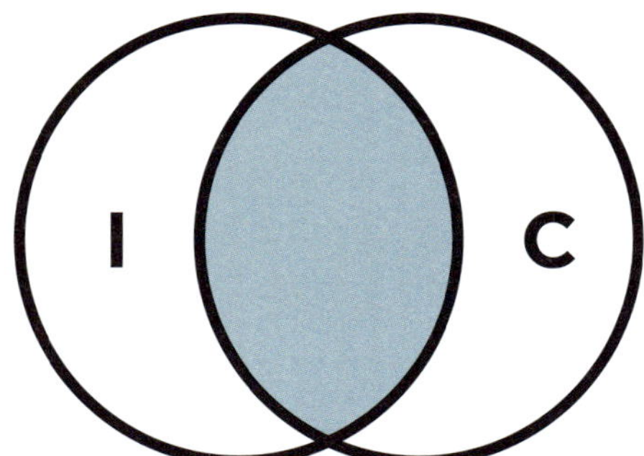

HIGH I / HIGH C
High I communicating with a High C

BSM: Fair

The High I will have few, if any, behavioral commonalties with the High C. This behavioral match is the toughest of all for the High I. Extrovert to an introvert. Feeling style to a data-oriented style. High risk to a low risk. Indirect style to a direct style. A trusting style to an untrusting style. The High C is the challenge for the High I. However, if both can capitalize on their behavioral strengths, this can be an incredible team. The High I will have to slow down, keep a tight rein on emotions and provide the necessary data to the High C. Personal talk is not allowed as the private life of the High C is exactly that — private. The High I will need to reduce gestures and definitely not touch the High C.

High C is looking for: INFORMATION

HIGH S BLENDING

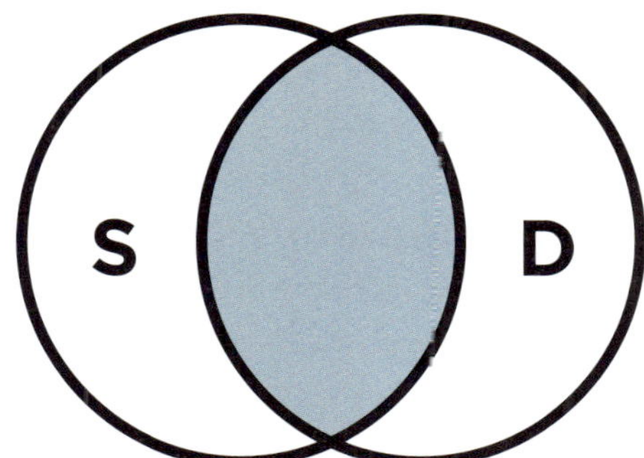

HIGH S / HIGH D
High S communicating with a High D

BSM: Fair
Slow pace dealing with a faster pace. People orientation compared to task orientation. Slow decision maker to a fast decision maker. The High S will need to adapt to communicate effectively with the High D. The basic adaptation will be to pick up the pace, cover only the high points and be more direct with the High D. The High D will usually like and respect someone who is direct and straightforward. The High S will have to make sure not to be overpowered by the High D. The tendency of the High S will be to go along for the sake of harmony and peace. Going along is fine, as long as the High S agrees on the direction the High D is going. It will be difficult, but the High S must stand up to the High D. The best approach is to utilize a questioning method, forcing the High D to defend their position.

High D is looking for: RESULTS/EFFICIENCY

© 1993-2018 Target Training International, Ltd.

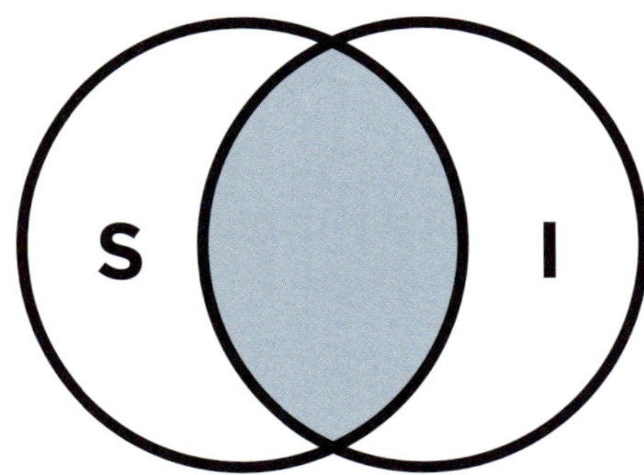

HIGH S / HIGH I
High S communicating with a High I

BSM: Good
Both of these styles share a need for warmth and interaction, as well as a need to verbalize. Both styles are also very people oriented and are concerned about the effect of their behavior on others. The High S prefers low risk, compared to the high-risk nature of the High I. The High S will tend to be a much slower decision maker than the High I, as well as being more methodical and systematic. The High S should loosen up with the High I to allow for more freedom and fun and at the same time, provide opportunities for the High I to verbalize. Find ways to support the ideas of the High I and encourage creativity and innovation. A good behavioral match, mostly because of their people focus, the High S and High I should interact well.

High I is looking for: The EXPERIENCE

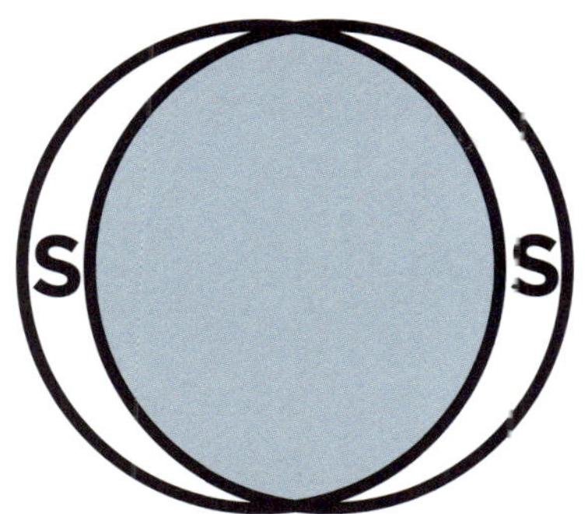

HIGH S / HIGH S
High S communicating with a High S

BSM: Good
An excellent behavioral match, two High Ss will get along great with each other. Both will be highly people oriented. Both will also have a strong need for closure. Their risk factor may be too low, which could cause them not to achieve their entire potential. Decision-making could also be too slow or too late; but in terms of compatibility, a High S–High S match very well.

High S is looking for: SECURITY

© 1993-2018 Target Training International, Ltd.

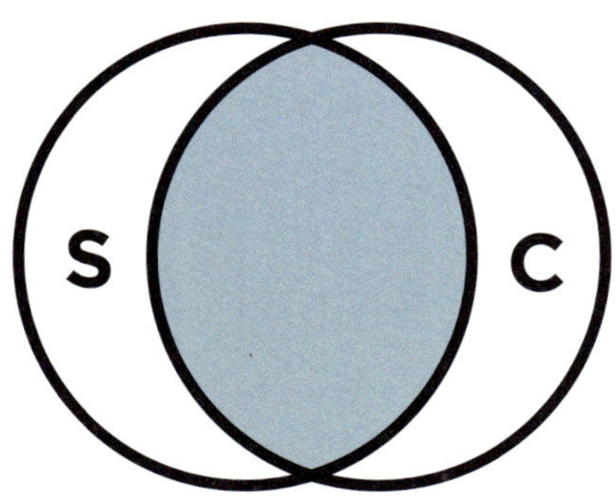

HIGH S / HIGH C
High S communicating with a High C

BSM: Good
The High S and the High C both share a need for a low risk, cooperative environment whether on the job or at home. Both tend to have methods and procedures they follow. The main difference between the High S and the High C is that the C is more focused on data and the S is more people oriented. When dealing with change, the High S will need enough information to feel comfortable with the situation, while the High C will need adequate data to prove the change is for the better.

High C is looking for: INFORMATION

HIGH C BLENDING

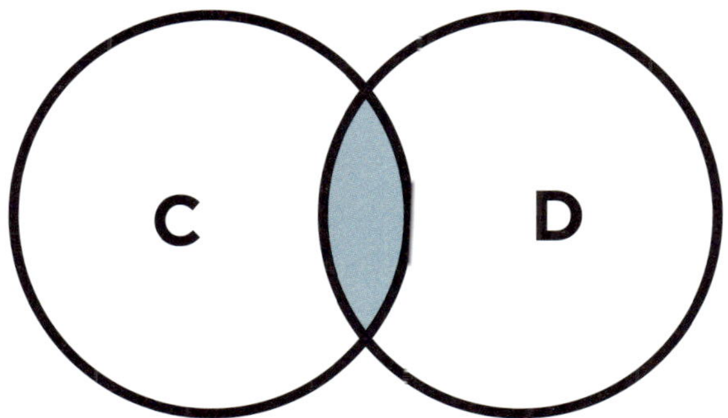

HIGH C / HIGH D
High C communicating with a High D

BSM: Fair
Both the High C and the High D are task oriented. The area of potential conflict lies in the arena of speed and risk orientation. The low risk of the High C versus the high risk of the High D. Slow decision-making requiring a great deal of data as opposed to fast decision-making requiring little data. Both are alike in that they have high expectations of each other, but this may cause the C to be too critical and the D to be too demanding (depending on their values). However, awareness of their behavioral differences can give birth to a fantastic team.

High D is looking for: RESULTS/EFFICIENCY

© 1993-2018 Target Training International, Ltd.

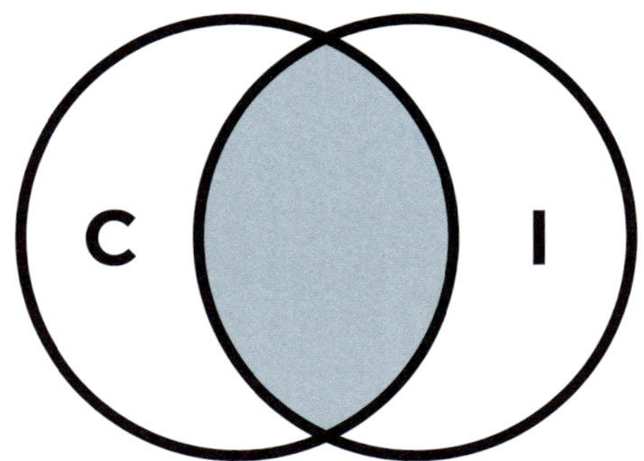

HIGH C / HIGH I
High C communicating with a High I

BSM: Fair

The High C - High I relationship is, behaviorally, the most difficult. Introverted to extroverted. Pessimistic to optimistic. Slow decision-maker to fast decision-maker. Low risk to high risk. Point after point seems to cause the High C and High I to clash. The High C will have to really loosen up and become more like a High I. By becoming more people focused, more fun and excited, the High C can adapt to create a winning communication with the High I. The High C must pick up the pace, using questions as a means to direct the High I to the desired conclusion. Move methodically to the desired goal allowing the High I to verbalize along the way.

High I is looking for: The EXPERIENCE

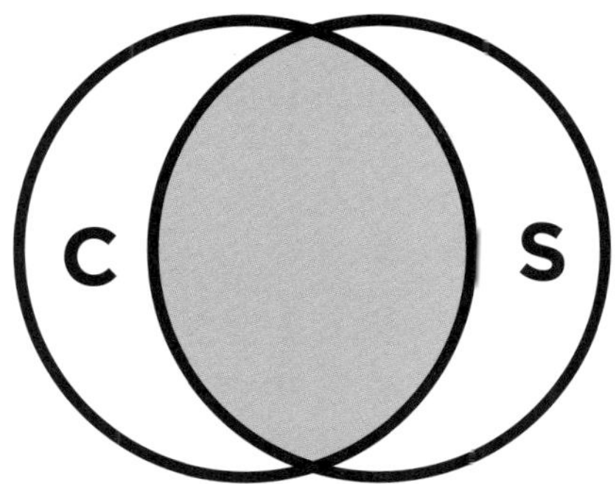

HIGH C / HIGH S
High C communicating with a High S

BSM: Good
The High C and the High S both share a need for a low-risk, co-operative environment whether on the job or at home. Both tend to have methods and procedures they follow. The main difference between the High S and the High C is that the C is more focused on data and S is more people oriented. When dealing with change, the High S will need enough information to feel comfortable with the situation, while the High C will need adequate data to prove the change is for the better.

High S is looking for: SECURITY

© 1993-2018 Target Training International, Ltd.

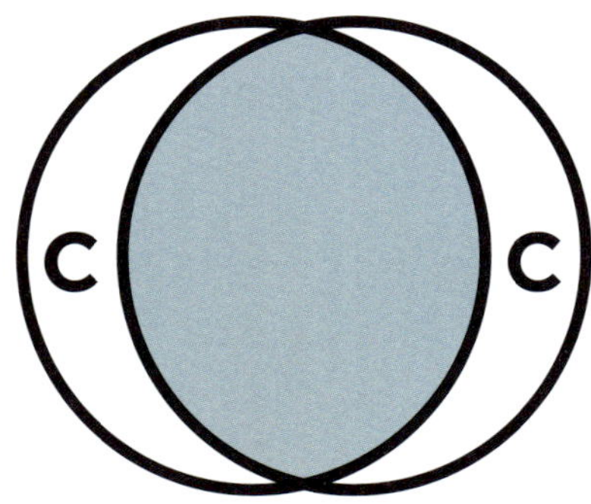

HIGH C / HIGH C
High C communicating with a High C

BSM: Good
Two High C's tend to have great relationships at home and on the job because they both share the strong tendency of needing procedure and order. Also, they have a need to gather data and thoroughly examine the facts before making a decision. Both low risk, slow decision makers and task oriented, the High C's tend to get along very well. However, frustration could appear due to their perfectionist tendencies. Overall, an excellent behavioral match.

High C is looking for: INFORMATION

OBJECTIVES REVISITED

Importance of Blending:

- People do not all communicate alike.
- Behavioral Style Matching indicates how styles initially blend.
- Interacting with people at all levels is an important skill to acquire.
- Understanding the behavioral needs of all styles and how to blend your style to each results in improved communications.

AUTHORS' NOTE:
All behavioral styles can learn to work well together. More of a behavioral tolerance and appreciation is developed when the individuals are aware of behavioral differences and understand the differences are not right or wrong. Breakdowns in relationships most often are a result of conflict in the area of values. Although this chapter defines need-related conflicts, these can and are overcome often, mostly through training on the DISC language. Through an awareness of potential communication problems, the student of the DISC language can immediately adapt their behavior for better communication.

© 1993-2018 Target Training International, Ltd.

WORKPLACE BEHAVIORS® & BENCHMARKING

Chapter Objective

To use the Workplace Behaviors assessment to explore the behavioral demands of a job, providing the employee and manager with valuable information used to meet those demands.

Chapter Contents

- Introduction
- Uses: Job Matching, Coaching, Development
- Master Job Graph
- Using the Report
- Objectives Revisited

"Put your personnel work FIRST because it is most important."

–General Robert Wood

© 1993-2018 Target Training International, Ltd.

INTRODUCTION

If the job could talk, it would clearly identify the appropriate behavior required to achieve superior performance with the least amount of stress. All jobs require activities that can be discussed in behavioral terms. By understanding these behavioral terms, we can match people to activities that will take advantage of their natural behavior.

During the Industrial Age, most jobs were tangible; and most tangible jobs don't require you to be all things to all people. As we have moved away from the Industrial Age, jobs have become more intangible and, thus, require us to look closely at behavior.

Today, organizations have created jobs that require a person to be all things to all people. That is, you must be in charge, provide service with a smile, follow up and follow through, like following procedures to assure that high standards are met at all times. **The problem with this type of job is that it requires a robot to do it, as people can only be all things to all people for a short time.**

The behavioral profile of a college student requires the student to:

1. Follow rules and regulations set by others
2. Follow up and follow through on all assignments
3. Talk only when asking or answering a question
4. Recognize that the professor is in charge

This job of being a student requires a certain behavioral profile, and our research proves that students who match this profile get the best grades. Students with a natural style opposite of this student profile have the lowest grade point average. So looking at a student being in a job that does not pay, we can see how a behavioral mismatch results in lower performance.

BIASES

Without a process to discover the behavior of a job, we end up with people's biases of the job. When people discuss a specific job that they currently are doing, we often hear about how they LIKE TO DO the job or how they ACTUALLY do the job.

The focus needs to be on HOW the job should be done. This is why you should follow our recommended process for benchmarking a job regardless of whether you are using one or multiple assessments (behavior, motivators, and skills).

To start, we need to discover what the job itself requires for superior performance. **If the job could talk, it would clearly define the behavior required to do the job.**

© 1993-2018 Target Training International, Ltd.

THE PROCESS

1. **Identify the job.**
2. **Identify Subject Matter Experts (SMEs).**
3. **Define the job's key accountabilities.**
4. **Prioritize key accountabilities in order of importance.**
5. **Weigh the key accountability in percentage of time required.**
6. **Focus on the one key accountability that requires the most time and respond to the Workplace Behaviors Assessment.**
7. **Combine the results and finalize the master job behavioral graph.**

For more details on this process, refer to **"Selecting Superior Performers Safely Under the Law"** on Page 263.

The Workplace Behaviors Assessment was developed to provide a systematic and comprehensive way of exploring the behavior demanded by various jobs. Most jobs have a job description or a list of duties and responsibilities. A job description rarely tells us anything more than what the person is to do in the job; it leaves out how he is to do it and when it must be done. The Workplace Behaviors Assessment identifies all the behavioral characteristics that are absent in job descriptions.

If we were to take the duties and responsibilities of any position and identify the amount of time spent completing each duty and responsibility in a given week, we could compile the amount of time spent on the various activities. By analyzing the activity and the behavior required for its successful completion, we could determine the amount of time spent dealing with the various behavioral characteristics. We could then discover the dominant behavioral characteristics that are present in the position. **The Workplace Behaviors Assessment allows us to analyze the behaviors required to be successful in that job.**

When a person is hired to do a job that requires the same behaviors he/she brings to the job, positive things happen:

1. The individual can immediately focus energy on completion of the job itself.
2. The individual will enjoy doing the job because of the natural match with his/her behaviors.

© 1993-2018 Target Training International, Ltd.

By contrast, those people who bring different behaviors to the job than what the job demands must first focus energy on adjusting their behaviors to the job. After expending this energy to bring about the behavioral change, they can then use what energy is left to perform the duties of the job. Some jobs can be so stressful in forcing individuals to behave in a manner that is not natural for them, that there is little energy left for the completion of the job.

An example of this type of conflict would be someone who is very aggressive and outgoing, has a tremendous sense of urgency, and likes to follow his/her own rules and regulations is placed in a position that requires attaining high quality, following many rules, following the system to perfection, and starting/finishing one activity at a time. The person described would be under stress in this environment and would only stay with the job if he/she could not find another one which met his/her natural behavioral style.

Anytime two people have different perceptions of the same job, the result will be a poor evaluation or substandard performance. **For example: Many people walk into performance reviews thinking one way about their performance and the manager thinks differently.** By both the manager and the employee understanding the job, the key accountabilities and the behavioral characteristics required for superior performance, the two can start the conversation from the same place of understanding.

This example is an indication that many managers lack the skills to assist their employees in meeting the behavioral demands of the job. This particular position was a certified one; and the person had met all the educational qualifications for the job, but by the manager's perception was not meeting the behavioral qualifications of the job.

WHO SHOULD USE WORKPLACE BEHAVIORS?

SMEs which includes both managers and their subordinates participate in this system. The manager's responsibility is to develop the Job Report using TTI's patented Job Benchmarking Process. This will allow a comparison of all people performing that particular job to the Job Report.

To establish a job graph, more than one person should respond to the Workplace Behaviors Assessment. People who know and understand the job should participate. If all SMEs see the job in the same light, then a report may be generated from that particular graph. If there are differing viewpoints, then the managers should negotiate each statement with the SMEs, and all respond to another Workplace Behaviors Assessment. Using the negotiated Workplace Behaviors Assessment, a job graph may be generated.

© 1993-2018 Target Training International, Ltd.

WORKPLACE BEHAVIORS FOR JOB MATCHING

STRESS EVALUATION

An employee whose behaviors fit the job requirements experiences less stress and is more productive. Workplace Behaviors can be significant in examining the behavioral and environmental indicators. For example, would a High D or High I feel uncomfortable in a High C job? Probably! Not only would they feel uncomfortable, but they may take more time off work for illness, be more accident-prone on the job, and have a lower productivity rate than the quality-conscious High C in the same job.

If you find a High D in a High C job, does it mean he/she should be fired? NO! It does mean there should be some discussion between managers and employees regarding job roles. Perhaps there can be adjustments in the manner in which the job is completed, or perhaps there are some modifications of the job, which could be made so a person with High D behavior would function more effectively.

DEVELOPMENT

REVITALIZING AND REDIRECTING PRESENT STAFF

Low productivity is often caused by a lack of understanding of the behavior the job requires. This may be addressed by developing a Job Benchmark and having all employees who perform that job respond to a Style Insights questionnaire. This will identify any area in which the employee has misdirected his/her energy.

PERFORMANCE EVALUATION

Managers evaluate performance based on their own perceptions. Subordinates tend to perform jobs based on their own perceptions. Performance evaluation provides a valuable opportunity to use Workplace Behaviors as a comparison of each person's perception of a job. If perceptions are different, the result is often poor evaluation and/or low productivity. By letting the instrument raise the critical issues, decisions can remain focused on the job. Performance evaluations can be done on a positive basis with new energy focused on the new action plan developed from the resulting dialogue.

© 1993-2018 Target Training International, Ltd.

COACHING

Every person brings both strengths and weaknesses to the job. It is important for people to compare their behavior to the behavior required by the job. **Then, and only then, can they develop a plan to identify these types of issues:**

- Does their current job utilize their behavioral strengths?
- Have they over-extended their behavioral strengths and turned them into a weakness?
- Does their current job require the use of their weaknesses?
- What activities in their current job stress them out?

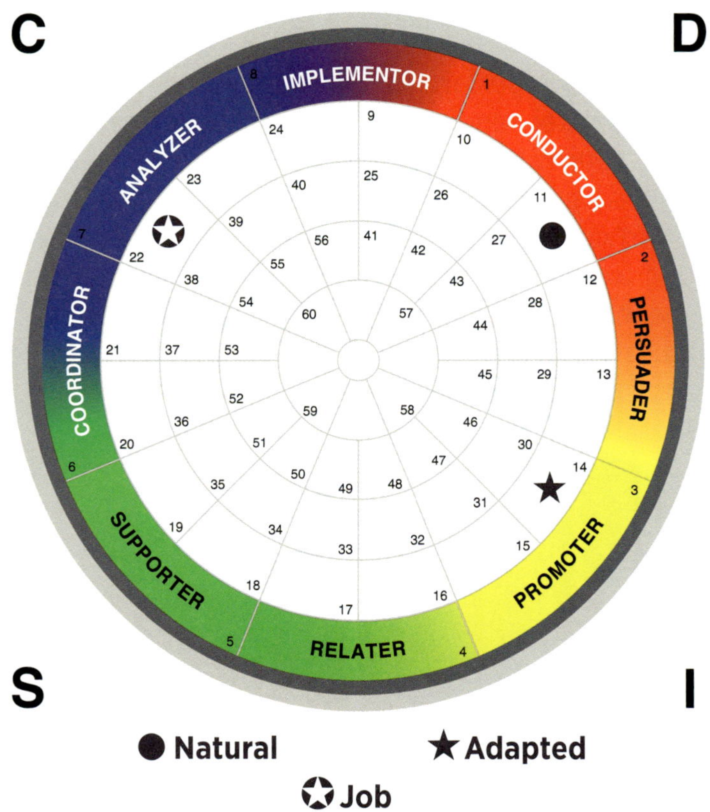

By looking at the above visual, you can see this person is adapting behavior that is not job related. Why? It could be on or off the job causes.

OBJECTIVES REVISITED

Importance of the Workplace Behaviors Assessment:

- Defines all the human factors absent in job descriptions.
- Allows us to define the behavior the person brings to the job and define the behavior required to be successful in the job.
- Helps the manager and subordinate have the same perception of the job.
- Helps managers assist employees in meeting behavioral demands of the job.

Authors' Note:
The Workplace Behaviors Assessment is a very powerful tool that should be used in every work situation. The power of the instrument lies in its ability to get everyone on the same page related to the behavioral needs of the job. How many problems are caused by managers and employees who see the job differently? Also, the ability to compare people's perceptions of the job facilitates communication and understanding.

© 1993-2018 Target Training International, Ltd.

Chapter Objective

To teach you how to "blend" your sales style with your customer's buying style for easier sales.

Chapter Contents

- Introduction
- Recognizing Behavioral Styles
- Buying Style Characteristics
- C Style
- S Style
- I Style
- D Style
- Blend Your Sales Style
- How to Build a Winning Sales Presentation
- Objectives Revisited

"Everyone is a salesperson. Everyone is selling something, every day."

–Bill J. Bonnstetter

© 1993-2018 Target Training International, Ltd.

INTRODUCTION

Research conducted by Target Training International, Ltd. has conclusively proven the following statements to be true:

1. People tend to buy from salespeople who have behavioral styles similar to their own.

2. Salespeople tend to sell to customers who have a behavioral style similar to their own.

3. Salespeople who are aware of their own behavioral style and learn to blend with their customer's style are able to increase their sales.

THE FORD OR THE CHEVY

A Chevy salesperson, with a High S behavioral style, was showing a new vehicle to a couple. Knowing the DISC language, the salesperson realized both the husband and the wife had High C behavioral styles. The couple expressed immediately that their desire was to buy a Ford, but merely wanted some information on a comparable Chevy model. The salesperson did not push them in any way, but offered them a variety of information they requested. Knowing that they were going to the Ford dealership up the street, the Chevy salesperson recommended them to a Ford salesperson who was a High D, and did NOT know the DISC language.

Why? The salesperson was hoping the High D would be pushy with the couple, and they would then come back and buy the Chevy. The High D salesperson was pushy and tried to close the deal immediately. After a few days of gathering more information, the couple came back and bought the Chevy.

NOTE **You may feel like the couple was manipulated. The point of including this true story is:** Whether we like it or not, people buy from people they like! They liked the laid-back, slow-paced Chevy salesperson and did not like the fast-paced, quick-closing Ford salesperson. The salesperson was more important than the brand of vehicle.

How many sales do we lose because of not behaviorally treating the customer properly? **PEOPLE BUY FROM PEOPLE THEY LIKE!** The problem is: **What do they like?**

Some buyers:

- Like you to be direct.
- Like to have fun.
- Like new products.
- Like proven products.
- Like a lot of data.
- Like to be touched.
- Like personal talk.
- Like time to think.
- Like to negotiate
- Like showy products.
- Like traditional products... and some DON'T!

© 1993-2018 Target Training International, Ltd.

If you, the salesperson, don't understand behavioral styles and do not have a good knowledge of the DISC language, you are saying goodbye to your valuable sales dollars. The single, best way for a sales manager to increase sales dollars and customer satisfaction is to train the sales team on the DISC language.

There are three steps to selling with DISC behavioral styles:

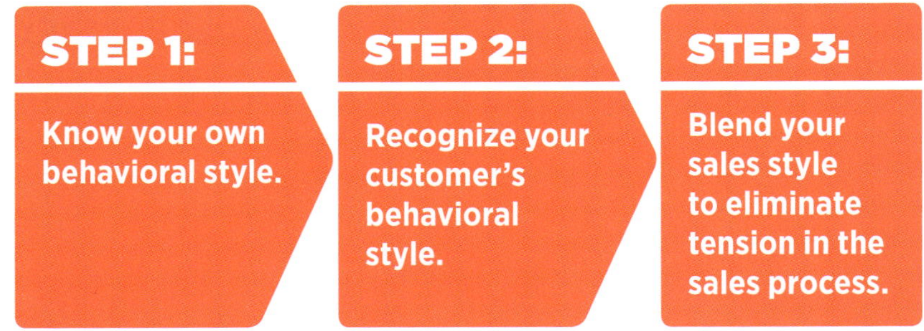

RECOGNIZING BEHAVIORAL STYLES

METHOD #1

This method, if used properly, can reveal your own behavioral style and that of your customer.

If you know someone who knows your potential buyer, ask him/her the following questions to help you prepare for the sales call.

1. **Is the person extroverted or introverted?**
   The High D and the High I factors are extroverted.
   The High S and the High C factors are introverted.

2. **Is the person people- or task-oriented?**
   The High I and the High S factors are people-oriented.
   The High D and the High C factors are task-oriented.

EXAMPLE **LEE TREVINO**

1. **Extroverted or introverted?**
   Lee Trevino is definitely extroverted, indicating he is a High D or a High I.

2. **People or task-oriented?**
   Lee Trevino is people-oriented, indicating he is a High I behaviorally.

Using this method to understand your customer's core style, simply ask the same questions in your mind as you observe the customer.

© 1993-2018 Target Training International, Ltd.

METHOD #2

This is the most accurate method of knowing your own and other's behavioral styles without using the Style Insight Instrument. Each of the four factors has an emotion associated with it. By observing the emotions of the four factors we can plot the entire graph.

STEP 1: PLOTTING THE D FACTOR

The High D emotion is anger. A High D will be quick to anger and tend to have a short fuse. A low D will be slow to anger and tend to have a long fuse.

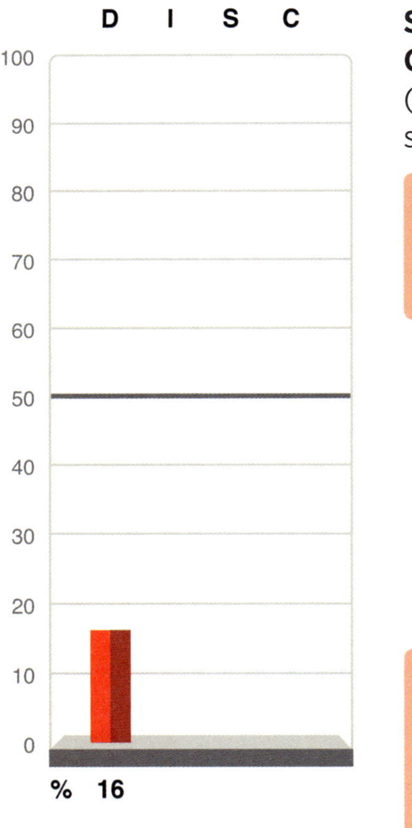

EXAMPLE

SAMPLE CONVERSATION:
(Person B trying to know the style of Person A)

Person A:
"People just bug me sometimes."

Person B:
"Really? Do you have somewhat of a "short fuse" or can you take a lot before you get angry?"

Person A:
"Oh, I can take a lot, but when I blow — watch out!"

Based on Person A's response we can plot the D factor below the energy line because Person A claims to have a long fuse. If Person A claims to have a short fuse, we can plot the D factor above the energy line.

STEP 2: PLOTTING THE I FACTOR

The High I emotions are optimism and trust. A High I will tend to be optimistic, have a positive outlook and be very trusting of others. A Low I will be pessimistic and skeptical with a tendency to distrust others.

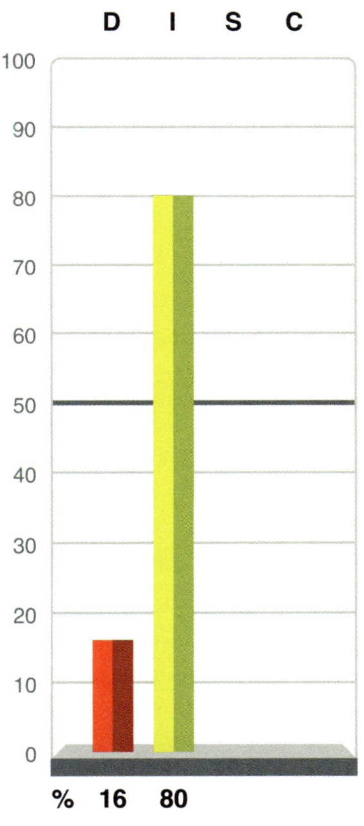

SAMPLE CONVERSATION:
(Person B trying to know the style of Person A)

Person B:
"I'm excited about my job. They like my work and said there was a future for me."

Person A:
"Really? That's great! I think you'll do just fine there. I'm glad they're taking care of you."

© 1993-2018 Target Training International, Ltd.

Based on Person A's response, we can plot the I factor above the energy line because Person A is showing optimism. If Person A had said something to the effect of "Yeah, right! I'd make sure I got that in writing," this would have indicated a Low I below the energy line. Based on the first two emotions, we know the approximate plotting point of the D and the I factor, as seen in the previous graph.

STEP 3: PLOTTING THE S FACTOR

The High S emotion is non-emotional. The High S feels emotion but hides it. A Low S will tend to show whatever emotion he/she is feeling. This particular factor is mostly observable. However, certain questions can reveal that you are talking to a High S.

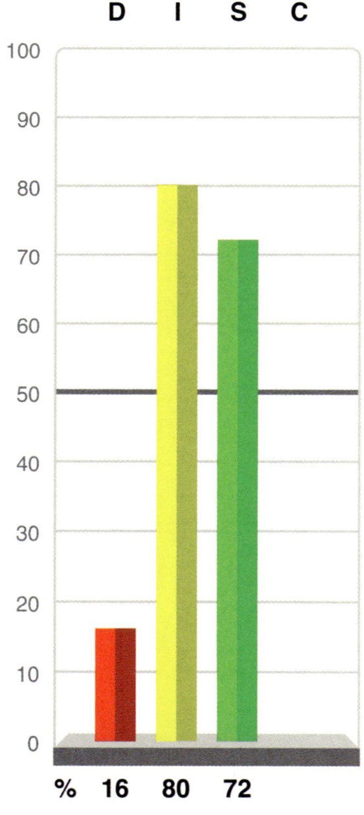

Questions to ask a third party who knows your potential buyer:

1. **Does the potential buyer like new products or traditional products?** New products are the Low S, traditional products are the High S.

2. **How does the potential buyer maintain his work area?** Neatly organized is the High S, a little on the sloppy side is the Low S.

3. **Does the potential buyer show emotion?** Hard to read is the High S, easy to read is the Low S.

STEP 4: PLOTTING THE C FACTOR

The High C emotion is fear. A High C will tend to respect rules and go by the book. A Low C will tend to exhibit no fear and not to follow rules and procedures or go by the book. The higher the C factor, the more the person will tend to be a better, safer driver.

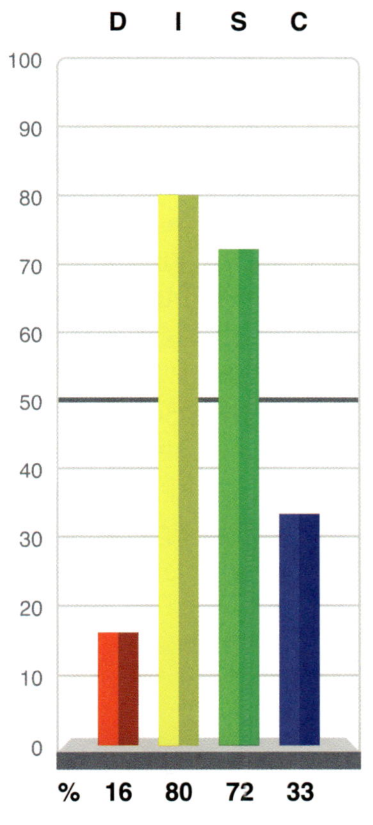

SAMPLE CONVERSATION: (Person B trying to know the style of Person A)

EXAMPLE

Person B: "Have you gotten many speeding tickets?"

Person A: "Heck, no! I never get caught. I know where all the cops hang out."

Based on Person A's response, we can plot the C factor below the energy line because Person A tends to break the rules of the road. Had Person A said he/she was a great driver, or if you noticed him/her driving safely while riding with him/her, you would have plotted the C factor above the energy line.

© 1993-2018 Target Training International, Ltd.

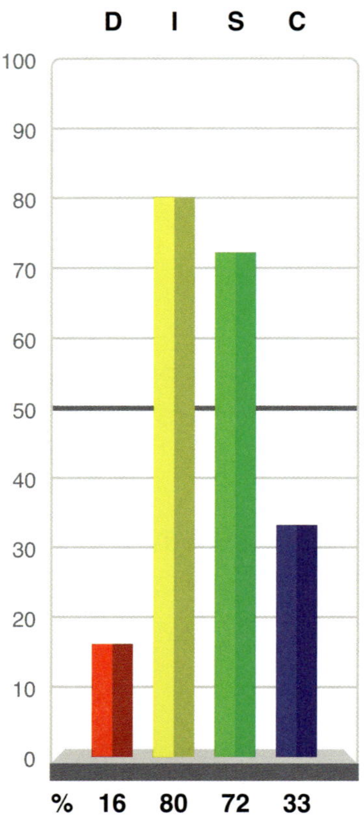

Based on the emotions of the four factors, we now plot the entire graph of Person A as seen on the left.

Behaviorally, Person A is a Low D and Low C with a High I and a High S. Utilizing Method #1 of extroverted or introverted, we notice that Person A is outgoing and friendly. Therefore, we know his/her highest point is the "I" factor.

Method #2 is very effective in reading the entire graph. It can also be used to identify the behavioral style of a person whom you haven't met by simply talking to someone who does know that person.

RECOGNIZING THE BEHAVIORAL STYLE

Actual phone conversation, using Method #2 of reading a person's style. (Jim's thoughts are in parenthesis).

Fred: "Jim, why don't you call Mike tomorrow?"

Jim: "Fine! I'll call in the morning! By the way, about Mike, is he optimistic and trusting?"

Fred: "Oh, definitely! And he is very patient with people."

Jim: (High I, Low D)

One simple question gave the caller very valuable information about the potential buyer before the sales call even started. This salesperson now planned his presentation for the High I buyer, realizing also that the "D" factor was below the midline. People who know your potential buyer can give you excellent clues about behavioral style.

Using Method #1 and/or Method #2 should allow you with practice to readily identify the behavioral style of your customers. Then, by understanding the characteristics of the four buying styles you can blend your style for increased sales.

© 1993-2018 Target Training International, Ltd.

HIGH C BUYING STYLE CHARACTERISTICS

TYPE OF PRODUCTS THEY TEND TO BUY

- Proven products

TYPICAL CHARACTERISTICS

- May be suspicious of you and your products.
- Does not make changes to new suppliers readily.
- Usually not too talkative.
- Is not an innovator. Will not readily try out new and innovative technology.

TYPE OF SALES PRESENTATION REQUIRED

- Needs a lot of proof, background information and proven results before making a purchase.
- Needs time to absorb details and digest facts before going to the next step.
- Highly suspicious of new and unproven products — use testimonials or plenty of research information to back up your presentation.
- Make sure testimonials are from others with a C behavioral style.
- Don't Rush! Don't waste time with small talk. Get right to the point with plenty of facts and figures. Answer all of their questions.

© 1993-2018 Target Training International, Ltd.

STATEMENTS THAT INFLUENCE A HIGH C

- "There has been a great amount of input into this idea, which ensures its quality."
- "Once you've taken the time to examine the facts, you'll see this is right for you."
- "You're in a position to examine the facts, interpret them and draw your own conclusions."
- "With something as important as this, let's set up several sessions where we can examine all possible alternatives."
- "I brought along all the information you'll need to thoroughly investigate this product and determine if it's right for you."
- "Others have found this to be the perfect solution to their problem. With your emphasis on standards, you will probably do it better."
- "You can see that our warranty eliminates any risk on your part. We stand behind the product 100%."
- "This is a proven product, having been on the market for years, so you know you have something you can rely on."

DRIVING FORCES FOR SELLING A HIGH C

- Set an environment where they will like and trust you.
- Present ideas in a non-threatening manner.
- Find ways to minimize risk.
- Do not hard sell!
- Give a complete proposal — explain details.
- Emphasize losses caused by delay.
- Stress security if they buy now or loss of security if they wait.
- Do not over-promise.
- Sales presentation must be consistent with sales material.

© 1993-2018 Target Training International, Ltd.

HINDERING FACTORS IN SELLING A HIGH C

- Getting personal about family if you don't know him or her.
- Touching or patting on back when you first meet.
- Loud, emotional sales presentation.
- Being shallow with answers to questions.

TYPICAL QUESTIONS ASKED BY THE HIGH C STYLE

1. Is it a proven product?
2. What else can you tell me about the product?
3. I don't have to decide now, do I?
4. What happens if it doesn't work?
5. Are you sure it lives up to all of your claims?
6. What is the warranty?
7. Is this the best on the market?
8. This isn't a new method, is it?
9. What are your qualifications?
10. Who are you?
11. How long has your company been in business?
12. Will you be able to meet my exact specifications?
13. What is everyone else using?

© 1993-2018 Target Training International, Ltd.

CLOSES TO USE WITH A HIGH C

The Puppy Dog — Try Before You Buy

By allowing the High C to use the product first and test it out, they begin to sell themselves, as well as experience the immediate benefits of the product.

The Think About It Deposit

Invariably, the High C buyer will not make the decision on the first presentation. A gently suggested deposit to hold the vehicle while the C has time to think about it is really a commitment. Even if the High C has the information where they feel comfortable, they will probably not make an immediate decision. **Here's how it works:**

EXAMPLE **SALESPERSON: "Mrs. Smith, you've invested a lot of your valuable time finding the right vehicle. I respect the fact that you need to think about it, but I want to make sure the car is still here when you decide to invest. You could help me out by placing a small deposit to hold the vehicle while you think about it. Of course, if you should decide not to purchase this vehicle, we'll gladly refund your deposit. I've also put together a packet of information for you."**

PEOPLE WILL BUY FROM PEOPLE THEY LIKE!

HIGH S BUYING STYLE CHARACTERISTICS

TYPE OF PRODUCTS THEY TEND TO BUY

- Traditional products

TYPICAL CHARACTERISTICS

- May be somewhat shy individual, but wants to be your friend.
- Not as suspicious as the C, but still very slow to make changes.
- Needs to trust the salesperson.
- Not an innovator. Likes a traditional way of doing things.
- Family-oriented.

TYPE OF SALES PRESENTATION REQUIRED

- Take it slow and easy. If you go too fast, you'll lose the sale.
- Provide plenty of proof and statistics.
- Earn their trust and friendship; visit about family and hobbies. May require additional visits for reassurances before the sale is made.
- Use facts and figures. Make repeat visits. Make sure you answer all their questions.

© 1993-2018 Target Training International, Ltd.

STATEMENTS THAT INFLUENCE A HIGH S

- "I feel you are open to a number of possibilities, and I want to recommend this plan of action."
- "Make some calls to others who have made the same type of change. I have a list that will help you."
- "By accepting this plan, you are investing in a great deal of security for you and your family."
- "Here is a comprehensive packet of information that will provide you with all the information needed to make a wise decision."
- "We'll make sure we take the time to investigate all the possibilities before we go ahead."
- "We've been a leader in the industry for _____ years, so we're going to be here when you need us."
- "You can see that our warranty eliminates any risk on your part. We stand behind the product 100%."
- "This is a proven product, having been on the market for _____ years, so you know you have something you can rely on."

DRIVING FORCES FOR SELLING A HIGH S

- Be sincere by using a quiet manner, simple explanations and explain details.
- Involve the family in decisions if they receive benefits.
- The S will make emotional decisions if family is involved.
- Do not hard sell!
- Give them time to think.
- Give assurances that their decision is right.
- Stress security if they buy now or loss of security if they wait.
- Full explanations.
- Show how your program will do the complete job, so they don't have to buy anything later.

© 1993-2018 Target Training International, Ltd.

HINDERING FACTORS IN SELLING A HIGH S

- Going too fast!
- Getting too friendly on the first meeting.
- Loud, emotional sales presentation.
- Being shallow with answers to questions, or not having answers.
- Hard selling or trying to close too fast.
- Bad mouthing current suppliers; they're probably friends.

TYPICAL QUESTIONS ASKED BY THE HIGH S STYLE

1. I always buy from another supplier; what's your price?
2. I buy from someone else and the service is good. Why should I switch to you?
3. This is a proven product, isn't it?
4. What happens if it doesn't work?
5. What does the warranty cover?
6. How long has this model been out? What's the track record?
7. Why don't you call me in a week? I'd like to think this over.
8. Will this do the job itself, or are there other things I'll need to buy with it?
9. There's no rush, is there?
10. What is everyone else using?

© 1993-2018 Target Training International, Ltd.

CLOSES THAT WORK WELL WITH A HIGH S

The Puppy Dog — Try Before You Buy

By allowing the High S to use the product first and test it out, they begin to sell themselves, as well as experience the immediate benefits of the product. Usually, the family of the S will develop an attachment to the product also.

The Think About It Deposit

Invariably, the High S buyer will not make the decision on the first presentation. A gently suggested deposit to hold the vehicle while the S has time to think about it is really a commitment. Even if the S has the information where they feel comfortable, they will probably not make an immediate decision. **Here's how it works:**

EXAMPLE **SALESPERSON: "Mrs. Smith, you've invested a lot of your valuable time finding the right vehicle. I respect the fact that you need to think about it, but I want to make sure that when you decide to invest that it is still here. You could help me out by placing a small deposit to hold the vehicle while you think about it. Of course, if you should decide not to purchase this vehicle, we'll gladly refund your deposit."**

PEOPLE WILL BUY FROM PEOPLE THEY LIKE!

HIGH I BUYING STYLE CHARACTERISTICS

TYPE OF PRODUCTS THEY TEND TO BUY

- Showy products

TYPICAL CHARACTERISTICS

- A friendly people-oriented person who would rather talk and socialize than do detail work.
- Will be glad to see you; will trade jokes and personal stories.
- Likes to try out new, innovative and showy products.

TYPE OF SALES PRESENTATION REQUIRED

- Spare the details; the I will not want to hear them. Will be a very quick buyer, usually on the first visit. BEWARE! Your competition can steal them away just as easy. So give plenty of follow-up service.
- Present new, innovative and showy products. The I likes to try new things.
- Allow time for socializing, perhaps over lunch.
- Have fun in the presentation. Tell stories. Its okay to touch the High I (upper forearm or back).
- Eliminate a lot of details. Just hit the high points.

© 1993-2018 Target Training International, Ltd.

STATEMENTS THAT INFLUENCE A HIGH I

- "It's the type of program that will utilize your ability to work with a new and innovative system."
- "This product allows you and your company to lead the way into the future."
- "This program puts you on the cutting edge of technology in your industry."
- "Yes, we have several companies that are looking at it, but most settle for the way things have always been. We felt you were more into moving into the future with the latest technology."
- "In fact, we'd like to showcase your business as one who is moving into the future with this latest advancement."

DRIVING FORCES FOR SELLING A HIGH I

- Provide recognition of their accomplishments.
- Let them talk for a while.
- Use their own words to direct the conversation back to business.
- Use testimonials and drop names!
- Provide friendly environment.
- Don't dwell on details.
- Support their dreams.
- Summarize major selling points.
- Don't get them lost in the facts.
- Be enthusiastic. Have fun!
- Close quickly, even on the first call.
- Give them choices of packages: three investments from large to economy.

© 1993-2018 Target Training International, Ltd.

HINDERING FACTORS IN SELLING A HIGH I

- Letting them talk so much that you lose the sale, or can't sell. Use their words and questions to keep them on track.

TYPICAL QUESTIONS ASKED BY THE HIGH I STYLE

1. Can you lower the price a little?
2. Are there any benefits for purchasing the product? Incentives? Like a free trip?
3. Would you mind if I told my neighbor about your product?
4. Have you had coffee yet? Let's talk over a cup of coffee. You bring the doughnuts.
5. What are your payment plans?
6. If I buy, who pays for the delivery?
7. Who else is doing this in my industry?

CLOSES THAT WORK WELL WITH A HIGH I

The Alternative of Choice

Give the I a choice of two options. By selecting either one, he indicates that he is going ahead with the purchase.

EXAMPLE **"You like both models I showed you, which one best meets your needs?"**

PEOPLE WILL BUY FROM PEOPLE THEY LIKE!

HIGH D BUYING STYLE CHARACTERISTICS

TYPE OF PRODUCTS THEY TEND TO BUY

- New Products

TYPICAL CHARACTERISTICS

- An entrepreneur with many interests. Often have several jobs or activities going on at once.
- Highly interested in new products and innovation.
- Usually have a fairly high ego factor.
- Does not like to waste time.

© 1993-2018 Target Training International, Ltd.

TYPE OF SALES PRESENTATION REQUIRED

- Don't waste time. The D buyer doesn't want a lot of facts and figures. Just hit the high points and get to the bottom line.
- You and your product must appear credible.
- Can be difficult to switch from present trusted suppliers, but once switched, will remain very loyal as long as you provide service.
- Does not want to see many testimonials, research, data, etc.
- Will be impressed with an efficient, businesslike approach.
- Will take interest in new products. Be concise and business like. Don't waste time with idle talk. Get to the point quickly, solve problems fast and make the sale.

STATEMENTS THAT INFLUENCE A HIGH D

- "You'll want to try this out. You're the type of person who can make this work."
- "This program will put you in the driver's seat. It will increase your current efficiency by _____%. This is totally new — there is nothing like it on the market."
- "You can easily see the advantages of using this method."
- "This puts you on the cutting edge of your industry, a leader in your field."
- "This provides you with an opportunity to get credit for what you do. It's something you can call your own."

DRIVING FORCES FOR SELLING A HIGH D

- Prepare your sales presentation for efficiency. Omit minor details.
- Flatter the ego. Concentrate on the immediate sale.
- Start with business — they will let you know if they want to chat.
- Ask questions so they can tell you about their operation.
- Stress opportunities for prestige, challenge and efficiency.
- Give direct answers.
- Emphasize results and the bottom line.
- Be efficient.
- Ask for the High D's opinion.

© 1993-2018 Target Training International, Ltd.

HINDERING FACTORS IN SELLING A HIGH D

- Being indecisive.
- Not answering objections directly.
- Explaining too many details.
- Don't give opinions, give options.
- Focus on the D. Do not work with three or four customers at once.

TYPICAL QUESTIONS ASKED BY THE HIGH D STYLE

1. What does it cost?
2. Is this the top of the line model?
3. Can I change it?
4. Is it new?
5. What is the warranty?
6. Are you sure you know what you're talking about?
7. Who else is using this model?
8. Can I get it now?
9. What are my payment options?
10. How much will it increase my efficiency?

CLOSES THAT WORK WELL WITH A HIGH D

The Alternative of Choice

Give the High D a choice of two options. By selecting either one, they are indicating that they are going ahead with the purchase.

EXAMPLE **"You liked both models I showed you, which one best meets your needs?"**

The Take Away

This close was developed to challenge the strong ego of the D profile. The close can backfire, but also can be very effective if done properly. Once the D has an eye on the product but is struggling with the money issue, the salesperson says:

EXAMPLE **SALESPERSON: "You know, Sue, I thought this was the right product for you, but maybe I made a mistake. Maybe we should look at your budget range. Let's look at this model."**

Those who have successfully used this close, state that the D will bounce back and buy the first one he/she was considering. By taking it away for a monetary reason, it sends a subtle message, which causes them to want to prove to you and themselves that they CAN afford it. Be careful when using this close. It is very effective, but must be sincere in its delivery. We present this close because it is a "behavioral close," but you need to examine it and decide for yourself if it is a close you would like to use.

PEOPLE WILL BUY FROM PEOPLE THEY LIKE!

© 1993-2018 Target Training International, Ltd.

We now have looked at the buying characteristics of all four styles. By "blending" your style with theirs, you will increase your sales. Guaranteed.

BLEND YOUR SALES STYLE

As you've seen, all customers are not alike. Each requires a different type of approach and responds to you in different ways. By "blending" your sales style with theirs, your sales presentations will attain maximum success. To do this, you must compare the strong and weak points of your own style with those of your different prospects and adjust yours accordingly. The following five reference pages give you the information you need for each style of salesperson.

BASIC PATTERNS AND APPROACHES

Learn to interpret patterns and the most common acts that go along with them. This will enable you to establish instant rapport that allows people to feel at ease with you. After the initial period you can relax and make minor adjustments.

STYLE TENDENCIES	*Greater*			*Lesser*
Tendency to use LOGIC:	S	C	D	I
Tendency to TRUST:	I	S	D	C
Tendency to BUY QUICKLY:	D	I	S	C
Tendency to be LOYAL:	S	C	D	I

BEHAVIORAL SELLING SKILLS - D

D - DOMINANT

<table>
<tr><td>

STEP 1
Know Yourself: D Salesperson

- Results oriented
- Wants to close fast
- Argumentative
- May try to overpower the person
- Likes to win
- May not follow up properly
- May be unprepared
- Can handle several customers at once

</td><td>

STEP 2
Read the Person You Are Speaking With:

Extroverted:
Friendly - I
Direct - D

Introverted:
Cooperative - S
Analytical - C

BEHAVIORAL STYLE MATCH (BSM):

1 - Excellent
2 - Good
3 - Fair
4 - Poor

</td></tr>
<tr><td colspan="2">

STEP 3
Use The Chart Below When You Are Selling to:

</td></tr>
<tr><td>

D — BSM - 2

The D is looking for: RESULTS

- Be direct
- Give alternatives
- Make sure you let them win (make sure you win, too)
- Disagree with facts
- Enjoy the "combat"
- Don't try to build a friendship
- Do not dictate to them
- Move quickly; they decide fast
- Do not try to overpower them

</td><td>

S — BSM - 3

The S is looking for: SECURITY

- Slow down presentation
- Build trust
- Focus on people
- Give them the facts they need
- Provide a logical presentation
- Get "little" agreements
- Listen carefully
- Show sincerity in presentation
- Don't control or dominate
- Do not close fast

</td></tr>
<tr><td>

I — BSM - 2

The I is looking for: THE EXPERIENCE

- Be personal, friendly
- Slow down, take time
- Joke around and have fun
- Allow them to talk
- Provide recognition
- Don't talk down to them
- Talk about people
- Follow up often

</td><td>

C — BSM - 4

The C is looking for: INFORMATION

- Give them the data
- Do not touch them
- Be patient, slow
- Use flyers with data
- Give more info than you'd like
- Keep control
- Do not talk personally
- Do not be pushy

</td></tr>
</table>

© 1993-2018 Target Training International, Ltd.

BEHAVIORAL SELLING SKILLS - I

I - INFLUENCER

<table>
<tr><td>

STEP 1

Know Yourself: I Salesperson

- Social
- People-oriented lack of attention to detail
- May over-promise
- May be "too talkative"
- May close too slowly, or not at all
- Enthusiastic
- Wordy, non-logical presentation

</td><td>

STEP 2

Read the Person You Are Speaking With:

Extroverted: Friendly - I, Direct - D

Introverted: Cooperative - S, Analytical - C

BEHAVIORAL STYLE MATCH (BSM):

1 - Excellent, 2 - Good, 3 - Fair, 4 - Poor

</td></tr>
<tr><td colspan="2">

STEP 3

Use The Chart Below When You Are Selling to:

</td></tr>
<tr><td>

D **BSM - 2**

</td><td>

S **BSM - 3**

</td></tr>
<tr><td>

The D is looking for: RESULTS

- Do not touch
- Stay business-like
- Be direct and to the point
- Do not over-promise
- Do not joke
- Let them win (you win also)
- Confidently close, not allowing them to overpower you

</td><td>

The S is looking for: SECURITY

- Give them the facts
- Slow down
- Be friendly, personal and earn their trust
- Provide assurances of your promises
- Get "little" agreements
- Let them talk; you ask questions
- Take necessary time before closing
- Follow up after the sale

</td></tr>
<tr><td>

I **BSM - 2**

</td><td>

C **BSM - 4**

</td></tr>
<tr><td>

The I is looking for: THE EXPERIENCE

- Have fun
- Don't waste too much time talking
- Make sure you close
- Give them the recognition
- Let them talk more than you

</td><td>

The C is looking for: INFORMATION

- Keep your distance
- Do not touch them
- Give them the facts, figures and proof
- Do not waste time
- Do not be personal
- Be friendly and direct
- Answer all questions, then close
- Be concerned with details

</td></tr>
</table>

BEHAVIORAL SELLING SKILLS - S

S - STEADINESS

STEP 1

Know Yourself: S Salesperson

- Natural salesperson, personable
- Steady and dependable
- Easily discouraged, low confidence
- Great on follow-through (may over service)
- May give away $$$ under pressure
- More enthusiasm may be needed
- May over use facts
- May wait too long to close

STEP 2

Read the Person You Are Speaking With:

Extroverted:	Introverted:
Friendly - I	Cooperative - S
Direct - D	Analytical - C

BEHAVIORAL STYLE MATCH (BSM):

1 - Excellent	3 - Fair
2 - Good	4 - Poor

STEP 3

Use The Chart Below When You Are Selling to:

D — BSM - 3

The D is looking for: RESULTS

- Be confident; don't be intimidated
- Close sooner than normal
- Disagree with facts, not person
- Do not be overpowered by them
- Let them win (you win too)
- Move faster than normal
- Come on as strong as "D" is, but friendly

S — BSM - 1

The S is looking for: SECURITY

- Give them the facts
- Provide the assurances they need
- Be yourself
- Close when you feel you have their trust
- Assure them of the right decision
- Introduce them to managers, service managers, etc.
- Follow up after the sale

I — BSM - 2

The I is looking for: THE EXPERIENCE

- Allow them to talk, but keep focus
- Provide minimal product info
- Provide follow up
- Give recognition
- Have fun with them
- "Jump" to close when ready

C — BSM - 1

The C is looking for: INFORMATION

- Answer questions with facts
- Do not be too personal
- Be direct and friendly
- Do not touch them
- Give them their space
- Do not fear their skeptical nature
- Follow through on details
- Give information, then close

© 1993-2018 Target Training International, Ltd.

BEHAVIORAL SELLING SKILLS - C

C – COMPLIANT

Step 1 –
Know Yourself: C Salesperson
- Knows data
- May over use data, over-evaluate
- Needs more enthusiasm
- May have trouble selling products below their own standards
- Well organized
- Good service
- Analysis paralysis

Step 2 –
Read the Person You Are Speaking With:

Extroverted:	**Introverted:**
Friendly - I	Cooperative - S
Direct - D	Analytical - C

Behavioral Style Match (BSM):

1 - Excellent	3 - Fair
2 - Good	4 - Poor

Step 3 –
Use The Chart Below When You Are Selling to:

D — BSM - 4

The D is looking for: RESULTS
- Touch upon high points of facts and figures
- Do not "over-data"
- Move quickly
- Be brief, to the point
- Satisfy their strong ego
- Allow them to "win" (you win, too)

S — BSM - 1

The S is looking for: SECURITY
- Move slowly
- Provide facts and figures
- Do not over-control, be too pushy
- Provide assurances
- Develop trust
- Focus on reliability and service
- Personal talk allowed

I — BSM - 4

The I is looking for: THE "EXPERIENCE"
- Focus on people; be friendly and fun
- Listen to them as they talk
- Ask questions
- Show excitement about products
- Close earlier than normal

C — BSM - 1

The C is looking for: INFORMATION
- Give data
- Remain in control
- Examine positives and negatives
- Close earlier than you would expect
- Follow through on promises
- Provide evidence

BODY LANGUAGE

Salesperson Do's

DO:
- Relax position, lean back in chair
- Maintain friendly eye contact
- Nod your head in agreement
- Pause before answering a question or objection
- Sit closer to "I" and "S", sit across from "D" and "C"
- If standing: Move around, gesture, open arms
- Give more space to "D" and "C"
- Use forearm or back touch with "I" and "S"
- Raise or lower your voice for effect
- Frown thoughtfully

Salesperson Don'ts

DON'T:
- Close your arms in front of you
- Perch on your chair
- Touch "D" or "C"
- Jingle coins or doodle with things
- Twist ear or stroke chin
- Tug nose
- Sit across from the "I" or "S"

Buyer's Eye Language: **An emotionally-charged person blinks more.**

Seating Positions & DISC

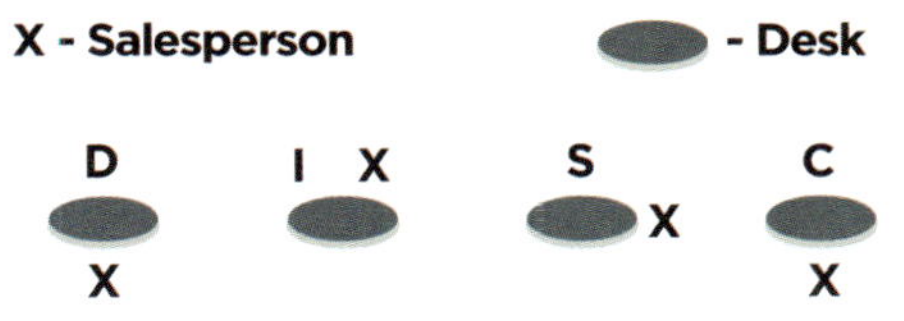

X - Salesperson **- Desk**

D	I	S	C
Desk, X across	Desk, X beside	Desk, X beside	Desk, X across

Impacting/Influential Communication

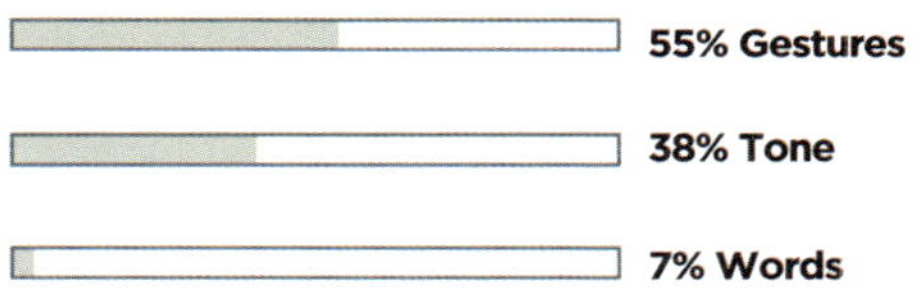

55% Gestures

38% Tone

7% Words

Buying Signals

- Bites lip/furrows brow
- Calls friend for advice
- Rubs chin
- Handles contract
- Scratches head
- Taps with pen
- Half closes eyes

Smiles

A real smile reaches the eyes.
A false smile reaches the lips only.

"I'm defensive."
- Arms crossed
- Face drawn
- Body rigid and tight
- Leaning back

"I disagree."
- Set jaw
- Shaking head from side to side
- Narrowed eyes

"I'm losing interest."
- Broken eye contact
- Slouching in chair
- Checking watch
- Changing posture
- Turning away body 45° to 90°
- Sighing

"You're too close."
- Body block
- Physical retreat
- Leg swinging or tapping
- Legs crossed away from you
- Broken eye contact

© 1993-2018 Target Training International, Ltd.

HOW TO BUILD A WINNING SALES PRESENTATION

Building a Winning Sales Presentation

STEP 1: EVALUATE

The first step in preparing your sales presentation is to list all the reasons your prospect will want to buy your products or services. **Put yourself in place of the prospect and list all the reasons for their making a purchase:**

1. ____________________
2. ____________________
3. ____________________
4. ____________________
5. ____________________

Rewrite the buying motives in order of their strength for each buying style:

Buying Style:

1. ____________________
2. ____________________
3. ____________________

Buying Style:

1. ____________________
2. ____________________
3. ____________________

Buying Style:

1. ____________________
2. ____________________
3. ____________________

Buying Style:

1. ____________________
2. ____________________
3. ____________________

Buying Style:

1. ____________________
2. ____________________
3. ____________________

© 1993-2018 Target Training International, Ltd.

List the characteristics of customers you like best:

1. ______________________________
2. ______________________________
3. ______________________________
4. ______________________________
5. ______________________________

What style would these customers tend to fall into?

List the characteristics of customers you don't like to sell or service:

1. __________

2. __________

3. __________

4. __________

5. __________

What style would these customers tend to fall into?

© 1993-2018 Target Training International, Ltd.

STEP 2: ANALYZING YOUR PRODUCTS OR SERVICE

Start by listing all the features that come to mind about your products or services. Add any additional features contained in your company literature. Then, take each feature and select the value or benefit each style will derive from the purchase.

1. Feature: ______________________________

Benefit for High D: ______________________________

____

____

Benefit for High I: ______________________________

____

____

Benefit for High S: ______________________________

____

____

Benefit for High C: ______________________________

____

____

2. Feature: ____________________

Benefit for High D: ____________________

Benefit for High I: ____________________

Benefit for High S: ____________________

Benefit for High C: ____________________

© 1993-2018 Target Training International, Ltd.

3. Feature: ______________________

Benefit for High D: ______________________

____

____

____

Benefit for High I: ______________________

____

____

____

Benefit for High S: ______________________

____

____

____

Benefit for High C: ______________________

____

____

____

STEP 3: DEMONSTRATIONS

List all the demonstrations you can use to emphasize the benefits of your product or service. Remember that your prospect will absorb your sales presentation through all five of their senses: sight, sound, scent, touch and taste. Try to incorporate as many of these senses as possible into your sales presentation and note the buying style that will be most influenced by each demonstration.

Buying Style: ______

1. ______________________________

____

Buying Style: ______

2. ______________________________

____

Buying Style: ______

3. ______________________________

____

Buying Style: ______

4. ______________________________

____

Buying Style: ______

5. ______________________________

____

© 1993-2018 Target Training International, Ltd.

STEP 4: MODEL SALES PRESENTATION FOR BUYING STYLE

DEVELOPING A TRUST RELATIONSHIP WITH STYLE

Climate: ____________________

Time: ____________________

Pace of Presentation: ____________________

____

What type of information would your provide? ____________________

____

What does this style know about your product? ____________________

____

List the emotional and rational factors that will appeal to this type of buyer:

____

What type of support does this buyer need to support their problem solving?

____

What does this type of buyer need to know to make a decision today?

____

What objections can you anticipate from this type of buyer?

1. ______________________________

2. ______________________________

3. ______________________________

PRESENTATION FOR:

Pre-approach: ________________________

Opening Statement: ________________________

Outline the order in which you want to present your benefits and make special notations beside the points that will be real hot buttons.

© 1993-2018 Target Training International, Ltd.

What closes will work best with this type of buyer?

1. ______________________________
2. ______________________________
3. ______________________________
4. ______________________________
5. ______________________________

Practice, practice, practice...

OBJECTIVES REVISITED

Importance of Selling with Style:

Understanding behavioral styles will help you gain valuable sales dollars. There will be less tension in the sales process.

Authors' Note:
All styles have their strong points. By blending your style with that of your customer, you are strengthening the points that will be impressive to your individual customers.

Also, keep in mind that the study of human behavior is not an exact science. The principles we have presented are guidelines only and must be modified accordingly. A person's observable behavior is the sum of all four factors: D, I, S, and C. Those who have studied and applied "blending" continue to report amazing success stories of increased sales and customer satisfaction. By learning the DISC language and applying it to your sales program, you will find it to be the most valuable sales training in which you have ever invested.

"People buy what they need from people who understand what they want."

–William T. Brooks,
Author of *The New Science of Selling and Persuasion*

© 1993-2018 Target Training International, Ltd.

ARTICLES & CASE STUDIES

Chapter Objective

To present evidence that TTI's assessments provide solutions for organizational people problems.

Chapter Contents

Research that validates the broad application of using assessments to provide solutions for people problems.

© 1993-2018 Target Training International, Ltd.

INTRODUCTION

TTI (Bill J. Bonnstetter) began research on behavioral tendencies in 1979. The first research project was identifying the buying styles of farmers based on the appearance of their farmstead. This research has been duplicated in Canada, Germany, France and several other countries. It continually proves that you can identify a person's buying style based on the appearance of their surroundings regardless of what country you live.

We continually do research related to performance; and some of those papers are included in this chapter. However, many of the earlier articles and research are posted on www.ttisi.com/research.

SELECTING SUPERIOR PERFORMERS SAFELY UNDER THE LAW 2009

By Bill J. Bonnstetter

INTRODUCTION

For the last 30 years, I have observed organizations hiring people that were not the best candidate for the position to avoid any potential liability from an EEOC claim. There is nothing in the law that says you must hire an inferior candidate. The law simply states that you, and any of the systems you use, cannot discriminate against the protected group(s).

This article is not intended to provide you with a way to get around the law, but rather to provide you with a system for hiring that does not allow typical human biases to enter into the process. We all see the world from our own view; however, sometimes this view may not be in the best interest of the position or the organization.

© 1993-2018 Target Training International, Ltd.

SOME OF THE ISSUES THAT KEEP US FROM HIRING SUPERIOR PERFORMERS

Bias: The Biggest Barrier (Challenge) in Selecting Superior Performers

Our own view point is influenced by how we value experience, knowledge, economics, aesthetics, altruism, power and tradition. When we are confronted by a person who sees the world differently, these views could be called biases. Neither right or wrong, nor good or bad, biases are simply a reflection of our personal viewpoint. Often, this personal viewpoint is unknowingly injected into the hiring process even when it is not relevant to a specific position or to the organization itself. When this happens, it creates a barrier, preventing us from selecting true superior performers.

Today we have laws that keep us from acting on our biases as they relate to gender, age and nationality, but there are still biases that get in the way. **Many people are also unknowingly biased on experience, education and intelligence, and this keeps them from selecting superior performers.** In addition, people bring much more to the job, including their passions, beliefs, personal skills and behaviors. Perhaps one of the most important personal skills is that of personal accountability, and most companies are not aware of its importance, nor do they have a way to measure it.

Exhibit 1 represents some of the things people bring to the job. Ninety percent of all people are hired based on what they say they can do or have done. We tend to hire for skills and fire for attitude. Keeping these factors in mind will help you understand our model.

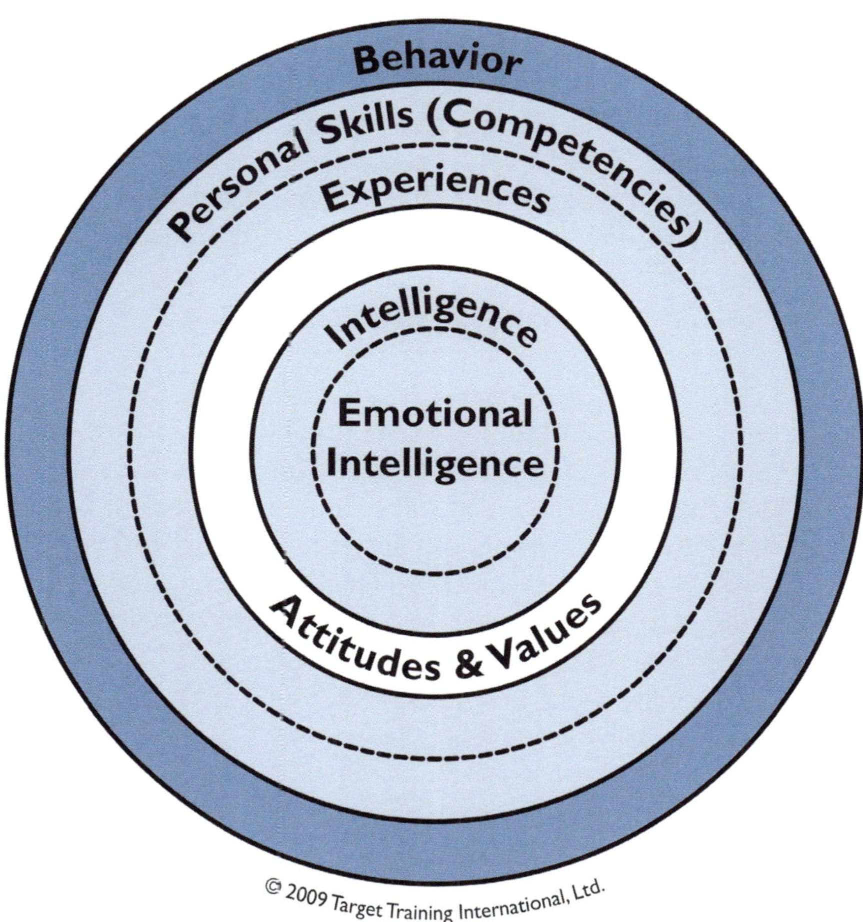

Exhibit 1

HIRING AND PERFORMANCE BARRIERS

In addition to bias, there are several other obstacles that prevent us from hiring superior performers. Sometimes these barriers are a result of inappropriate standards, as many organizations attempt to clone their top performers. At one time, I too thought this was possible; but after years of research, I have proven that there are serious problems with this approach:

1. **A strong brand like Dell, Xerox or IBM, can actually carry a weak sales force.** When you benchmark using your top performers, you end up comparing candidates to a C- sales force and set a standard that is also C-. When this occurs, the top and bottom sales people tend to look alike from the standpoint of behavior, motivators, skills, etc.

   Our research has proven this two different ways. Years ago when we were attempting to benchmark using the top 10 salespeople and the bottom 10, both groups looked alike. In fact, the top 10 did not contain one candidate that fit our opinion of what we would expect as a superior performer in a small, unbranded company. Once we helped the strong branded companies hire to our standard, the candidates we recommended were the sales award winners the following year. This validated our opinion that you must benchmark jobs, not people.

2. **Mismanagement can ruin a great hire.** If you are currently hiring superior performers but not managing them correctly, they will leave. I have asked these questions in all of my international speeches on retention:

   - Have you ever been mismanaged?
   - What was your performance like while you were mismanaged?
   - What did you do about it?

Over 95% of all people will state they have been mismanaged. They will tell you that their performance was sub-par during this period. Eventually they all left the company because of the one issue — mismanagement.

3. **When you benchmark the top 10 to 20 people in a position, the standard is reduced.** My research indicates that you can quite often identify the top three people in a position, and many times in actual order of 1, 2 and 3, based on performance. Considering that the rest of the group actually waters down what you're trying to discover, you will sell yourself short by hiring someone who is believed to be a superior performer but only meets a low standard. What do people have or bring to the job that makes them a superior performer? This is easy to determine by looking at behaviors, attitudes and personal skills of everyone.

4. **Failure to use assessments as a part of your hiring or screening process limits your ability to accurately select superior performers.** Assessments have been given a bad rap, and there are a few that should not be used. However, not all assessments should be dismissed because of the reputation of a few. Four-quadrant behavioral assessments when used as the only assessment will make everyone look good at the start but will eventually fail because behavior only describes "how" you do what you do. It is possible for successful people to differ on "how" they do the job.

   Discovering "why" successful people do a job will provide a better understanding. When a person's intrinsic passions are fulfilled on the job, they will perform better than those who do not receive intrinsic rewards. Cloning the identical behavior of your top performer will not get the same results if they have different attitudes. Our research proves that using only behavioral assessments for hiring sales and executive positions will result in hiring mistakes. For many jobs, a person's passion is key to performance. I can prove

© 1993-2018 Target Training International, Ltd.

very quickly with a four-quadrant behavioral system that a company will have superior performers in sales from all four quadrants as long as they have the correct motivators and passion for the job.

5. **Failure to let the job talk.** If the job could talk, it would clearly identify the knowledge, personal skills, hard skills, behavior and intrinsic rewards that are needed for superior performance. Unfortunately, our personal biases keep most people from hearing the job talk. It wasn't until I acknowledged my personal biases that I started to discover the truth about jobs that leads to the selection of superior performers. I don't work alone in my research on performance anymore because of this one issue. Everyone involved in the selection process must be willing to admit their biases and be open to other views. It is important that this session be led by an experienced job benchmarking facilitator. To do this, pretend you are building a robot to do the job. What would we have the robot do? It is when we think of a person in the position that our biases also enter the process. Over the last 30 years, every time the use of assessments in selection is questioned it's because biases have entered the decision. The purpose of this paper is to assist you in selecting superior performers safely under the law. Don't dismiss assessments until you see, hear and touch the evidence to be presented.

6. **Typically, organizations hire for skills and fire for attitudes.** This often happens because people are biased on the value of skills and do not fully understand attitudes. If skills always led to success, then all people who have passed skill or knowledge tests would be successful. For example, we know that not all medical doctors, lawyers, CPAs, nurses and chiropractors are successful. They have all passed an exam that certifies their knowledge and skills, but there is much more that contributes to success. In fact, we would be more successful in selection if we hired for attitude and focused on developing skills. To understand our biases about skills, identify the skills you want all candidates to bring to the job and then be truthful about the time and cost to develop them on the job. Typically, software managers want to hire programmers with at least five years of experience; but with technology changing at such a rapid pace, more often than not the tools being used in the position haven't been around for five years. So why is the experience important? A few years ago, I hired a programmer straight out of college who was refused an interview because he lacked the "right" experience. He worked directly for me, and I made sure that he got the right experience so I could ultimately transfer him to the programming department. Today, he's still with the company and is one of our best programmers.

© 1993-2018 Target Training International, Ltd.

Before I explain the process, let's read about successes from this process. **See Exhibit 2 below.**

CASE STUDY:
Job Benchmarking Provides Foundation for Success

With our patented job benchmarking, one associate was able to revolutionize talent management at two different companies. In the first company, Corey, a sales manager, called me and shared a problem he had with his sales force. That problem was 74% turnover. We proceeded to benchmark the job using our patented, job-related process. Corey then compared all current and former sales people against the benchmark as well as new sales people. Everyone was put on a personalized development and management plan based on TTI's concept. The results were 0% turnover for the next 24 months. The company was sold, and Corey moved on to another company.

At this second company, he inherited a sales team that ranked No. 22 out of 22, or dead last. Again, Corey benchmarked the sales position using our process and compared his current sales people to that benchmark. He quickly discovered that 75% of his sales force did not match the benchmark. Corey replaced that 75% with people who matched the benchmark, and now his team is currently No. 1 out of 22 sales teams. Corey's new company had been using a competitor of TTI to screen candidates, which apparently didn't work, as people got through the system that were not qualified candidates.

Exhibit 2

YEARS OF RESEARCH WENT INTO DEVELOPING THIS PROCESS THAT ALLOWS YOU TO DO TWO THINGS:

Select Superior Performers and Have Real Evidence to Support the Job Requirements.

Avoiding the issues associated with the typical benchmarking process involving top performers is important in selecting the right candidate. To start, we need to discover what the job itself requires for superior performance. If the job could talk, it would clearly define the knowledge, the behavior, how the job helps satisfy people's intrinsic passions and the personal skills needed to do the job.

In addition, ensuring you hire superior performers safely under the law requires a system that clearly identifies what is required by the job and how each candidate compares to those job requirements. Based on over 30 years of research, I have created a job benchmarking system that addresses the common biases associated with selection, gives the job a voice and provides a benchmark that is job related. In 2007, this benchmarking system was patented (#7,184,969), making it a truly revolutionary process. The job benchmarking system incorporates seven major steps that must be followed for the best results:

1. **Identify the job to be benchmarked.**

   Meet with key members of the organization to determine what position(s) should be benchmarked. A great starting point is to determine which positions have high turnover, low productivity or management difficulties. Another angle to look at is what positions you would like people to strive for, or whether you would like to increase performance even though the performance is already high. Talk about the positions that are critical to the organization's success. These are the jobs you want to start with.

© 1993-2018 Target Training International, Ltd.

2. **Identify key subject matter experts.**

   Subject matter experts are critical to an accurate benchmark and properly selecting the right people to participate is important. Subject matter experts should be people who interact with the position being benchmarked on a daily or weekly basis. An ideal mix would be the direct manager, the manager's direct supervisor, two people who are performing well in the position or have successfully held the position within the past six months, and two people in lateral positions. The benchmarking process allows for up to ten subject matter experts; but three to seven is ideal, as it is better to have fewer people who really know the job than many people who do not.

3. **Subject matter experts meet and identify key accountabilities.**

   Key Accountabilities are essential to superior performance and are the foundation of the job benchmark. Similar to performance objectives, they are a more detailed description of why the job really exists. Through a facilitated brainstorming process, the subject matter experts will establish three to five key accountabilities to ensure that all participants have the same clear picture of how the job should be done. Later the key accountabilities will be integrated into job descriptions, performance evaluations, interview processes and commitment and accountability programs.

4. Prioritize key accountabilities and determine time commitment.

Once each key accountability is established, the group of subject matter experts prioritize those key accountabilities in order of importance to success on the job, then assign an approximate percentage of the work week to be spent on each key accountability. **See Exhibit 3 below.**

SAMPLE KEY ACCOUNTABILITIES

Priority Key Accountabilities

1. Effectively prospect, qualify, demonstrate and close according to company guidelines to ensure sales goals are met while maintaining company's integrity and brand image — **40% of Work Week.**
2. Follow up with customers to ensure their needs are met and up-sell additional products — **20% Percent of Work Week.**
3. Keep abreast of industry-related knowledge and competition to adapt sales presentations and marketing efforts — **10% Percent of Work Week.**
4. Work closely with other sales representatives in adapting and improving the sales strategy for specific products — **10% Percent of Work Week.**
5. Other activities — **20% Percent of Work Week.**

TOTAL: 100% of Work Week

Exhibit 3

© 1993-2018 Target Training International, Ltd.

5. **Subject matter experts respond to the job assessment.**

   Once the key accountability session is complete, each of the subject matter experts will respond to an online job assessment, keeping these key accountabilities in mind. The assessments will be combined to create a Job Benchmark Report, detailing the position's requirements for superior performance from 37 views: 8 behavioral factors, 6 motivators and 23 personal skills.

6. **Subject matter experts review results.**

   The subject matter experts then meet a second time to discuss the results revealed in the Job Benchmark Report. In this step, it is important that all of the subject matter experts agree on the final Master Job Benchmark Report.

7. **Complete the Ideal Candidate Form.**

   The hiring manager and everyone involved in the hiring process should complete the Ideal Candidate Form to document additional job details before the selection process begins. This is a very important step, and one that should be given careful consideration, as the recruitment and screening process highly depends upon the decisions made in this step of the process. **Clearly define the experience required so that you don't miss out on Superior Performers who might lack this experience but that meet or exceed all the other requirements.** Discuss how long it will take to give them the desired experience and how much it will cost.

IDEAL CANDIDATE FORM DETAILS

Pre-Employment Assessment Requirements

- Personal Skills (top 5-7)
- Motivators (2-3)
- Ideal Behaviors

Educational Requirements

- Level required and degree type
- Certifications necessary

Experience Requirements

- Specific job and industry experience
- Number of years preferred

Custom Phone Screen Questions

Custom Applicant Pre-Qualifier Questions

Resume Screen Preferences

- Job hopping
- Employment gaps
- Over qualifications

Recommended Background Check Package

Compensation Package

Marketing the Position Using Information in this Form

Exhibit 4

SAMPLE INTERVIEW QUESTIONS

PERSONAL ACCOUNTABILITY:
A measure of the capacity to be answerable for personal actions.

1. Tell me about a time when it was necessary to admit to others that you had made a mistake. How did you handle it?

2. Give an example of a situation where others had made an error or mistake and you had to take the blame for their actions. How did you feel about doing that?

3. What is the worst business decision you ever made? What made it the worst? Would knowing what you do now have helped you to avoid making that decision?

Exhibit 5

© 1993-2018 Target Training International, Ltd.

SAFELY UNDER THE LAW

In a recent US Court of Appeals for the Tenth Circuit from the District of Colorado, Susan K. Turner v. Public Service Company of Colorado, Case Number 07-1396, Judge Tymkovich ruled in favor of the Public Service Company of Colorado. Ms. Turner brought a gender discrimination suit in regard to their hiring practices. The court held, among others, that the criteria used to rate candidates were not excessively subjective because each applicant answered the same job-related questions.

TTI has over 6800 job benchmarks. These benchmarks come from Fortune 100 companies all the way down to businesses with fewer than 50 people. The specific jobs are from all industries and many from Mexico, Europe and Asia. TTI has compared benchmarks from different companies, but with similar key accountabilities and job descriptions. They are never identical, but often very similar. Most often they require the same skills but in a different hierarchy.

TTI has the evidence to support and defend our process against any challenge. The fact that we have never been challenged for an EEOC claim speaks loudly to our factual evidence. All of the 6800 job benchmarks have all 37 factors ranked, including definitions and interview questions. Perhaps the best evidence lies with the people who were actually hired because they were a perfect fit for the position. Last year, 92 percent of people who were hired based on our job fit were still in the job 12 months later. Many have received special recognition based on superior performance.

Every company needs a selection system that all hiring managers can follow and that has documented evidence that the people hired using the system are above average or superior performers. **That system should contain the following:**

1. A view of the job — key accountabilities defined, analyzed and prioritized to determine the knowledge, personal skills, intrinsic rewards, hard skills and behavior that would lead to superior performance:

   - 23 personal skills
   - 8 behaviors
   - 6 intrinsic rewards that will match a person's passion

2. A complete description of all 37 factors, which can be compared to similar positions from other companies. For example, we have benchmarked hundreds of outside sales positions and find they are all similar, but not exact. Definitions of 37 factors available upon request.

3. All interview questions are job-related.

4. Superior performance research that supports benchmarking of the job, not people.

5. Gap Report to support both superior performance as well as those who are inferior performers.

6. A complete system for onboarding all new hires including a development plan that is personalized and totally job-related that leads to performance and retention solutions.

7. A performance management system modified to incorporate all the job related activities discussed through this system for current or new employees.

© 1993-2018 Target Training International, Ltd.

THE RESULTS

By adhering to an established, job benchmarking process, you will have the following detailed information to support your selection criteria, ensuring evidence to defend any EEOC challenge. Your results can be compared to potentially hundreds of benchmarks using the same process.

- Job description
- Key accountabilities
- Ideal candidate identified
- Interview questions for key success factors
- Top performer comparison
- Ineffective performer comparison
- Gap between job requirements (▲) and talent (★).

Good Match:

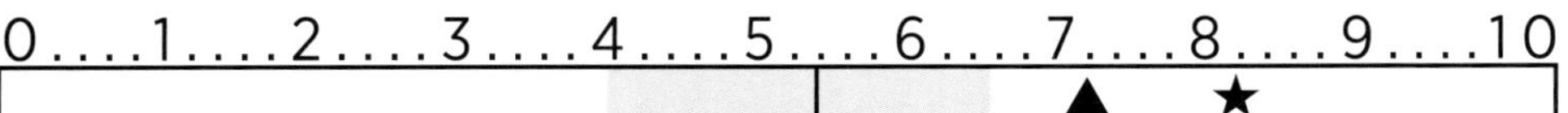

Bad Match:

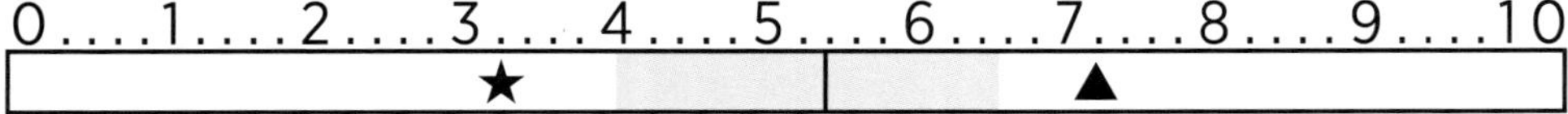

IF THE JOB COULD TALK... 2000

By Bill J. Bonnstetter

JOB TALK

If a job could talk, it would explain precisely what was necessary to achieve superior performance. We could ask it to tell us about the:

- Knowledge a person needs,
- Personal attributes required to drive success,
- Rewards for superior performance,
- Hard skills vital for the job,
- Behaviors necessary to perform at peak levels and
- Intrinsic motivators.

But we all know that jobs can't talk. If they did, we would certainly hear the real story.

THE PROBLEM

Instead, we must get the truth from another source — subject matter experts. These are the people in and around a given job. But even asking people about a job presents a challenge.

Before we can learn the true meaning of superior performance for any particular job, the experts must remove their natural biases. Bias is an unfair preference or dislike of something. Bias can create a blind spot — blocking out a single thing — or act like a set of blinders — making only one thing visible.

Unfortunately, biases get in the way of truly understanding job requirements. Over the years, we have learned that it is difficult — if not impossible — for subject matter experts to completely ignore their own bias. We also know that once subject matter experts do slice through their bias, they are able to hear the job talk. Once that happens, they can identify the key accountabilities or competencies for the job.

© 1993-2018 Target Training International, Ltd.

Only after they remove those natural biases can they deliver a true definition of superior performance for the given job.

THE SOLUTION

Removing bias can be the most formidable challenge in defining superior performance. In fact, we know that it is impossible to strip away the bias without an impartial facilitator. An expert can spur a group into unbiased, fair discussion and act as a catalyst for developing a clear understanding of what superior performance looks like. In short, an expert facilitator will help subject matter experts hear a job talking.

THE RESULTS

The process leads to an understanding of the knowledge, intrinsic motivators, personal attributes, behaviors and hard skills required of each key accountability for the job in question. After the process, businesses can compare all current and new staff members to the results and provide a developmental plan for each person. Development plans that are job related are much better than those based on one person's opinion.

GROUND BREAKING RESEARCH 1998

WHAT'S INSIDE TOP SALES PERFORMERS IN THE UNITED STATES AND EUROPE

By Bill J. Bonnstetter,
President and CEO Target Training International, Ltd.

Research studies of top salespeople in both the United States and Europe confirm that top sales performance can be predicted. These findings confirm that top performing salespeople are similar in very specific ways. This research carries significant implications for people who are considering sales as a career, are currently selling or are accountable for sales performance. **The net conclusion of the research shows that top salespeople around the world place a high value on efficiency, utility and economics.**

The most successful organizations in the world already know that hiring the right sales people has the potential of becoming one of the most powerful secret weapons in their arsenal of competitive strategies. What they may not know is that hiring the right salespeople can be as simple as following a recipe based on recent findings from an international study I conducted with Frank Scheelen of Institut.

As global competition and increased customer demands require organizations to improve in key performance areas such as customer service, quality, reducing costs and customization, aggressive organizations must be ever vigilant in the identification, acquisition, development and integration of innovative technology. The type of innovative technology is now available to select top performers.

© 1993-2018 Target Training International, Ltd.

As a result of our 20 years of research, development and distribution of assessment tools to measure performance, we have been telling organizations that it is what's on the inside, not the outside that counts, especially in sales performance. **What we are fighting is the myth that hiring good looking and intelligent sounding people correlates to sales performance.**

Much of the research conducted in the past on top salespeople has been focused on behavior. Behavioral research has been popular because, like looking good and sounding good, behavior can be observed. Little, if any significant study has been focused on what goes on inside a top salesperson. Our ground breaking research in the United States and Europe now confirms that attitudes far outweigh looking good, sounding good or behavior in distinguishing top salespeople.

Two of our most significant assumptions were confirmed by the two studies:

1. Top performing salespeople around the world are similar; and...

2. Motivators are more important than behavior in sales performance (Refer to Study One and Study Two in the following pages)

In both studies, only top performing salespeople responded. In the United States study and a separate German study, top salespeople responded to two assessments. One was based on internationally validated DISC behavioral model and the other was based on the Personal Interests, Attitudes and Values model.

The DISC assessment identifies eight basic patterns that define how people tend to behave. **Listed below are brief descriptions of the eight behavior patterns:**

1. **Conductor** – Direct and results-oriented.

2. **Persuader** – Optimistic and flexible.

3. **Promoter** – Verbal and trusting.

4. **Relater** – Cooperative team player.

5. **Supporter** – Accommodating and persistent.

6. **Coordinator** – Cautious and self-disciplined.

7. **Analyzer** – Precise and detail-oriented.

8. **Implementer** – Creative and indecisive.

The PIAV assessment measures six distinct attitudes that provide the context for motivation or why people act the way they do. **Listed below are the six attitudes with a brief description of the focus of each:**

1. **Utilitarian/Economic** – A focus on practicality, efficiency.

2. **Theoretical** – A focus on education, learning and truth.

3. **Aesthetic** – A focus on beauty, harmony and balance.

4. **Individualistic** – A focus on controlling one's own destiny or the destiny of others.

5. **Social** – Putting a cause or others before self.

6. **Traditional/Regulatory** – A focus on a system for living.

The results of the United States DISC behavior study of top salespeople in 178 firms are illustrated with pie charts.

© 1993-2018 Target Training International, Ltd.

As you can see on the next page, top sales performers tended to be spread across four behavioral patterns. In the German study, top sales performers tended to be spread across three of the same behavioral patterns. In view of these results, it is reasonable to conclude that salespeople with most, if not all, behavioral patterns can be top performers.

However, when it comes to what is on the inside of top performing salespeople, both the United States study as well as the German study confirm it is hands-down, a Utilitarian attitude. The implications for the global sales community, whether they are salespeople or those who must hire, manage, develop and motivate them, are clear. The most important selection criteria when hiring salespeople is a high Utilitarian motivator. Once salespeople with a high Utilitarian attitude are hired, the job satisfaction and motivation buttons that need to be pushed are efficiency, practicality and return on investment of time, talent and resources.

Studies of attitudes also reveal that when a person's highest attitude is fulfilled, they will begin to be motivated toward their second highest attitude. For instance, a top performing salesperson whose highest attitude is Utilitarian and second highest attitude is Aesthetic will begin to be motivated by beauty and harmony only after they have made as much money as they want, or need for security, through the most efficient and practical methods. This provides important insight into incentives. Income and other financially related incentives will yield the best effects with high Utilitarian salespeople, unless the salesperson is completely satisfied in those areas. Although financial rewards are always a safe bet, incentives should be tailored to each salesperson's motivations.

TOP SALES LEADERS: USA VS. GERMANY

Study One – Top Sales Leaders, USA: N = 178

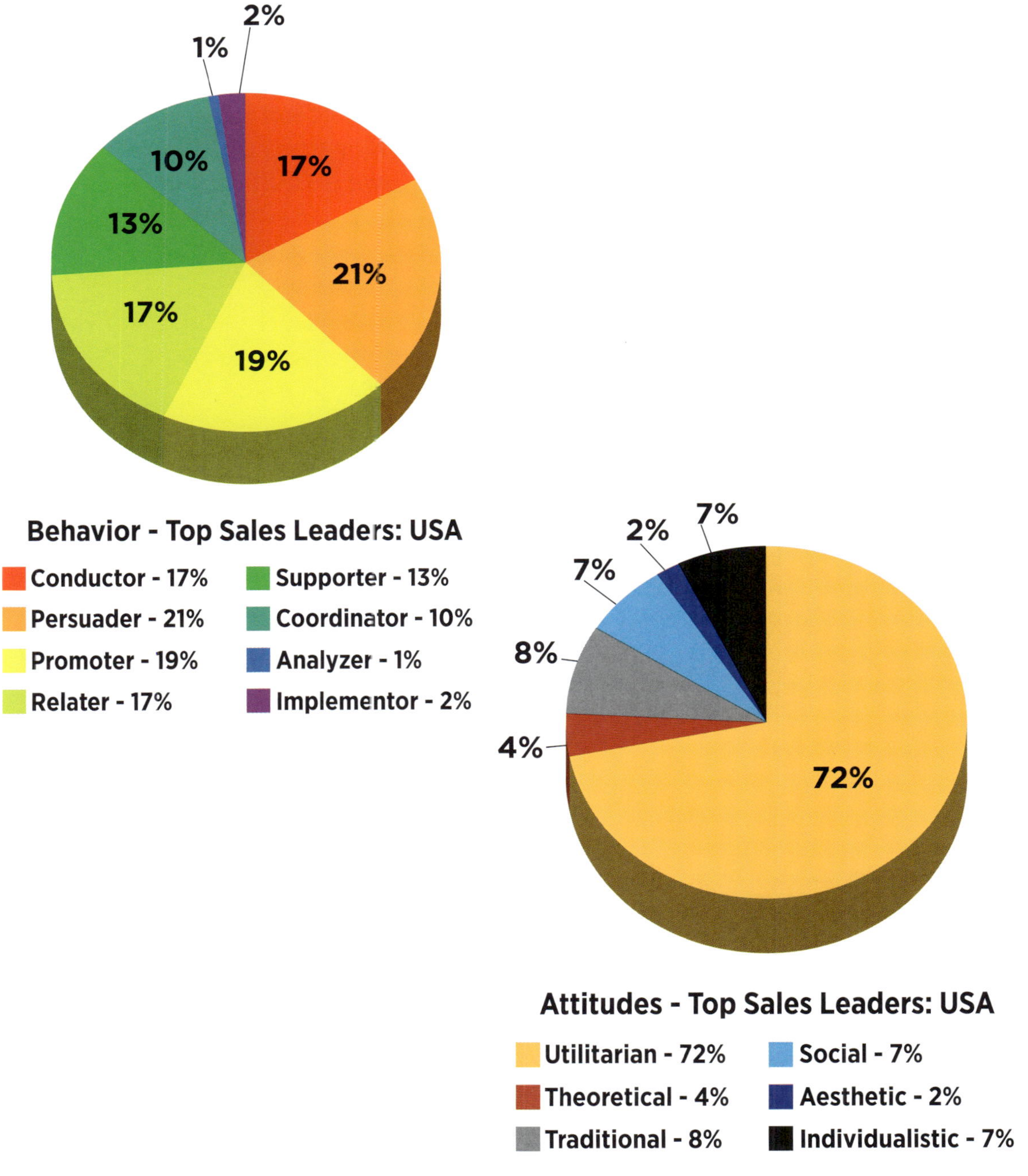

Study Two – Top Sales Leaders, Germany: N = 492

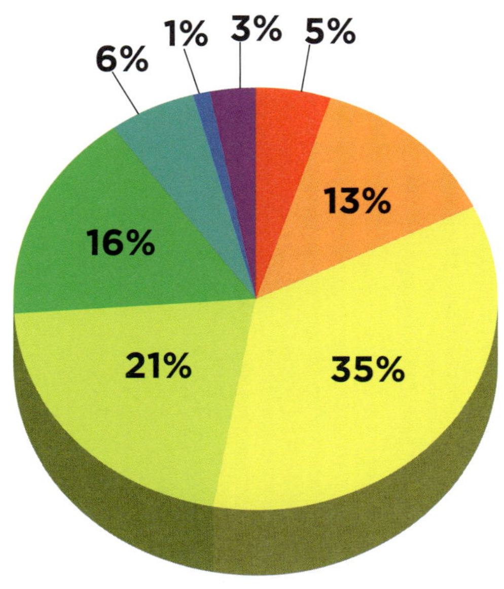

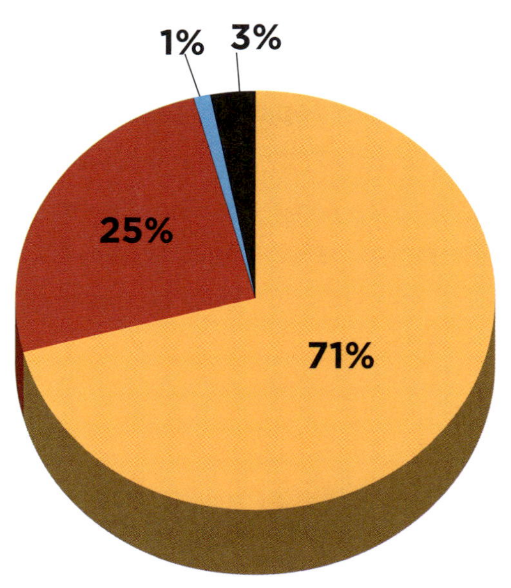

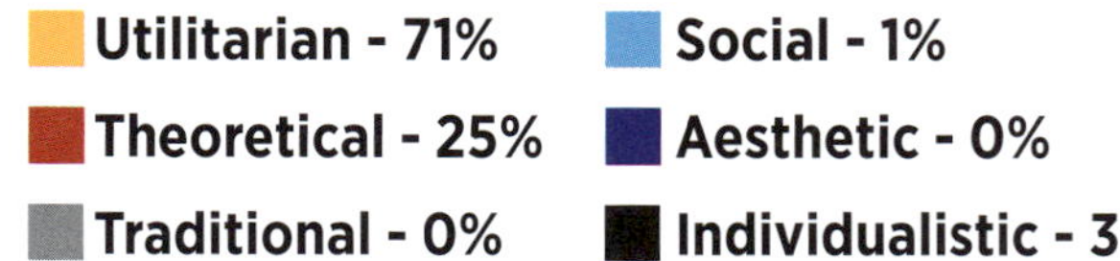

GERMANY: N = 492

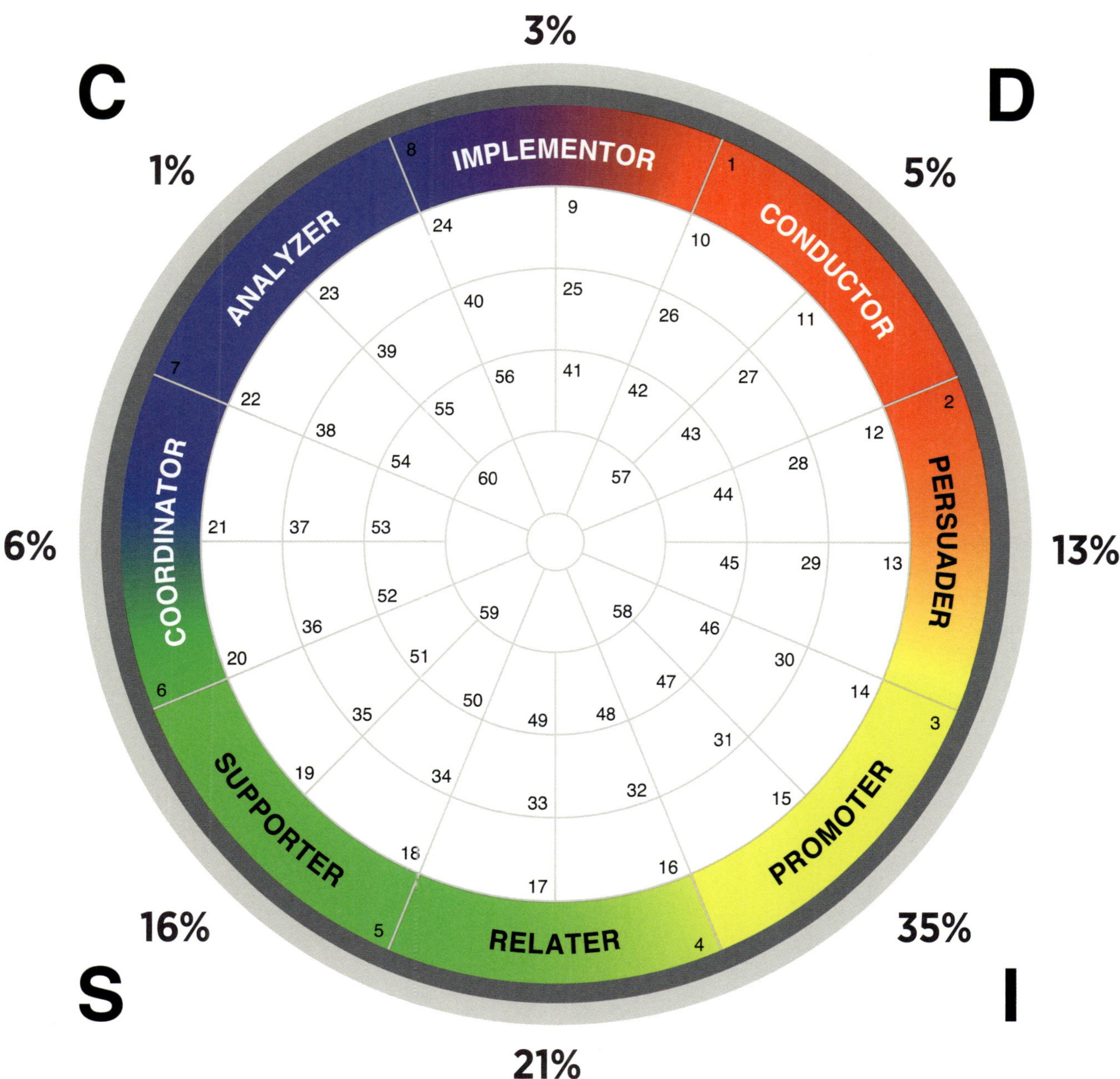

USA: N = 178

2%
C
D
1%
17%
10%
21%
13%
19%
S
I
17%
IMPLEMENTOR
CONDUCTOR
PERSUADER
PROMOTER
RELATER
SUPPORTER
COORDINATOR
ANALYZER

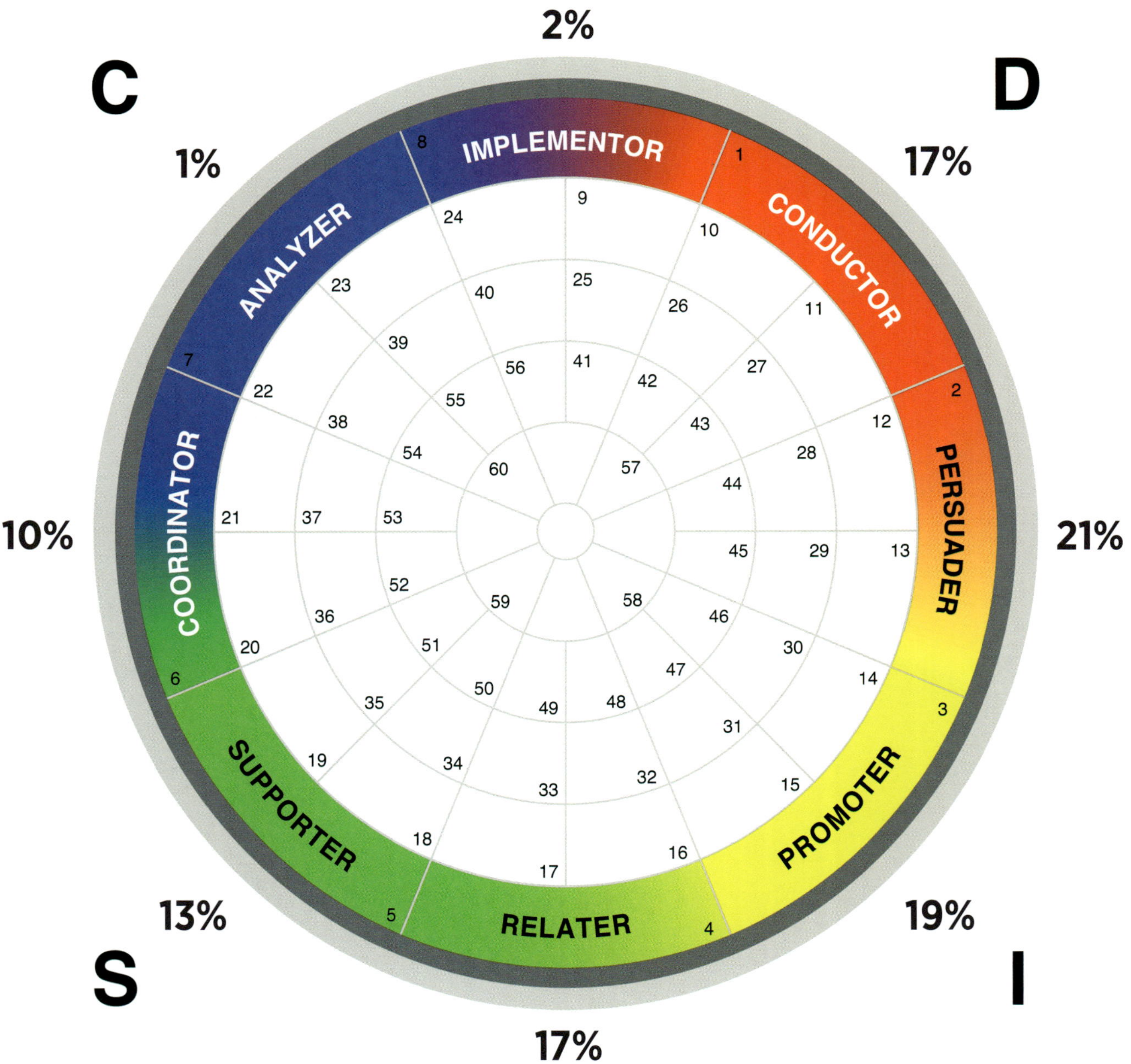

DO YOU HAVE WHAT IT TAKES TO BE A SERIAL ENTREPRENEUR? 2010

By Dr. Ronald J. Bonnstetter & Bill J. Bonnstetter

The sources of new job creation have taken on enormous importance as millions of jobs have been lost around the globe. The Kaufman Foundation found that U.S. startups (firms less than one year old) create an average of three million new jobs annually and "without startups there would be no net job growth in the U.S. economy." In fact, even when startups are excluded, young firms (one to five years old) account for approximately two-thirds of job creation. **This shows that it is not just small businesses, but startup businesses in particular that have long been the engines of job creation, making entrepreneurs crucial drivers in the race to put people back to work.**

This makes it urgent that the strategy for stimulating global economic growth includes reliable ways to identify those individuals who have the characteristics to succeed at building a viable business. Venture capitalists and other funders in particular will benefit from being able to compare the attributes of a funding applicant to a successful entrepreneur's profile before investing.

© 1993-2018 Target Training International, Ltd.

WHY SERIAL ENTREPRENEURS?

This article focuses on serial entrepreneurs, who are defined as those who have created more than one successful business which employs others. Concentrating our study exclusively on this subset of serial entrepreneurs is intentional, the better to distinguish the defining characteristics of successful entrepreneurship. We have intentionally excluded people who might normally be considered entrepreneurs but who are, in fact, running their business more like a hobby than a bona fide business and are therefore not likely to employ many others. Franchisees are not considered here because they have chosen a path designed to reduce risk by purchasing a proven brand name or an already established system rather than creating a new one.

These serial entrepreneurs potentially have three to five times the economic impact of a person who would normally be classified as an entrepreneur or small business person for the following reasons:

1. They have already experienced success and usually failure, too.

2. They tend to learn from both, developing the professional skills vital for success.

3. They have personal funds from previous ventures or have the ability to raise funds based on past successes.

4. Their track record makes them more likely to create gazelle companies, which tend to grow bigger, faster and thus employ more people than a typical start up.

5. They have demonstrated the ability to sustain a business past the first year, into the high growth job production years of a young firm.

Our group of serial entrepreneurs earned impressive track records, having on average built five different businesses and sold two of them. Most have experienced failure at some point (66%) but persevered to achieve solid successes that have them in the 36% tax bracket (80%).

What exactly characterizes a serial entrepreneur? Data was collected in three specific areas relevant to performance: attitudes, behavior, and professional soft skills. Attitudes tell us why entrepreneurs are motivated to do what they do, behavior is how they are doing it, and professional skills reveal what they do well. Since serial entrepreneurs are clearly doing something right, it behooves us to understand them. Recognizing the characteristics they have in common will not only enlighten the funding process, it also makes it possible for us to identify the potential entrepreneurs among us so we can actively cultivate them.

© 1993-2018 Target Training International, Ltd.

MOTIVATING A DRIVE FOR PROFIT

We examined the attitudes that motivate serial entrepreneurs based on six fundamental value areas common to all people. Knowing a person's motivators illuminates why they hold certain attitudes and, thus, why they choose to act. These motivators are what initiate our behavior.

The six basic motivator areas are:

Aesthetic: A drive for beauty, form and harmony in objects, nature or experiences.

Traditional: A drive for an orderly, well-established, unified structure for living.

Social: A selfless drive to help others.

Utilitarian: A drive for a practical return on time or money spent to accumulate wealth and what is useful.

Theoretical: A drive for knowledge, discovery and continuous learning.

Individualistic: A drive for personal power, influence and control over surroundings.

Every person ranks these six basic motivators with varying degrees of importance, and for many people there are one or more additional areas that are highly cherished.

For the purpose of this research, we identified the single highest or primary value of these serial entrepreneurs, which were:

Serial Entrepreneurs	U.S. Adult Mean
1. Utilitarian - 62%	38%
2. Theoretical - 21%	15%
3. Individualistic - 10%	9%

Remembering that motivators are the drivers of behaviors, it is significant that serial entrepreneurs are dramatically more utilitarian than is average in the U.S. population. It's their defining characteristic, revealing a consistently results-oriented practicality in their decision-making processes. With fundamental, practical considerations as a guide, they are always looking for the most efficient and effective way to accomplish the business at hand. The first consideration before proceeding is that any investment of energy, staff or resources will produce a worthwhile return on investment. This means that serial entrepreneurs will, by nature, remain focused on achieving a profitable bottom line. The utilitarian value also tempers the serial entrepreneurs' theoretical and individualistic motives.

A theoretical value means that a business person is motivated to be a continuous learner who actively seeks to be knowledgeable about their industry and is open to the best solutions available. This person won't have to be prodded to keep up with technological advances or evolving business practices that will affect their enterprise. Acquiring new information as it becomes available comes naturally to them, because they place a high value on knowledge. A person with a theoretical approach to business will do the homework necessary to be prepared before taking action. But they are highly

© 1993-2018 Target Training International, Ltd.

unlikely to act on information or impulses that don't result in an economic return. For example, the highly utilitarian person would not purchase new business equipment or software, no matter how superior research shows it to be, until it can be directly connected to achieving goals related to profits. For other people who put a high premium on the theoretical value, knowledge can be valuable just for its own sake, but for the serial entrepreneur, the value of knowledge is in its usefulness for achieving goals.

An Individualistic value indicates a higher than normal drive to have power and to exert control over what goes on around them. For someone planning to start a business, holding this value prepares them to direct those around them and means they have the willingness to be responsible for the calculated risks required to succeed. These are people who gravitate toward positions of leadership in most fields, in their quest for personal power, influence and renown.

People with a strong UTILITARIAN attitude:

- Will protect organizational or team finances as well as they do their own.
- Are profit-driven and bottom-line oriented.
- Are highly motivated to achieve and win in a variety of areas.
- Pay attention to return on investment in business or team activity.
- Are highly productive.
- Show a keen awareness of the revenue clock — their own and the organization's.

People with a THEORETICAL attitude:

- Like to develop quick utilities or procedures that are a new way to look at a situation.
- Are active problem solvers.
- Have a strong knowledge-driven ethic.
- Ask many of the necessary questions to gain the maximum amount of information.
- Have a very high interest level, always questioning and always learning more.
- Actively engage in problem solving and strategic solutions.
- Could be considered intellectuals.
- Are good at integrating the past, present and future.

People with an INDIVIDUALISTIC attitude:

- Have a strong drive for control.
- Bring creative ideas.
- Have no fear of taking calculated risks.
- Desire to be an individual and celebrate differences.
- Realize that we are all individuals and have ideas to offer.
- Enjoy making presentations to small or large groups and are generally perceived as engaging presenters by the audience.

© 1993-2018 Target Training International, Ltd.

BUSINESS BUILDING BEHAVIOR THAT WORKS

Next we examined their behavior, the components of their make-up that are easily observable in day-to-day actions. Looking at serial entrepreneurs from a behavioral standpoint, we start to see their uniqueness. For the purpose of this research, we looked at their primary **behavior** as it relates to eight dimensions of normal behavior:

1 Very competitive
2. Not very competitive
3. High trust
4. Low trust
5. Slow to change
6. Quick to change
7. Rule follower
8. Rule breaker

89% of our serial entrepreneurs fall into one of five categories:

Serial Entrepreneurs	U.S. Adult Mean
1. Very competitive - 33%	12%
2. High trust - 18%	20%
3. Low trust - 9%	8%
4. Quick to change - 7%	1%
5. Rule breaker - 22%	12%

The entrepreneur's ability to adapt to change and to comply with regulation is only slightly higher than average, as is their tendency to establish relationships based on trust. How we see serial entrepreneurs strongly distinguished from the general public is by their likelihood to have a highly competitive nature. The numerous setbacks that are par for the course when starting a new business may deter others. But when entrepreneurs undertake to bring a new product or service to the marketplace, they will confidently stand up to opposition and ignore naysayers because they genuinely relish the challenge to prove the worth of their ideas.

This competitiveness is the source of their resilience, since it is grounded in a solid self-confidence that says, "I can win at this!"

Based on their behavior, these are words that describe a serial entrepreneur:

- Bottom-line organizer
- Forward looking
- Places high value on time
- Challenge oriented
- Competitive
- Initiates activity
- Challenges the status quo
- Innovative
- Tenacious
- Creative problem solver
- Motivates others toward goals
- Positive sense of humor
- Negotiates conflict
- Verbalizes with articulateness
- Independent
- Change agent
- Rule breaker
- Optimistic and enthusiastic

© 1993-2018 Target Training International, Ltd.

SUPERIOR PROFESSIONAL SKILLS

The next area we studied was their mastery of professional skills using a validated assessment. This assessment measures a person's mastery level of 23 universally recognized, work-related competencies. Most adults have mastery of about 5 or 6 skills. As a group, the serial entrepreneurs are above the mean (average) on 14 of the 23 professional skills.

Serial Entrepreneurs exhibit above average mastery of the following professional competencies:

- **Leadership** - Achieving extraordinary business results through people.
- **Goal Orientation** - Energetically focusing efforts on meeting a goal, mission or objective.
- **Presenting** - Communicating effectively to groups.
- **Employee Development/ Coaching** - Facilitating and supporting the professional growth of others.
- **Interpersonal Skills** - Effectively communicating, building rapport and relating well to all kinds of people.
- **Persuasion** - Convincing others to change the way they think, believe or behave.
- **Personal Effectiveness** - Demonstrating initiative, self-confidence, resiliency and a willingness to take responsibility for personal actions.
- **Management** - Achieving extraordinary results through effective management of resources, systems and processes.
- **Flexibility** - Agility in adapting to change.
- **Creativity/Innovation** - Adapting traditional or devising new approaches, concepts, methods, models, designs, processes, technologies and/or systems.
- **Decision Making** - Utilizing effective processes to make decisions.
- **Negotiation** - Facilitating agreements between two or more parties.
- **Conflict Management** - Addressing and resolving conflict constructively. The ability to resolve different points of view constructively.
- **Futuristic Thinking** - Imagining, envisioning, projecting and/or predicting what has not yet been realized.

Serial entrepreneurs were only slightly below the national average on 3 of the 23:

- **Customer Service** - Anticipating, meeting and/or exceeding customer needs, wants and expectations.
- **Continuous Learning** - Taking initiative in learning and implementing new concepts, technologies and/or methods.
- **Analytical Problem Solving** - Anticipating, analyzing, diagnosing, and resolving problems.

Serial entrepreneurs were below average on the following 6 of the 23:

- **Teamwork** - Working effectively and productively with others.
- **Written Communication** - Writing clearly, succinctly and understandably.
- **Diplomacy** - Effectively handling difficult or sensitive issues by utilizing tact, diplomacy and an understanding of organizational culture, climate and/or politics.
- **Self Management** - Demonstrating self control and an ability to manage time and priorities.
- **Planning & Organizing** - Utilizing logical, systematic and orderly procedures to meet objectives.
- **Empathy** - Identifying with and caring about others.

According to serial entrepreneurs, the desire to create a business has been powerful:

At what age did you dream about starting your own business?

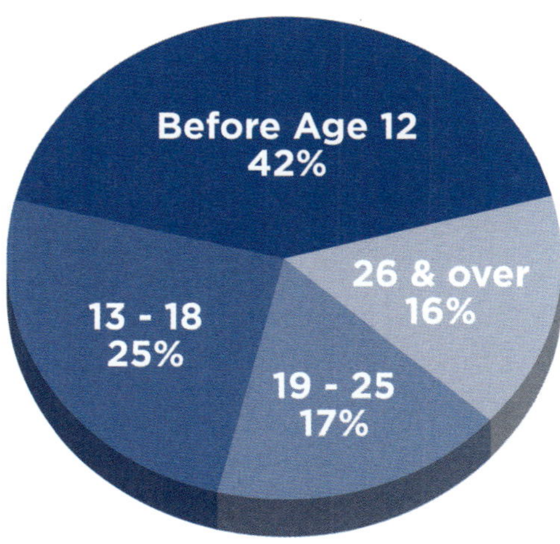

How many times per week did you think about starting your own business?

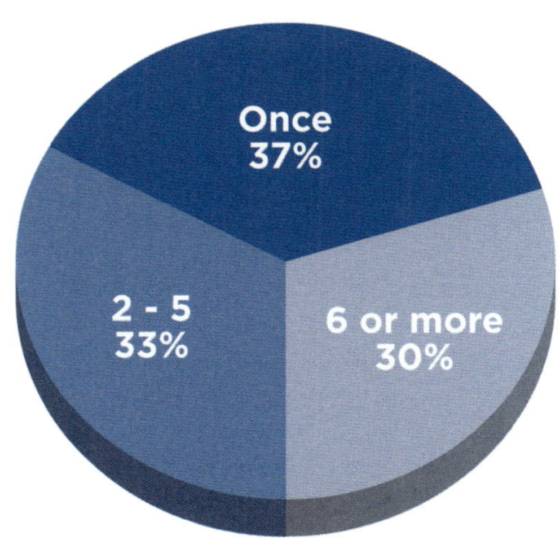

© 1993-2018 Target Training International, Ltd.

What emerges is a picture of someone highly motivated to achieve and resilient enough to succeed, in part because they have the flexibility and decisiveness to adapt to the frequent change inherent in growth.

Serial entrepreneurs tend to be competitive, self-motivated people with an optimistic view of possibilities. While most aren't likely to have the highly detailed nature of an engineer or technician, they do have the communication skills necessary to enroll others in their vision and will tenaciously push past obstacles on the path to achieving it.

They were youngsters when they began envisioning themselves as successful business owners. Fully 88% of the serial entrepreneurs we studied began dreaming about starting their own business before the age of 25, and an astounding 42% of them were imagining it before the age of 12. Considering that 37% of them were thinking about it weekly, this was more than a passing interest. Another 33% returned to the idea again and again (2 - 5 times a week) and 30% dwelled on it daily (6 or more times per week), so these serial entrepreneurs harbored an intense focus from an early age.

Based on our research over the years, serial entrepreneurs already have the requisite behavior and motivators prior to building their first business. These weren't developed as a result of their various ventures, but it's likely that they did develop some of their professional skills in the process. The jury is still out on precisely how people develop soft skills, but we've proven that these 23 job related competencies are not curriculum based. Professional skills may be introduced and understood through a lecture learning process, but they are gained and mastered through practice.

IDENTIFYING ENTREPRENEURS WITH SUCCESS POTENTIAL

Research will continue beyond 2011 as we partner with 18 universities across the U.S.A. to study college students in order to identify those that have the characteristics of entrepreneurs. Our goal is to learn more about what happens to entrepreneurial-minded individuals as they progress through the educational system, and to learn more about how college students build personal skills.

We believe that everyone is a diamond in the rough until they find the right job, career or venture. And just as every person is unique, we see unique patterns in given groups of people. Over the years the data has shown clear distinctions in the profiles of superior performers who are, for example, in the financial planning field as contrasted to engineering or sales. With that in mind, we will also be studying high school valedictorians and drop outs for indications of entrepreneurial tendencies.

© 1993-2018 Target Training International, Ltd.

The most important use of the serial entrepreneur profile is to establish a baseline against which to compare first-time entrepreneurs, a particularly useful tool for angel investors, banks, private equity firms and venture capitalists who are evaluating the success potential of applicants. Are they funding projects with people who have what it takes? It would be enlightened self interest for these firms to start collecting this kind of data on the new business owners they finance and track them with longitudinal studies.

Given that nascent entrepreneurs dream of starting a business early in life, it would be wise to fuel their entrepreneurial intensity early by steering them toward useful industry experience and by bringing a sense of urgency to developing education that includes the experiential opportunities necessary to develop crucial practice-based professional skills.

In the aftermath of the global economic crisis it's been widely acknowledged that new job creation is the key to reviving the housing market in America and to jump-starting economies around the world. Considering their potential to move us back to solid financial ground, we need to identify and mentor people in high school, in college and in every workplace who have the mindset of serial entrepreneurs. Entrepreneurs are critical to our immediate economic recovery and long-term future. We need to identify and fast track them.

EMPLOYER BRANDING 2010

By Ashley Bowers

INTRODUCTION

Every company is known by the public via two distinct brands, its employer brand and its consumer brand. Understanding what distinguishes the employer brand and how it may affect attracting and retaining superior performers can be the difference between spring-loading out of a recession and not recovering at all.

EMPLOYER BRAND MATTERS - What is Employer Brand?

Simply put, your employer brand is the perception the world has about your company as a good or bad place to work. Having a good employer brand means your company is perceived as an employer of choice, known in your industry and region as a highly desirable place to work. Having a poor employer brand could mean losing star performers and experiencing an uphill climb to replace them.

Signs that the economy may be on the upswing are encouraging for businesses hoping to increase sales, but they may also portend the next big challenge: an eminent shuffling of key talent.

In one 2010 study, more than half of US employers anticipate that retaining key talent will be more difficult next year.[1] Financial hardship and fear currently have workers pursuing or temporarily staying in second or third choice jobs, but make no mistake: they are sustained by the hope that recent signs of economic growth mean they can soon move on to greener pastures. Employers who don't offer a value-added employment experience may lose superior performers.

© 1993-2018 Target Training International, Ltd.

How is it Different from Consumer Brand?

Employer brand is distinct from the company brand that serves to attract buyers for products and services. While creating a hip persona may be effective for attracting consumers to products, employer branding is not as simple as clever ads, trendy office decor or a website posture that says, "We're cool." Talented job seekers have become adept at using a variety of communication channels to cooly evaluate an employer's value offering and will reject clever spin for verifiable facts.

Establishing your company as an employer of choice will require a sophisticated strategy. It requires using an awareness of changing workplace considerations from the employees' perspectives to formulate a value proposition to employees that clearly answers the age-old question, "What's in it for me?"

The employer brand is made up of a constellation of factors that contribute to an employee's experience inside a business. These include everything from the obvious (such as compensation and benefits) to factors which, while more subtle, profoundly affect an employee's quality of life after hire. Strategically shaping these factors can help retain strong performers while attracting new talent, by showing you've taken steps to create a work environment where they can thrive.

YOUR Image is THEIR Image

Company branding and employer branding aren't the same, but they may intersect to fuel each other. A good place to work may also be perceived as a worthwhile place to buy, and vice versa. Many of the same characteristics that attract socially responsible consumers to patronize a given business with their dollars — factors such as producing high quality products and services, using environmentally friendly manufacturing, fair trade policies, gender neutral pay practices, diversity in hiring, reducing the carbon footprint and providing healthy working conditions — are also considerations for job seekers. A review of the employer brand should verify that your company's stance on these issues is communicated across channels like blogs, newsletters, websites, etc.

More than ever, consumers stop to consider whether a company's demonstrated motivators are aligned with their own before opening their wallets. Similarly, employees want to be identified with companies that have a great reputation. They want to feel proud of their company.

WHO CONTRIBUTES?

Treat Prospective Employees Like External Customers of Your Employer Brand

Remember that prospective job candidates are customers who spread information by word of mouth about your company. Interviewers who are inattentive, uncommunicative or downright rude will unwittingly erase the hard work you do to position your company as an employer of choice.

On the other hand, a thoughtful recruitment strategy which includes job benchmarking and candidate behavioral and motivation assessments in tandem with a clearly communicated employer brand is a truly valuable career experience for the job applicant. Unlike some application processes, one that uses assessments is uplifting and affirming.

Even candidates who don't get the job offer will leave with valuable insights. The unique assessment report provided to them is an independently validated tool for understanding themselves as an employee. Recognizing both their strengths and potential areas for development enables them to better communicate their value to potential employers.

© 1993-2018 Target Training International, Ltd.

Examine each step of the hiring process to assure that it gives applicants an appreciation for what it would be like to work inside your business, and your company shines as a positive experience during their job hunt.

It Starts with a Great Fit

Momentum for retaining key players starts when they're hired. Minimize potential losses of both talented employees and their productivity by using assessments to ensure that each person is in the position that's the right fit for that individual. Assessment tools help hiring managers deploy employees in positions where they potentially have the biggest impact on the bottom line. Employees who are in the job that is best suited to their unique set of skills and inclinations are happier, and thus more likely to stick around.

Win Good Word of Mouth from Happy Employees

Job seekers and potential customers alike are increasingly well-informed consumers, using a variety of technology channels to investigate a company's offerings. This makes the strategy of how best to promote a favorable company image all the more important when the goal is to attract the best talent.

Smart companies consciously treat current employees as the internal customers they are, providing a value added career experience and letting human nature take its course. Satisfied employees then become goodwill ambassadors who are a reliable source of high quality hires.

Apply What You Know About Customer Satisfaction to Employer Branding

Dissatisfied customers tend to engage in more word of mouth than satisfied customers. Disgruntled employees may, too. With the rise of social networking, astute steps toward enhanced employer brand perception is a necessity, not an option. Like it or not, cynical workers have an abundance of channels for broadcasting their opinions of the company. The number of people using tools such as Facebook and Twitter to air their loves and hates to the world challenges the degree of control companies have historically had over public perception.

Until recently, traditional marketing and public relations efforts focused on channels such as television and print advertising, allowing companies to present a carefully shaped picture of products and services. Today the enormity of website, blog, Facebook, and Twitter options have relocated your company's employer brand to the digital public domain. The talented job seekers your company hopes to attract have ready access to what current customers and employees alike are saying about their experience of your company and its products, just as consumers do.

Your brand perception is owned in the public domain. You cannot control what is being said but you can substantially influence it by communicating the facts about life inside your company and how employees feel about it. Evaluating and upgrading the employee value proposition is the indispensable first step to creating favorable buzz about working for your company.

© 1993-2018 Target Training International, Ltd.

CULTIVATE & MAINTAIN

Why it's Not Just About Pay

Recent economic events have caused a shift in the way people evaluate the importance of their career to overall life goals. Sleepless nights and prolonged stretches of unemployment—whether their own or a loved one's—provoke a serious evaluation of priorities. So does the experience of being stuck in a poor job fit because of a stunted economy. It's never been so obvious that the quality of one's work life profoundly shapes overall quality of life.

Outstanding Benefits Aren't Just About Health Insurance and Vacation Days

Talented people want work/life balance and schedule flexibility, and with an array of technologies, it's easy for management to provide them while maintaining productivity and communication. When asked, "How important is it to you to have flexible hours as long as you get the job done," 51.48% of respondents in one study said it was important or very important, with another 32% citing it as somewhat important.[2] Allowing employees some flexibility in choosing their work schedule makes an enormous impact on quality of life, particularly if they commute through heavy traffic or have growing families to care for.

Encouraging wholesome lifestyle habits by providing a functional kitchen, work site exercise or discounted gym memberships contributes to employees' health while strengthening the employer's brand. Working for a company that makes it possible to seamlessly fulfill one's work and family responsibilities while remaining healthy is high on job seekers' shopping lists.

Express Your Organizational Values

Defining and expressing the company's values has become an important consideration for both retaining and attracting talent. Company values are not just an expanse of lofty text on the website: they help create the company culture and are the ground of your decision making process when plans affect staff. They are the ruler against which all decisions should be measured and should be consistently evident in all company communications, particularly those with employees

Are you able to succinctly articulate your company's values? Can your employees see them demonstrated in concrete actions? For example, involvement in community, charitable and environmental causes is increasingly viewed as making work and life more meaningful. When companies give employees the opportunity to 1) choose the nature of the involvement and 2) participate together, they allow staff to help build the company's culture from the bottom up. Employee surveys can be customized to measure how successfully company values are conveyed, while identifying logical next steps.

Soften Secondary Effects of the Recession that Impact Performance

It could be called the Poison Pill Effect: Layoffs don't just affect departing staff. How well or poorly a company treats laid off workers has a profound effect on remaining staff, too (and of course these stories are broadcast outside the company.) Employees are already speculating about their own chances of being laid off, so they will pay close attention to how management treats departing workers. In the post-recession economy, your staff—including critical top performers—may be affected by the pervasive gloom that has 64% of employees feeling stressed at the possibility of losing their job.[3] In an atmosphere of uncertainty, fear takes over and employees may speculate scenarios which are then repeated as if they have validity.

Be sensitive to how the current economic climate affects your employees outside of work. Even people lucky enough to have a job are

© 1993-2018 Target Training International, Ltd.

feeling the pain when they get home at night to spouses, children, friends or parents who may be unemployed and depressed. Just as they are being asked to produce more at work with a smaller staff, they may be carrying a heavy load at home.

The diminished housing market may also have a devastating and lasting effect on workers' prospects and self esteem. They may be reluctant to discuss personal financial matters at work, but some are quietly losing their homes to foreclosure, while others anticipate years of financial fallout from badly damaged credit.

With widespread job losses, even those who are working may feel grim about the future. Many can't anticipate pay raises or job stability in the near future, but they face the prospect of maintaining inflated payments on a devalued home. Your staff's morale and thus their performance on the job may be affected.

Leadership Communication Matters Now More Than Ever

Counter fear and stress with clear, intentional communications that consider employees' viewpoints in even the smallest matters. If this year's strategic plan has been communicated, they will have an accurate view of where the company now stands and what has to happen in the near future to avoid more layoffs. Now is not the time to leave employee prospects to speculation. It is imperative that communications with staff are frequent, consistent and honest. Employees need to know specifically how their own performance can positively or negatively affect the success of the company's 2010 plan.[4]

A survey designed to include an assessment of employees' current perspectives will provide useful feedback for leadership about how effectively they are reassuring staff when communicating the game plan for moving from survival to growth in the aftermath of the financial downturn.

The Curative Power of Professional Development

Professional development boosts performance toward the goals companies must accomplish to turn the corner this year. It also acts as a realistic antidote to the stress employees feel in the post-recession economy. From Millennials to Baby Boomers, the lack of potential for advancement this year is particularly frustrating for the superior performers companies hope to retain. They recognize that the current economy is a roadblock to the career growth their performance warrants. Despite knowing that companies are hard pressed to increase salaries or provide bonuses now, in the absence of mitigating factors, high performers may be tempted to look elsewhere for increased opportunity.[5]

Provide growth opportunities as part of the employer brand, because professional development dollars perform double duty. Investing in employee development can help retain talented workers. They correctly perceive growth opportunities as a demonstration that the company values them and is investing in their future. Training that guides them to the next level of effectiveness doesn't just positively impact productivity and the bottom line. It gives superior performers the sense of progress they crave now and may encourage them to be patient as business rebounds.

© 1993-2018 Target Training International, Ltd.

Paying for Health & Productivity Initiatives Pays Off

Many of the actions that build a strong employer brand perception bring favorable economic returns, too. Health and productivity programs have been shown to lower absenteeism, boost revenue per employee and have even been correlated to elevated shareholder returns.[6] It seems that tending to the well-being of employees is also tending to the bottom line, so expenditures for employee health and professional development is money well spent.

IN SUMMARY...

Rampant stress and job discontent is fertile ground for savvy businesses to position themselves as an employer of choice in preparation for the coming top performer shuffle. Against the backdrop of a slowly recovering economy, companies who strategically use their resources to provide a superior employment experience will stand out more dramatically than ever when compared to competitors with a poor employer brand. Going forward, company survival, staff development and employee job stability are entwined, as businesses compete not just to maintain a foothold in their industries, but to retain the top talent that will help them thrive.

FOOTNOTES – EMPLOYER BRANDING

1 51% of responding US companies expect retaining key talent to get more difficult in the next year. From Recession to Recovery: How Far, How Fast, How Well Prepared? Towers Watson, March 2010, p. 4.

2 Target Training International Performance Systems, Ltd. Job Seeker Survey, April 2008.

3 "Excessive work hours (75%), lack of work/life balance (65%) and fears about job loss (64%) are the foremost sources of stress affecting organizations today." 2009/2010 North American Staying@Work Report: The Health and Productivity Advantage, Towers Watson, December 2009.

4 "Even if company-wide recognition processes have been eliminated, effective managers find ways to recognize their workers' individual and collective accomplishments and convey publicly how their work has advanced the larger agenda of the department and organization." Monster.com/Monster Intelligence, "Managing and Motivating Your Team in Stressful Times" by Joanne Murray, Monster Contributing Writer http://hiring.monster.com/hr/hr-best-practices/workforce-management/hr-management-skills/managing-in-stressful-times.aspx

5 "If companies don't act now and plan strategically, they could face a double talent exodus: first by the employees who see no room or potential for advancement, and second by the baby boomers who will, inevitably, retire." From Recession to Recovery: How Far, How Fast, How Well Prepared? Towers Watson, March 2010 p.2.

6 "Companies with the most effective H&P programs experienced superior human capital and financial outcomes: 11% higher revenue per employee, lower medical trends by 1.2 percentage points, 1.8 fewer days absent per employee and 28% higher shareholder returns." 2009/2010 North American Staying@Work Report: The Health and Productivity Advantage, Towers Watson, December 2009.

© 1993-2018 Target Training International, Ltd.

MOVING HIGH POTENTIALS INTO STAR PERFORMERS 2010

By Ashley Bowers

INTRODUCTION

One measure of an organization's health is the state of its talent pipeline. Whether preparing for executive succession, filling open management positions as the need arises, or staffing new roles created by restructuring or growth, how ready is your company to fill key positions with star performers? The answer may fall somewhere between how many superior performers you have now and how many high potentials you are cultivating.

Forward thinking leaders don't rely just on hiring superior performers or poaching established talent from competitors. They are mining their talent pool now, to deepen the engagement of existing stars while causing a whole new group of superior performers to emerge from the ranks.

These market leaders are getting a profit boost by making use of talent management systems. There is a wealth of expertise available to help employers better deploy talent, and data shows that strategic talent management pays off handsomely. Results from Ernst & Young's *Global Talent Management Survey* show that companies that integrate and align business strategies with talent management deliver higher shareholder value. Those with the best alignment "had significantly higher financial performance [a 20% higher annual return on equity (ROE) over a five-year period] than those that did not."[1]

Going forward, successful competition in the marketplace is increasingly correlated to a company's ability to attract, retain and develop talent.

BENCH STRENGTH STARTS WITH A BENCHMARK

The foundation of a strong talent pool is properly bench-marked jobs, since accurately measuring performance in a specific job is only possible after a standard for performance has been established. Ideally every position in a business is benchmarked, assuring that uniform, unbiased criteria define the accountabilities, skills, attitudes, motivators, behavioral style and experience that each job calls for.

It's best to let the job speak for itself, rather than having one or two people write a job description that will unavoidably reflect their own idiosyncrasies. An effective benchmarking process [2] will call for assembling a team of subject matter experts to collaborate on voicing the job. The expert team should include the top three performers currently occupying the position, top performers who have occupied the position within the last six months, the position supervisor, the manager, and one or two people in roles that interact with the job being benchmarked. The team should not include every person occupying the position, since that would lower the bar, resulting in hiring for and accepting diminished performance expectations.

The benchmarking process is a logical opportunity for realigning each position with the most up-to-date strategic business initiatives. The team will clarify why the job exists and how it fits into the company's strategy going forward. As they define, weigh and prioritize key accountabilities, a clear picture emerges. The behaviors, motivators, personal skills and task preferences required for success in the position can now be used to screen a suitable candidate. A bonus is that the benchmarking process may also close past accountability gaps between positions that gave rise to recurring deficiencies in communication or productivity.

Planning for upcoming leadership needs starts with identifying priority management and executive positions for benchmark-

© 1993-2018 Target Training International, Ltd.

ing. These would be the ones generally considered most at risk for vacancies and those with a known likelihood of someone leaving, followed by future positions planned to anticipate growth. It's important to assess the existing team against the benchmarks produced so that any gaps in the current team can be accounted for when planning for new positions, training, or succession.

The benchmark produced will provide unbiased marching orders for HR's hiring efforts, making it an invaluable tool for *Selecting Superior Performers Safely Under The Law.*[3] Once jobs have been benchmarked, the critical competencies and attributes required for each job are used as guidelines both for hiring and for training high potentials to excel.

HIRE FOR HIGHER PERFORMANCE

With jobs benchmarked, the next step is assessing staff to get the most detailed picture of each individual's profile. Beyond intelligence and experience, individuals bring a unique combination of attitudes, behaviors, and skills to the job. Each of these factors has a direct impact on performance, determining whether the employee is average or exceptional in that particular role.

While a person's behavioral profile is crucial for determining that they are an appropriate fit for the job, it's a mistake to rely on behavioral match only. Just as hiring candidates with prior relevant experience is not enough to guarantee top performance, assessments that only describe workplace behaviors are not inclusive enough to most accurately predict potential performance.

According to the president of one of TTI's Value Added Associate consulting firms, "Hiring managers commonly hire for behavior only. This can be intentional or unintentional. And it often results in turnover because the candidate wasn't truly aligned with the position. You have to look from the outside in and from the inside out. From the outside in you see the person's experience, and maybe you like them (behaviors). From the inside out, you have the TriMetrix® [4] results (talents, motivators and behaviors). Smart people developed TriMetrix. Use the system because the system works. Believe your diagnostics, act on them, develop your people and you will experience terrific results and happy employees." See Case Study 1 for a creative use of motivational indicators to deploy and retain talented managers.

A comprehensive assessment process includes an analysis of the underlying attitudes and world view that motivate a person to action. When a job addresses the vital motivations equated to a meaningful life, job satisfaction and the potential for superior performance goes up. Before they can become stars, employees with high potential must be deployed in positions that align to their deeply held intrinsic motivations. The result is invigorated job satisfaction that leads to better retention, and with development, better performance.

The assessment must also include an analysis of the person's competence in 23 universally-recognized job skills. Proficiency with these skills, seen in Table 1, is what determines a person's ability to work effectively with others, to manage themselves and to align with evolving company strategies so that key outcomes are achieved.

TABLE 1
Personal Skills

- Accountability For Others
- Conceptual Thinking
- Conflict Management
- Continuous Learning
- Customer Focus
- Decision Making
- Developing Others
- Diplomacy & Tact
- Empathetic Outlook
- Flexibility
- Goal Achievement
- Influencing Others
- Interpersonal Skills
- Leading Others
- Objective Listening
- Personal Accountability
- Planning & Organization
- Problem Solving
- Resiliency
- Results Orientation
- Self-Management
- Self-Starting
- Teamwork

© 1993-2018 Target Training International, Ltd.

CASE STUDY 1 - National Retailer

One of TTI's Value Added Associates was hired by the new division of a successful national retailer to assist filling management teams for the division's new chain of stores. Their goal was to set the new chain apart from the parent company by establishing a company culture that expressed their distinct consumer market appeal.

- TTI benchmarks were created for Assistant Manager, General Manager and District Manager positions.
- TTI TriMetrix Reports were used to assess candidates for Assistant Manager and General Manager positions, as well as managers already hired.
- Development programs were put in place using TTI University Online's Rx development options, making it possible for managers to address their own unique growth needs.

The client had already hired both a General Manager and an Assistant Manager before benchmarks were created. Assessments revealed that the GM was strongly motivated by the desire to give back to society and help others. Her job description was adjusted accordingly, to include the responsibility for creating store events that would generate revenue while contributing to the surrounding community and enhancing employee job experience.

The Assistant Manager completed an assessment which indicated his strong motivation to achieve aesthetic harmony. His job description was adjusted to include responsibility for new store launches, particularly aesthetic aspects such as signage and product placement.

Potential hires were assessed, with GMs compared to the GM benchmark, while Assistant Managers were compared to both benchmarks. The results indicated that some candidates could be fast-tracked, because their profile more closely matched that of a GM. In fact, some AMs were promoted to General Manager within two months.

The result after 10 months has been zero turnover in a market where turnover rates are currently at 30% and historically at 50%. Hiring right-fit employees and adjusting jobs to fit their strengths have supported retention to give the chain a strong start. As a result, the Value Added Associate has been tasked with staffing 30+ new stores in 2010.

IDENTIFYING POTENTIAL STARS

A high potential is an employee who fits the benchmark for the position and measures above the mean on at least 18 of the 23 universally recognized personal skills. For example, strong personal initiative can be an indicator of a high potential candidate. As another Value Added Associate, and author of "The Target — The Secret to Superior Performance" points out, **"Mediocre performers show up on time and meet deadlines without having to be prodded. Star performers go well beyond that, to work in the white spaces of their job description. If they recognize a problem, even if no one else knows about it, they attempt to solve it. They volunteer to help others when they see they have the knowledge that's needed."** This ability to be self starting is one of many qualities revealed in an assessment that measures the application of personal skills on the job.

Cultivating high potentials who are already within the ranks to become superior performers means they will be ready to step up as positions open. Promoting internal candidates who have been specifically developed to the needs of the next-step position also offers an opportunity for the business to ramp candidates up to full productivity more quickly upon entering the new position. Time to effectiveness in the new role is abbreviated for the employee who is already acclimated to the company culture and goals, in addition to saving the time and resources that would have been spent on a candidate search.

© 1993-2018 Target Training International, Ltd.

CASE STUDY 2 - Engineering Firm

A TTI Value Added Associate was hired by an engineering firm struggling with low productivity. Despite a corporate philosophy of only hiring the best, they still weren't as productive as some of their industry peers. The initial evaluation confirmed that in fact, 77% of them were mediocre performers, 6% were low performers, and only 17% were star performers.

- The consultant started by assessing employees and managers with a comprehensive tool that included an essential piece — measurement of EQ (emotional quotient.)[5]
- He created a tailored coaching manual using each engineer's TriMetrix assessment report to create a unique development plan. This identified their specific strengths and managers used it to coach them on how to leverage their strengths in that particular work environment.
- Managers followed a regimented routine for the coaching session, meeting with each employee for one hour a month to focus on the 23 skills, EQ awareness, and work strategies. Development plans included teaching employees to understand how their emotions impact those around them at work.

The result was that when employees were assessed after one year of training, 20% had moved from mediocre to superior performance status. Billable hours were up 30%, while profit after tax increased by a staggering 25%. Our consultant reports, "Even those who started out as skeptics ended up as raving fans."

NOT THE SAME OLD TRAINING DAY

Anyone who's ever wasted a day sitting through a completely unnecessary training, especially one they could easily have taught from the front of the room, will concede that great employee development is not a one-size-fits-all solution. **Time and money are wasted when training isn't personalized to each individual's verified needs, causing some individuals to tune out or become frustrated.**

In the past, development often meant delays in delivery because of timing issues. Employees who genuinely needed immediate training for job effectiveness might be forced to wait months until the other seats could be filled. Getting all the right people in the room at the same time could be easily thwarted by travel, sick leave, vacations, etc., and in the meantime, performance stalls.

Sophisticated talent management systems offer development options that address the distinct needs of each individual, many of which can be accessed immediately. An internet delivery system combined with component-style trainings offers 24/7 access so high potentials can move forward faster. With their own unique set of strengths and weaknesses identified, employees use the system at will.

Rather than being a course or class, each individual training component in TTI University Online's Rx^6 development program is a stand alone information system that will identify more detail about a particular skill, with tips and suggestions about how to incorporate skill development into daily work life. They are designed to result in a consistent understanding of personal skills throughout the company and to help employees value having them in their working repertoires.

© 1993-2018 Target Training International, Ltd.

Managers refer employees to these components but don't have to memorize the definitions. Otherwise, development would become a tremendous burden on managers. They can choose between prescribing a training path or simply monitoring one that the employee self-manages. Either way, both the employee and manager can focus development efforts on assuring that the high potential employee is boosting performance in the current position while building the strengths necessary to perform well in the next one.

CASE STUDY 3 - Food Manufacturer

After three consecutive years of poor performance, the client hired a TTI Value Added Associate. In 2008 alone, losses totaled $2M, and the company's lender had given them 18 months to reverse the trend.

- The turnaround process began with a comprehensive assessment process that correlated to benchmarked jobs. TTI's associate is adamant in saying, "There is no 'wiggle room' for hiring bias. For example, don't hire a candidate just because you like them. A benchmarked position is a must because it's the foundation for superior performance. If the candidate doesn't align with the benchmark, it's a no-go."
- Two new sales people were hired, and the VP of sales was replaced. The Value Added Associate made sure that the entire sales team was a good match to the skills, behaviors and motivators that the sales benchmarks called for. Results from TTI assessments showed that the revised team fit the profile required for star performance potential in the job.
- Development plans were customized for each employee, using TTI University's online Development Rx's as a tool for each person to address the skill gaps that their assessment identified. Using these resources expanded employees' understanding of their own capacity beyond their current performance.
- In some work groups, TTI Professional Development Series weekly seminars were used to establish a common language of performance that established consistency. For other teams, our consultant delivered Dynamic Communication and Your Attitude is Showing single event seminars to quick-charge skills for an immediate return, such as when new employees need quick access to team communication.

The consultant acknowledges that moving high potentials to star performance is a process that requires reaching every dimension of an individual's capacity. The first priority is assuring that there is alignment between the candidate and the company culture, because the individual must have the ability to develop relationships within the company that make it possible for them to utilize available resources in their entirety. They must also be willing to put in the required effort.

By the time the client reached their lender's deadline, the Value Added Associate had guided the company through a process that resulted in a $2.2M turnaround, posting a profit of $200K for 2009. Going forward, the consultant team ensures that on-boarding of new hires automatically has a development focus.

© 1993-2018 Target Training International, Ltd.

SUMMARY

As businesses around the globe see improvement in the marketplace, we're finding out what defines the new business-as-usual. For many it has been shaped by lessons learned in an economy that requires making every dollar and every person count. More than anything, the new normal is defined by how effectively businesses deploy available resources, especially staff.

Fortunately, available resources include metrics that offer deep insights into every aspect of business that we care to examine, including people and performance. It's possible to know more, sooner, than ever before. If knowledge is power, which information can power increases to the bottom line?

Workforce analytics are demonstrating that the successful alignment of a company's talent with its business strategies fuels growth. Those that foster a continuous learning culture find that developing talent pays big dividends. Market leaders gain a competitive edge when they hire, retain and develop today's high potential employees into the superior performers they will need tomorrow.

FOOTNOTES – MOVING HIGH POTENTIALS INTO STAR PERFORMERS

1 "Sophisticated Talent Management Programs Drive Business Results", Ernst & Young, May 24, 2010 www.ey.com/US/en/Newsroom/News-releases/Sophisticated-talent-management-programs-drive-business-results

2 Target Training International, Ltd. and Performance Benchmarking, Inc., www.ttidisc.com/products.php?product=jb

3 "Selecting Superior Performers Safely Under the Law," Research Report by Bill Bonnstetter, Target Training International, Ltd., October 2009 http://www.ttiresearch.com/articles/Selecting_Superior_Performers.pdf

4 TriMetrix® is a combination assessment report that measures world view, behaviors, motivations, values, and skills. By producing a 'Gap Report' between the individual and the job benchmark, it identifies both strengths and areas for improvement that can lead to enhanced performance.

5 "TTI Emotional Quotient™ Leveraging Emotional Awareness for Effectiveness in the Workplace," www.ttied.com/images/4/40/Flyer_TTIEQ.pdf

6 TTI University Rx Online provides simple online delivery of independent learning opportunities at the employee's convenience. For more information, contact a TTI Solutions Specialist at 800-869-6908

© 1993-2018 Target Training International, Ltd.

BEHAVIORAL INTERVIEWING 2002

By Bill J. Bonnstetter

Behavioral interview questions that are job related are far more accurate forecasters of future success as they seek results from past experience.

Statistics bear this point out. According to research, behavioral interviewing is more than five times more predictive of success than traditional interviewing techniques.

The real goal of any interview — behavioral or not — is to uncover answers to two, central questions:

- Is this candidate the right one for our company?
- Are we the right company for this candidate?

Because of its high-level of accuracy, behavioral interviewing will do a better job of answering those questions than conventional interviewing. Behavioral interviewing is not just asking a candidate to talk about a specific circumstance or situation in his or her past. It requires an in-depth conversation aimed at uncovering evidence of past performance that will act as a predictor for future success.

To be truly useful, questions should be geared toward an individual's personal attributes, behaviors and intrinsic motivators. Once the interviewer is assured of a candidate's talents, he or she can zero-in on the specific ones that will be required in the job.

Zeroing-in becomes even easier when the key accountabilities (key competencies) are already identified by a job benchmark before the interviewing process even begins. Finding the right people to interview is simple when hiring managers know what questions to ask each prospective employee. After developing behavioral interview questions for each job you're trying to fill, select three or four and use them as telephone screening questions. This will cut down on the interview time to fill a job and help eliminate bias.

A SIMPLE LESSON, WELL LEARNED 2005

By Bill Brooks

Joe Smith was a top performer in his first sales position right out of college. In fact, he won every sales award there was to win in his first three years. Competitors, headhunters and other sales organizations outside of his industry constantly contacted him for his sales expertise. Until the day Joe Smith came face-to-face with a simple lesson, well learned.

The product Joe sold was a brand new, state-of-the-art computer solution that addressed serious business issues. The major competition he faced was a lack of awareness about his company and product. Sometimes a tough sale... But at least it was on an uncluttered battlefield.

After he was sales representative of the year in his fourth year he painfully decided to take one of the many sales positions that had been coming his way for the past three years. The one he took gave him a third more salary and double the commission and bonus opportunity.

Joe took the job and was miserable after six months and fired within one year. The reason for his failure was a single issue that he ultimately couldn't solve.

© 1993-2018 Target Training International, Ltd.

JOE WAS IN OVER HIS HEAD

Joe's new job was selling another high-tech and high-ticket product. Joe was smart enough to know that he wanted to stay in a similar industry. And isn't it true that sales is sales? His new product had been on the market for almost a decade and his new employer had developed an exciting new upgrade to the product that promised great things for both new and existing customers.

Joe's problem was that he entered a crowded battlefield — a marketplace loaded with highly competitive products and crushing price demands. Joe had to forget about a simple sale and start to dislodge competitors from accounts where they had been for as long as a decade.

It may be true that sales is sales, but you do need to understand the differences in the varied environments where you do the selling. That's the painful lesson that Joe learned too late.

In his case, his problem was a lack of skill and understanding as it related to two issues: How to dislodge existing vendors and how to sell against price pressure.

These two realities are quite often intertwined. In fact, they are often so interdependent that one without the other is virtually impossible. Look at how to dislodge a competitor when they are in an account you're trying to enter.

Some Strategies NOT to Implement:

- Don't disparage or bad-mouth your competition.
- Don't try to buy the account with low pricing.
- Don't give your product/service away to create demand.

Some Strategies TO Implement:

- Determine why your prospect is buying from your competitor, whether it's price, service, compatibility of equipment or loyalty. Study it and be able to do it better.

- Develop ongoing opportunities for you to have a physical and psychological presence in the account. Send updates on products, progress or new services you provide.

- Don't try to convince the prospect that having only a single supplier is bad business. You might displace your competitor and become a sole supplier, too.

- Position yourself as an unflappable professional who provides only high-quality service and products — someone your customers can trust to implement meaningful solutions quickly and efficiently.

- Don't use low-ball pricing to dislodge your competition. You are only establishing a precedent for low pricing and the inevitable loss of this account to another discounter.

- Study your competitors. Then develop a strategy that does what they do even better. Remember, your prospect bought from them for some reason — simply redefine that reason and take it to another level.

- When studying your competition, do your best to determine their vulnerability. Remember that no one is perfect. Learn who, within the prospective account, is close to having enough and will serve as your internal ally.

- Position yourself as a true industry expert — someone who others in the know rely on for advice. Word gets around — and will likely find its way to your prospect.

© 1993-2018 Target Training International, Ltd.

It was too late for Joe. He did find another job. But this time he returned to a marketplace that was less reliant on dislodging current suppliers from existing accounts.

Joe Learned a Few Valuable Lessons:

- All sales and sales management positions are not the same.
- Dislodging current suppliers is long-term, strategic and opportunity-seeking work.
- He would work hard to retain his customers in his new job because eventually, someone would try to dislodge him, too.

Remember — not all sales positions are created equally. Always work to understand your sales position and its requirements.

DO YOU HAVE WHAT IT TAKES TO BE AN ENGINEERING STUDENT? 2008

By Bill J. Bonnstetter & Dr. Ronald J. Bonnstetter

What does it take to be a successful engineering student? You may think it's having a high level of interest in engineering or achieving a high GPA in high school math and science. If you have an engineer in the family, you might wonder if this means that you are genetically predisposed to being an engineer. This begs the question: Are there factors that show you are predisposed to perform well at something?

Yes, there are. Without knowing about your family history or your performance in high school math and science, we can predict your likelihood of successfully completing freshmen engineering courses — and we can predict it with a high level of accuracy. In one study conducted on freshmen engineering students at the University of Nebraska at Lincoln, we predicted with 76% accuracy which students would fail the course. How did we do that?

We started by identifying the behavioral characteristics that are optimum for professional engineering jobs. After all, if engineering students are to become working engineers one day, they will need these characteristics, too. Then we examined the behavioral styles of incoming freshmen engineering students. By comparing the students with the professionals, we confirmed that there is an ideal behavioral style for being a successful engineering student.

This ideal style may be natural for a person, or the person may need to adapt their behavior to more closely match it; but either way, the ideal behavioral style for an engineer is the one most commonly found among professional engineers and students who perform well in engineering courses.

© 1993-2018 Target Training International, Ltd.

FRESHMEN ENGINEERING STUDENTS

When we compared incoming engineering students to an average of the general national workforce, we learned several things:

- Students entering the engineering program tend, on average, to be far more quality conscious than the national workforce average — about four times more so.

- Students entering the engineering program tend, on average, to be less people-oriented and more task-oriented than the national workforce average.

What do these tendencies mean when it comes to being an engineering major? To appreciate the characteristics of incoming freshmen and professional engineers, we examined how they operate in certain key areas of life. Knowing how you approach life helps us understand how you approach school.

UNDERSTANDING BEHAVIORAL STYLES

Understanding what it takes to be successful as an engineering student (or successful at anything) requires that you understand aspects of behavior that all people share.

There are four areas of life that we all experience:

1. **Dominance/challenge:** How you address problems and challenges.

2. **Influence/contacts:** How you handle situations involving people and contacts.

3. **Steadiness/consistency:** How you demonstrate pace and consistency.

4. **Compliance/constraints:** How you respond to rules and procedures set by others.

Understanding a person's natural way of operating in each of these areas gives a reliable indication of how they will tend to behave on the job — in this case, the job of being an engineering student. When you've answered the questions in our online assessment process, you'll have your own unique profile plotted on a graph like the one below, along with a full report of your unique profile. This insight into yourself will help you ensure that you're making optimum choices about what to study and how to study, and choosing a profession that suits your natural inclinations.

© 1993-2018 Target Training International, Ltd.

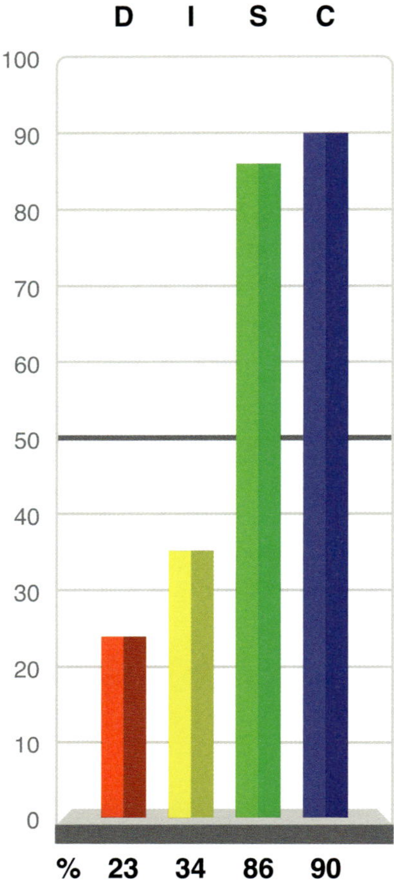

Figure 1 - High C DISC Graph

A person's behavioral style is recorded as scores on four DISC Graph vertical category lines (Dominance, Influence, Steadiness or Compliance). There is a distinct bar for each category, showing how you prefer to respond in that aspect of life.

Various scores in this system aren't better or worse, they're just different; so a lower bar is no more worthwhile than a higher bar. They are merely a graphical snapshot of how a person tends to function in life.

PRIMARY BEHAVIORAL STYLE

A person's primary behavioral style is the score that is furthest from the midline (50) on the chart, in either the up or down direction. This is the indicator that best describes how they tend to approach life. In Figure 1, the furthest score above the midline was a 90 in the C (Compliance/constraints) category, so this person could be said to have a high C primary style.

The primary style is significant, but so is the secondary style — the one that is the second furthest from the midline, also in either direction. Each of the categories yields useful information about how the person behaves.

It's easy to assume that a graph with high bars is better, but it's not true. There is no superior graph, just a different graph for each person. What can be better or worse is the "fit" between that particular person and a specific job or role. For example, a person whose natural style makes them well suited to be an engineer might not be well suited to being a jazz musician. Everyone has a behavioral style that helps them to excel in certain situations and prepares them to perform capably in some others, but their behavioral style may also mean that they will be challenged to just keep up sometimes. It's important to remember that every behavioral style has a natural head start towards performing well in certain situations.

© 1993-2018 Target Training International, Ltd.

WHAT DISC MEANS: THE HOW OF YOUR ACTIONS & COMMUNICATIONS

Figure 2 shows the essentials about each major aspect of behavioral style. There is more detailed information available when you've completed an assessment and are ready to delve into what it means. Looking at the basic descriptions in Figure 2, it's easy to see how our tendencies in each of these areas affect the way we communicate with those around us and why others sometimes seem so different.

D	I	S	C
Will assertively accept problems ↑ How a person solves problems or	Will actively seek out people to interact with/or influence ↑ How a person influences people or	Will initially resist change; Steady pace ↑ How a person sets the pace or	Will follow rules set by others ↑ How a person responds to rules or
Accepts challenges ↓ Will accept challenge in conservative manner; Avoids conflict	Interacts with others ↓ Will use more skeptical, logical approach to influence	Reacts to change ↓ Will actively seek change; Fast pace	Procedures and constraints ↓ Will actively attempt to set their own rules

Figure 2 - What DISC Categories Represent

OPTIMUM ENGINEER BEHAVIOR

Based on benchmarks of actual engineering jobs, the ideal behavioral pattern for engineering success is high S and C combined with low D and I. What this means is that being highly detail-oriented, adhering to established practices and following the rules or procedures (high C) is an important part of engineering work. Having a high S means that the person is very consistent, can be relied upon to deliver the work at a predictably steady pace and will complete it in established ways. Think about it. Would you want to be the first to drive on a bridge designed by someone who wanted to throw out the rule book on testing procedures and change things up without regard for tried and true safety precautions?

OPTIMUM ENGINEERING MAJOR BEHAVIOR

If the job of being an engineering major were to be bench-marked, it would also be classified as a high C position. Sure enough, entering UNL engineering freshmen did exhibit far fewer high I scores, and four times more high C scores than the national workforce average. Many of them have chosen a field that is a successful match to their natural inclinations.

So it should be no surprise that the students who performed well in their first semester of classes showed this tendency. In fact, 61% of students with a 3.0 or better GPA also had high C as their primary behavioral style, while only 20% of the 2.0 or less GPA students did.

© 1993-2018 Target Training International, Ltd.

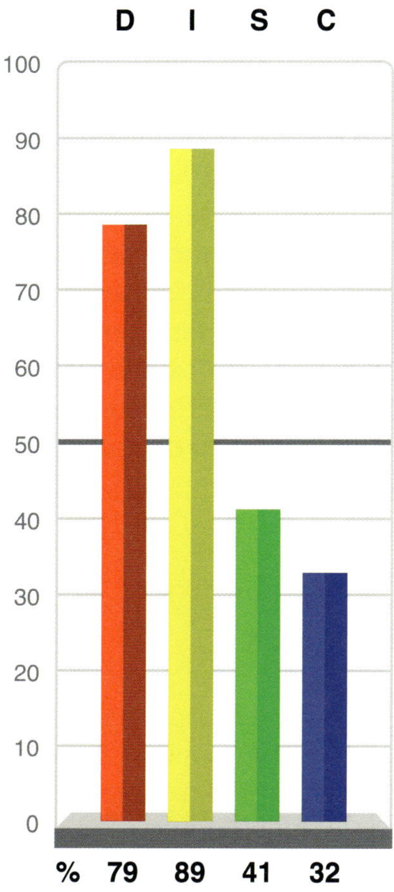

Figure 3 - High I DISC Graph

In contrast, we find that lower grades correlate with the higher I scores (influence/contacts), shown in the graph to the right. Words that describe the primarily high I group include: sociable, talkative, emotional, personable, good mixer, popular, and confident. Fifteen percent of students with less than a 2.0 GPA had high I as their primary behavior, while only 6.3% of students with a grade point of 3.0 or better had high I dominance.

So, while the high Cs were working for perfection, the high Is were socializing, confident that their old high school success would no doubt follow them into college. Clearly, these people-oriented skills are not the ones that help a student perform well in engineering studies.

A low I may well be just as important a predictor of a high grade point as the C factor. A person with a low I could be described as detached, analytical, reflective, calculating and critical. Sixteen percent of those students with a GPA of 3.0 or better also had a low I as their primary style, while only 12% of the 2.0 or less students had a low I. Similar concerns can be seen when comparing the primary S and D styles. Many of these grades suggest that students were not adapting for success.

ADAPTED BEHAVIOR VS. NATURAL BEHAVIOR

Is it possible to naturally have a style that's not the ideal style for a successful engineering student and perform well anyway? Yes. A person can adapt their behavior from what comes naturally to what the situation calls for. People do it all the time.

Every person has both a natural and an adapted behavioral style. The natural one is an unconscious, gut reaction, while the adapted style is the set of behaviors they use to rise to the occasion — the skills they must employ to do the job. If the job requires skills that don't come naturally, then the student must be able to adapt for success.

When we looked at freshmen engineering students, only 68% of them naturally had the preferred style (of high S and C combined with low D and I), but 74% of the students with top grades were demonstrating these ideal behaviors. Therefore, the top GPA group contains an additional 6% of students who were high performing because they adapted themselves to the preferred behavior. Only 26% of the group were able to succeed without these skill sets.

Simply stated, the more you adapt to the ideal behaviors, which translate to effective study and classroom habits, the better your engineering grade point average will be. The key is adapting. Once a high D or high I student recognizes the need, they can learn how to adapt these new skills for success.

Adapting works very well when a person is willing to do what it takes to perform well in a course, but what would it be like to adapt oneself in a career? That depends on how much adapting the person needs to do to succeed. It's normal to make small adaptations to any environment. But if a person's natural style is not fairly close to the style required by the job, they will find that adapted behavior has limitations. The person may feel stressed, even though they are in a situation they chose. They will have to expend a significant amount

© 1993-2018 Target Training International, Ltd.

of energy just adapting to the situation before they can begin to put energy into accomplishing the work at hand. The energy spent adapting could have been spent on accomplishing results in an environment more closely fitted to their natural inclinations.

This is why someone who is well suited to being an engineer might not be happy working as a jazz musician, a role that requires a high level of change and constant variation from established norms. The person with a naturally low C low S behavioral style will delight in discovering endless variations on a musical theme, while the high C high S musician will struggle to keep up.

So you could say that while some adaptation is useful, too much adaptation is inefficient. Our progress is enhanced in an environment where our natural style is the one that best matches a successful profile. To be successful at any undertaking, it's important to adapt to a successful behavioral style when necessary and choose a career area we are naturally well suited.

STATISTICS RELATING TO DRIVER ANALYSIS SYSTEM EFFECTIVENESS 1984

By Bill J. Bonnstetter

In 1984, TTI benchmarked the job of an over-the-road truck driver and continued this study for several years. We discovered that understanding the job requirements allowed us to hire drivers who would have fewer accidents when matched to the job than drivers who did not match the job.

These safe drivers delivered better fuel mileage, and compensation claims dropped because of fewer accidents. Drivers with the desired traits maintained their vehicles better than those who did not match the job requirements, resulting in huge savings for the companies.

Additional research identified different job requirements for company drivers versus owner/operators with regard to performance.

RESULTS FROM HIRING DRIVERS THAT MATCHED THE JOB

COMPANY #1
Prior Turnover: 180%

First Year Results:
Turnover reduced to 37%
Accidents reduced by 65%
Compensation claims reduced by 80%

COMPANY #2
Prior Turnover: 108%

First Year Results:
Turnover reduced to 70%

Second Year Results:
Turnover reduced to 43%
Accidents reduced by 50%
Compensation claims reduced by 50%

COMPANY #3
Prior Turnover: 130%

First Year Results:
Turnover reduced to 67%
Accidents reduced by 50%
Compensation claims reduced by 65%

COMPANY #4
Prior Turnover: 180%

First Year Results:
Turnover reduced to 160%

Second Year Results:
Turnover reduced to 87%
Accidents reduced by 60%
Compensation claims reduced by 50%

COMPANY #5
Prior Turnover: 120%
Turnover reduced to 45% in four years

OBJECTIVES REVISITED

At this time you should feel comfortable that all TTI assessments are not only valid, but TTI is committed to research and does it on a regular basis.

© 1993-2018 Target Training International, Ltd.

QUESTIONS & ANSWERS

Chapter Objective

To provide answers to the most common questions the authors are asked and to clarify any questions you may be asking yourself at this point.

Chapter Contents

Questions & Answers

"My greatest strength as a consultant is to be ignorant and ask a few questions."

–Peter Drucker

© 1993-2018 Target Training International, Ltd.

QUESTIONS & ANSWERS

1. AREN'T THERE 16 CLASSIC STYLES THAT MAKE UP 95% OF THE POPULATION?

Yes, there are 16 classic styles. Some companies have incorrectly stated that these 16 classic styles make up 95% of the population. Research conducted by TTI has shown these 16 styles only comprise 54% of the population. The other 46% of the population are forced to fit into one of the 16 styles. Graph II literally has over 19,000 different combinations that are possible. TTI computerized reports generate 384 different reports, giving a much more accurate analysis.

2. WHY DON'T YOU USE GRAPH III?

Research by TTI has proven conclusively that when there is a disparity between Graph I and Graph II, Graph III does not give accurate information regarding behavior, and therefore is not valid. Graph I is your adapted behavior and Graph II is the natural behavioral style. How can we average the two together and get a Graph III? The only way we can use Graph III is if Graph I and II are similar, in which case Graph III is still unnecessary because it will then mirror Graphs I and II. Consultants still using Graph III need to update their material.

Systems that produce products based on Graph III should never be used for selection.

3. AREN'T YOU LABELING PEOPLE?

Yes, behaviorally we are. We are taking similarities seen in people as early as 400 B.C. and putting them into a useful observable language. DISC is a relationship language. If I know some of your needs and adapt my behavior to meet them, I can encourage better communication. On first meeting people, we immediately begin to form impressions of them and make value judgments. Many of the traits we judge as good or bad are merely behavioral traits. DISC, when properly used, is a language that actually decreases labeling and increases understanding of ourselves and others.

4. WHICH STYLE IS THE BEST?

There is no best style. Each style brings different strengths to the table. A highly successful team needs all four styles actively participating. Some managers have intentionally hired styles similar to their own. The result is a team that is weak in many of the areas that the neglected style would be strong in. Surveys of successful CEO's have shown the presence of all four styles.

5. ARE YOU USING THE LANGUAGE OF DISC TO MANIPULATE PEOPLE?

That is not the goal of this manual. The DISC language should be used to promote better communication and relationships. It is a powerful language that is neither good nor bad until it is utilized by someone. An individual with a strong set of motivators will use the language for the good of others. However, some people will try to use the language in win/lose scenarios.

© 1993-2018 Target Training International, Ltd.

6. DO OPPOSITES ATTRACT?

Two rules seem to apply; "birds of a feather flock together" and "opposites attract". One person informed the authors that "birds of a feather flock together" applies to business, and "opposites attract" applies to relationships — especially marriage. We'll let you decide.

7. DOES THE DISC MODEL INDICATE ABNORMAL BEHAVIOR?

No, the Style Insights is not a clinical instrument. However, it is used by many clinicians to assist people in the understanding of normal behavior. Two unique patterns can occur which indicate possible problems. These are discussed in Chapter 5. The psychology behind the instrument is based on Marston's book, *Emotions of Normal People*.

8. WHY IS THE DISC LANGUAGE NEUTRAL?

If a High D person is good or bad, it has nothing to do with the fact that a person is a High D. A person's behavioral style is just that — a person's behavioral style. DISC measures HOW people act, not WHY (motivators). Some people have argued that when people are in a "survival" mode, the bad side of behavior comes out. In some cases that may be true, but again it is based on motivators. A High D who notices a fire may save himself and his things, or he may go in the building and risk his life to save others. This book is the first to state the DISC language as being neutral. History records men and women who faced death with a smile and a song, not the negative side of behavior. Why? Their motivators did not allow them to mistreat others even though they were mistreated. DISC is a neutral language.

9. IS THE STYLE INSIGHTS INSTRUMENT A PERSONALITY TEST?

Emphatically, NO! Personality extends far beyond the scope of the DISC instrumentation. Personality consists basically of everything we are. The DISC model measures "how" we act. It is the language of observable behavior. We therefore refer to the Style Insights Instrument as a "Behavior Analysis Instrument."

10. CAN I USE TTI'S DISC FOR SELECTION?

Yes, TTI's DISC can be used for selection. However, we recommend a complete job benchmarking process including the use of other TTI assessments in the process.

11. GRAPH I AND GRAPH II DISPARITY, WHAT DOES IT INDICATE?

When Graph I is significantly different from Graph II, it indicates the person is altering their behavior to meet the demands of the environment. What is the effect of altering the behavior? Research by Judy Suiter and Dr. David Warburton indicates increases in job dissatisfaction, health problems and stress all related to Graph I and Graph II disparity.

© 1993-2018 Target Training International, Ltd.

12. CAN I CHANGE MY NATURAL BEHAVIOR? (GRAPH II)

Graph II is "you." Your Graph II behavior will only change as a result of a significant emotional event. Why would you want to change a part of you that is distinctly "you"? You will be most energized when you are exhibiting Graph II behavior, because it is part of your basic design. The wisest approach for effectiveness and success is to learn your behavioral style and then learn to adapt to others' styles. You can easily learn to change Graph I by adapting to the environment, but Graph II cannot be changed. Graph II rarely changes unless a person goes through a major life change.

13. HOW LONG DOES IT TAKE TO EFFECTIVELY LEARN THE LANGUAGE?

You can learn the basics quite easily and begin to read other people's behavioral style. DISC is literally a language. How-ever, it is a language of observation. Once you learn the basics of the language, you must make a conscious choice to use it daily. Write letters, emails and other correspondence with DISC in mind. Communicate. Review and use it just as you would any other language. We have seen excellent success in as little as five hours of training. This book, if reviewed often enough, will give you all you need to know in order to use the language effectively. The authors have a combined total of thousands of hours using and applying the language, and we are still learning.

OBJECTIVES REVISITED

You should now have the answers to the most common questions asked of the authors, and clarity about any questions you may be asking yourself at this point.

© 1993-2018 Target Training International, Ltd.

VALIDITY

Chapter Objective

To prove to distributors and their clients that TTI only sells time-tested, valid and proven assessments.

Chapter Contents

- Information from the Experts
- Articles
- Adverse Impact
- Validity
- Objectives Revisited

"First we will be the best, and then we will be the first!"

–Grant Tinker,
American TV executive

© 1993-2018 Target Training International, Ltd.

STYLE INSIGHTS® DISC INSTRUMENT VALIDATION

Since 1984, TTI has always used outside, independent statisticians to validate all their questionnaires. Revalidation takes place every few years and the following study was completed in 2011. The intent is to provide a verifiable pattern of evidence that establishes the Style Insights instrument as a sound, reliable, valid, and usable instrument for a variety of purposes in personal and organizational development and for organizational and corporate use in a number of venues.

The research and statistics have been written and conducted to the specifications published in Standards for Educational and Psychological Testing (1999) cooperatively by the American Educational Research Association, American Psychological Association and the National Council on Measurement in Education. The guidelines provide the standards against which many US-based and international assessments are designed and validated. It is the purpose to respect those specifications and to encourage the reader to explore the standards in more detail. The reader is also encouraged to ask active questions about other assessments in the marketplace and to discover the extent to which those assessments followed similar guidelines to the Style Insights instrument and reports.

MEASUREMENT OF ONE'S "STYLE" — A BRIEF HISTORY

The Style Insights instrument is generically loaded into a category of assessments sometimes called "personality tests." TTI prefers the use of the term "style" instead of "personality" for a variety of reasons. First, the term "personality" is a very complex and global term indicating a wide bandwidth of behavior and applications of the entire individual. Second, the term "style" as originally suggested by Fritz Perls, relates more to the specifics of how someone does something, and is therefore more applicable to the purposes and goals of the Style Insights instrument and reports.

Historically, there are a variety of ways by which one's "personality" and "style" have been measured. Early work by Kraepelin (1892) with the free association test involved the subject being given a list of stimulus words to which the subject was asked to provide the first word that came to mind. The free association methodology has been used for a variety of assessment purposes and it remains in use today.

Some criticism of the method remains with issues of scoring, inter-rater reliability and malingering by the subject.

In answer to the critical issues of scoring and inter-rater reliability came the self-report inventory. A very early form of this assessment technique was developed by Woodworth during World War I (DuBois, 1970; Goldberg, 1971; Symonds, 1931). The original purpose was that of a screening test for identifying those unfit for military service. The War ended before the model was deployed; however, civilian forms were developed for both adults and children. The Woodworth Personal Data Sheet served as a prototype and early model for many inventories to follow. Some designs explored specific areas such as vocational adjustment, school adjustment, home, etc. Other assessments explored interpersonal responses in social settings, and later came assessments focused on interests and attitudes. It is in the self-report genre that the Style Insights® instrument and reports are based.

The "performance" or situational test is another commonly used assessment method. With this model, the subject is asked to perform a task, and is measured based on their performance. The specific purpose for some of these tests is concealed from the subject. An early application of this model was developed by Hartshorne and May, et al., (1928, 1929, 1930),

© 1993-2018 Target Training International, Ltd.

and standardized on school children. Situational tests for adults were developed during World War II by the Assessment Program of the Office of Strategic Services. These tests were high in complexity for the time, and needed some detailed staging and skilled administration. Even so, issues of inter-rater reliability and interpretation of responses were rather subjective.

Another methodology is that of the projective test design. In this method, the subject is presented with an ambiguous or open-ended task or description to provide of a stimulus card or process. Again, the purposes of these tests are somewhat disguised from the subject to reduce the potential of the subject creating a preferred response, or malingering. As with free association and some situational tests, there is room for inter-rater reliability errors and variability in scoring due to the subjective nature of the instrumentation.

The Style Insights instrument and reports use the self-report methodology that eliminates inter-rater reliability issues because of the objective scoring method of the instrument. Using the self-report method, the instrument captures one's own self-perception and records responses. While inter-rater reliability is eliminated, an inherent issue with all self-report instruments is the accuracy of one's responses and the focus of their self-perception. Therefore, the respondent is always encouraged to be honest in their response and clear in their situational focus when they respond. This methodology has been widely used and adopted in many academic and commercial applications.

CONNECTION OF DISC TO TARGET TRAINING INTERNATIONAL'S PUBLISHED INSTRUMENTS

In 1983 - 84 TTI acquired a DISC-based instrument under a license agreement. Since that time TTI has invested substantial amounts of attention, energy, and resources into the continued statistical validation of the instrument and the reports. Changes have been made to the newer versions of the instrument to keep pace with current terms and descriptors in use, and to up-date those terms and descriptors that were useful decades ago, but are less valid in the 21st century. TTI is rare among DISC providers in that their statistical validation work features current scores from the 21st century that are based in the language/cultural groups using an instrument. This allows for increased reliability and validity of the report printouts by comparing one's scores against a large, well-defined, contemporary, culturally relevant database.

VALIDITY & RELIABILITY

Reliability based on response processes and internal structure

The issue of instrument reliability is the initial question asked when exploring how "good" an instrument is, or if it is actually useful. The word "reliability" always means "consistency" when applied to instruments and tests. There are several procedures that are commonly used for this routine statistical treatment. Test-retest reliability is the consistency of scores obtained by the same persons when re-tested with the identical instrument. Alternate-form reliability provides the subject with two similar forms of the instrument. Both test-retest and alternate-form reliability documentation should express both the reliability coefficient and the length of time passed between the first and second testing events. Both of these procedures focus on the consistency of measurement. Such consistency and the "learning the test" advantage is a major concern with ability and knowledge measurements. The Style Insights is not subject to an advantage from repeated administration because it asks for self-reports. The instrument's scales are as stable as the individual's perception of situational demands and self-concept is constant.

© 1993-2018 Target Training International, Ltd.

Split-half reliability involves a single administration of the instrument, and uses the technique of "splitting" the instrument in half, e.g., odd and even question items, and determining a correlation between the two sets of scores. This technique reduces some of the concerns of test-retest and alternate-form reliability by eliminating the passage of time between testing events. Kuder-Richardson reliability is also based on a single form and single administration of the instrument and measures the consistency of responses to all items on the test. The Kuder-Richardson formula is actually the mean of all split-half coefficients based on different splittings of the test.

The Spearman-Brown reliability formula is another statistical treatment that provides a reliability coefficient and is frequently used with the split-half procedures.

Spearman-Brown differs by including a method for doubling the number of items on an instrument as a part of its formula. By doubling the number of items on the instrument, reliability usually increases. Some critics of the Spearman-Brown formula say that it may artificially raise the reliability coefficient of a test. Each of the reliability coefficients discussed so far are ones that can be calculated by hand or using a simple calculator.

The alpha coefficient is the expression of an instrument's reliability and ranges from 0 through +1.00. An instrument with a perfect reliability would have an alpha coefficient of +1.00, and no instrument has yielded that score to date. Additionally, there is no standard, agreed-upon "levels" of what makes a good or bad correlation for testing purposes. However, there is general agreement on a minimum standard for alpha equal to .6 or greater, with some experts advocating use of a .7 or higher standard. Obviously, the higher the alpha coefficient the stronger is the coherence of items. Cronbach's alpha (α) (Cronbach, 1951) is considered by many to be the most robust reliability alpha to date (Anastazi, 1976; Reynolds, 1994). "Coefficient α is the maximum likelihood estimate of the reliability coefficient if the parallel model is assumed to be true" (SPSS, pg. 873). For dichotomous data, "Cronbach's alpha is equivalent to the Kuder-Richardson formula 20 (KR20) coefficient" (SPSS, pg. 873). Cronbach's alpha is used to determine all of the reliability coefficients used to assess the Style Insights instrument. The reader is encouraged to compare the reliability coefficients presented in this manual to the reliabilities of other instruments, and also to ask how other vendors compute their alpha numbers.

Validity Based on Context & Relationships to Other Variables

Validity helps answer the question, "Does the instrument measure what it is supposed to measure?" It also asks a deeper quality-related question: "How well does the instrument make these measures?" These questions are obviously more difficult to answer and may leave room for subjectivity. With regard to any questions of validity, the critical issue is the relationship between performance on the instrument and other observable facts about the behavior being studied. When someone says, "The test wasn't fair," the comment is usually directed to the test's validity, not reliability. A more accurate way to state the same expression is, "The test wasn't valid." There are three primary forms of validity: Content, criterion-related, and construct validity.

Content validity examines the instrument's content to determine if it covers the behavioral topic being measured. Simple examination of items in a biology or chemistry test should indicate questions related to the topic or subject being studied.

When used in the development of the DISC themes, it is important that all four descriptor categories are represented in rather equal proportion for selection of D, I, S, or C descriptors. Additionally, it is important to explore social desirability as an

© 1993-2018 Target Training International, Ltd.

element of content validity. If there is an imbalance between words that are socially desirable versus descriptors that are less desirable, then content validity is affected. The Style Insights instrument is screened for content validity and since its initial printing some descriptors have been replaced to boost both the content validity and the reliability of the instrument.

Criterion-related validity refers to the ability of an instrument to predict a participant's behavior in certain future situations. One's scores on an instrument are compared with any variety of external "criterions." In the use of the Style Insights instrument and reports, there are a variety of studies available from TTI that have clearly linked specific scores and patterns of scores to job success in specific, well-defined areas. Criterion-related validity has two forms: concurrent validity and predictive validity. Concurrent validity examines one's scores and compares them to external criterion at the same time as taking the instrument. Predictive validity explores one's instrument scores against criterion after a specified time interval. Both methods provide robust support for the Style Insights instrument and reports.

Construct validity examines the ability of an instrument to measure a theoretical construct or trait. Construct validity is built from a pattern of evidence and multiple measures across a variety of sources. Some constructs explored in behavioral trait analysis include: Developmental changes of participants responding to the instrument at different ages and stages of their lives or under different response focus points. Correlation with other tests is a form of construct validation.

One very important technique within construct validity activity is a factor analysis. This is a technique that "refines" an instrument by comparing and analyzing the inter-relationships of data. In this process the interrelationships are examined and "distilled" from all initial combinations, to a smaller number of factors or common traits. Through factor analytic work using other instruments, it has been discovered that instruments from some other vendors have specific descriptors that actually factor-load into different categories than the ones in which they are scored on the instrument (Golden, Sawicki, & Franzen, 1990). The Style Insights instrument has been refined through the factor analysis process and has made subtle scoring changes that increase both the overall validity and reliability of the instrument and reports.

REVISED SCALE RELIABILITY

Scale reliabilities were calculated using Cronbach's alpha (α). Cronbach's α is considered the most appropriate statistical test for calculating reliability. The statistic models internal consistency, based on the average inter-item correlation. These evaluations are a more rigorous approach than a traditional split-half statistic. Cronbach's α is a statistic bounded by 0 to 1. In general an α equal to or greater than .6 is considered a minimum acceptable level, although some authorities argue for a stronger standard of at least .7.

The following table compares reliabilities using Cronbach's α. These findings document the Style Insights 2011.i as an instrument with solid scale construction and reliability. This revalidation is based on the new method of responding to the questionnaire by ranking 1, 2, 3, 4 rather than choosing "most" or "least".

Cronbach's Alpha (α) – Scale Reliabilities: N=16,950								
	Adaptive D	Natural D	Adaptive I	Natural I	Adaptive S	Natural S	Adaptive C	Natural C
SI.2011.i	.885	.884	.850	.845	.856	.834	.826	.826

© 1993-2018 Target Training International, Ltd.

TTI PERFORMANCE SYSTEMS ON ADVERSE IMPACT

WHAT IS ADVERSE IMPACT AND/OR DISPARATE IMPACT?

Under the Disparate Impact rule, an employer may not use an employment practice (e.g., a pre-employment aptitude test) that, even though neutral on its face and applied to all applicants or employees, disproportionately excludes members of a protected category. An employer can defend its reliance on such an employment practice only if the employer proves that the challenged practice is job related for the position in question and consistent with business necessity.

Applicants for employment, promotion, or other employment benefits who challenge the denial of the benefit to them will have to prove that the specific employment practice at issue has a disparate impact, unless the applicant proves that the elements of the employer's decision-making process are not capable of separation for analysis, in which case the entire decision-making process may be analyzed as one employment practice.

The Equal Employment Opportunity Commission (EEOC) has long advocated the 80% rule to assess when a particular employment practice has an unlawful disparate impact. Some standard is necessary because all employment criteria will exclude some applicants or employees.

Essentially, the EEOC has determined that if the selection rate of a particular employment practice for a protected category is less than 80% of the selection rate for the relevant comparison group, that employment practice has a disparate impact. While the administrative 80% rule has not been incorporated into statute, the EEOC and the courts look to the rule as a guide in determining disparate impact challenges.

WHAT IS A PRE-EMPLOYMENT APTITUDE TEST?

An aptitude test by definition is any of various tests given to measure abilities, as manual dexterity, visual acuity, reasoning, or verbal comprehension, and used to assist in the selection of a career. By definition it is assumed that a pass/fail rating is determined for such tests.

HOW ARE ASSESSMENTS FROM TTI DIFFERENT?

Overall TTI assessments are not pass/fail assessments. While on the surface some of the assessments appear to have ten as the best "score" this is not the case. Each factor of measurement can be strength on either end of the scale (a zero all the way to a ten). This is because of our job-related process. TTI does not recommend using assessments in hiring unless you have completed our job benchmarking process.

The job benchmarking process is designed to provide clarity as to the position requirements, key accountabilities, skills, behaviors and motivators for each position within an organization. While TTI has over 7000 job benchmarks available, it is recommended to complete the process within each organization for each position.

Because the TTI assessments are not pass/fail, the 80% rule has to be applied differently. To illustrate TTI's compliance with this standard, we look at the mean of the measured factors for the general population as well as male/female, veteran status, disability status and ethnicity. The following charts will demonstrate that the TTI assessments do not have more than a 20% difference in how protected groups score versus the general population.

© 1993-2018 Target Training International, Ltd.

ADVERSE IMPACT STUDY COMPLETED IN 2010

Conclusion — There is no evidence to suggest any of the TTI assessments (DISC, Motivators, Hartman Value Profile) could cause adverse impact with regard to gender, race, disability or veteran status. Even though the means of the subgroups are statistically different from the means of the general population, they are all well within the EEOC guideline of 80% and well within the first standard deviation from the population mean.

BEHAVIORAL/DISC FINDINGS AS OF SEPTEMBER 2010

RANDOM SAMPLE N=35389

Measurement	Mean	Standard Deviation
Dominance	51.74	24.33
Influence	57.58	25.75
Steadiness	47.87	27.62
Compliance	52.81	23.75

MALES N= 21814

Measurement	Mean	Standard Deviation	% Difference from Random Sample
Dominance	55.56	23.53	3.82%
Influence	54.71	25.7	2.87%
Steadiness	43.72	27.02	4.15%
Compliance	53.47	23.18	0.65%

FEMALES N=13575

Measurement	Mean	Standard Deviation	% Difference from Random Sample	% Difference from Non-Protected Group*
Dominance	45.60	24.33	6.14%	9.96%
Influence	62.18	25.17	4.61%	7.48%
Steadiness	54.53	27.27	6.66%	10.81%
Compliance	51.76	24.61	1.05%	1.71%

*The percentage difference from the non-protected group compares the protected subgroup to the non-protected subgroup within the same EEOC category.

BEHAVIORAL/DISC FINDINGS AS OF SEPTEMBER 2010

CAUCASIANS N=14355

Measurement	Mean	Standard Deviation	% Difference from Random Sample
Dominance	52.32	25.39	0.58%
Influence	58.79	26.50	1.22%
Steadiness	48.35	28.69	0.48%
Compliance	51.63	24.20	1.18%

AFRICAN AMERICANS N=2005

Measurement	Mean	Standard Deviation	% Difference from Random Sample	% Difference from Non-Protected Group*
Dominance	48.51	22.36	3.23%	3.81%
Influence	51.04	23.57	6.53%	7.75%
Steadiness	52.07	26.45	4.20%	3.72%
Compliance	57.65	20.44	4.84%	6.02%

HISPANIC N=1047

Measurement	Mean	Standard Deviation	% Difference from Random Sample	% Difference from Non-Protected Group*
Dominance	50.19	22.76	1.55%	2.13%
Influence	56.30	25.57	1.27%	2.49%
Steadiness	47.91	27.15	0.04%	0.44%
Compliance	55.30	22.92	2.49%	3.67%

*The percentage difference from the non-protected group compares the protected subgroup to the non-protected subgroup within the same EEOC category.

BEHAVIORAL/DISC FINDINGS AS OF SEPTEMBER 2010

ASIAN N=705

Measurement	Mean	Standard Deviation	% Difference from Random Sample	% Difference from Non-Protected Group*
Dominance	47.89	23.89	3.85%	4.43%
Influence	50.28	25.22	7.29%	8.51%
Steadiness	50.78	27.56	2.91%	2.43%
Compliance	59.77	22.90	6.95%	8.13%

HAWAIIAN/PACIFIC ISLANDER N=75

Measurement	Mean	Standard Deviation	% Difference from Random Sample	% Difference from Non-Protected Group*
Dominance	47.43	20.69	4.31%	4.90%
Influence	55.48	28.00	2.10%	3.31%
Steadiness	52.64	27.61	4.77%	4.29%
Compliance	55.67	23.84	2.85%	4.03%

DISABLED N=255

Measurement	Mean	Standard Deviation	% Difference from Random Sample	% Difference from Non-Protected Group*
Dominance	49.60	25.51	2.14%	4.21%
Influence	50.59	25.53	6.69%	9.77%
Steadiness	52.05	28.46	4.18%	3.99%
Compliance	57.99	24.53	5.18%	7.03%

*The percentage difference from the non-protected group compares the protected subgroup to the non-protected subgroup within the same EEOC category.

BEHAVIORAL/DISC FINDINGS AS OF SEPTEMBER 2010

DISABLED VETERAN N=125

Measurement	Mean	Standard Deviation	% Difference from Random Sample	% Difference from Non-Protected Group*
Dominance	57.11	24.21	5.37%	5.97%
Influence	52.18	26.12	5.40%	5.73%
Steadiness	42.66	27.02	5.22%	6.52%
Compliance	54.69	21.22	1.87%	1.92%

VIETNAM VETERAN N=402

Measurement	Mean	Standard Deviation	% Difference from Random Sample	% Difference from Non-Protected Group*
Dominance	55.53	25.22	3.79%	4.39%
Influence	50.77	26.08	6.80%	7.13%
Steadiness	45.34	29.26	2.53%	3.84%
Compliance	55.68	22.72	2.86%	2.91%

OTHER VETERAN N=1414

Measurement	Mean	Standard Deviation	% Difference from Random Sample	% Difference from Non-Protected Group*
Dominance	55.45	24.03	3.71%	4.31%
Influence	53.11	25.78	4.46%	4.79%
Steadiness	44.80	27.85	3.07%	4.38%
Compliance	54.44	22.89	1.63%	1.68%

*The percentage difference from the non-protected group compares the protected subgroup to the non-protected subgroup within the same EEOC category.

OBJECTIVES REVISITED

At this time you should feel comfortable that all TTI assessments are not only valid, but are revalidated on a regular basis.

© 1993-2018 Target Training International, Ltd.

BIBLIOGRAPHY

Bonnstetter, Bill J.
Buyer Profile Blending Factors
Freiberg-Frederick & Associates, 1982

Burnet, J.
Greek Philosophy: Thales to Plato
MacMillan, 1964

Hartman, Robert S.
Hartman Value Profile: Statistical Validation of the Hartman Theory of Value Structure
by Evaluation Systems

Hippocrates/Galen
Great Books of the Western World
Encyclopedia Brittanica, 1952

Jung, Carl J.
Psychological Types
Princeton University Press, 1971

Marston, William M.
The Emotions of Normal People
Richard R. Smith, 1938

Spranger, Eduard
Types of Men
Max Niemeyer Verlag, Halle (Saale), 1928

© 1993-2018 Target Training International, Ltd.